Plays By
Jonathan Reynolds

Broadway Play Publishing Inc
New York
BroadwayPlayPub.com

Plays By Jonathan Reynolds
© Copyright 2002 Jonathan Reynolds

Assistant to the Publisher: Michele Travis

Cover photo: Peter Cunningham

First printing: September 2002
I S B N: 978-0-88145-207-5

Book design: Marie Donovan
Copy editing: Sue Gilad
Typeface: Palatino

CONTENTS

ALSO BY THE AUTHOR

Sidekick
Vitreous Floaters
The Scrotum Monologues (one-act)
Lines Composed Above Tintern Abbey, Part II (one-act)
Geniuses
Styne After Styne (musical)
Whoopee! (musical, adapter)
Tunnel Fever or The Sheep is Out
Escape (play for television)
Micki and Maude (screenplay)
Switching Channels (screenplay)
Leonard Part 6 (screenplay)
My Stepmother is an Alien (screenplay, co-author)
The Distinguished Gentleman (co-author)

ABOUT THE AUTHOR

Raised in New York City, Jonathan Reynolds trained as an actor at Denison University under William O Brasmer, at The Eagles Mere Playhouse under Alvina Krause, and at The London Academy of Music and Dramatic Art (LAMDA). In 1967, he left the cast of *Rosencrantz and Guildenstern Are Dead* halfway through its Broadway run to join the presidential campaign of Eugene McCarthy. He stayed with the McCarthy campaign through the Chicago convention and then went on to become press representative for the congressional candidate Stanley Sheinbaum of Santa Barbara.

Following that tumultuous year, he became a producer for David Frost's television show and then for Dick Cavett's. His first plays, *Yanks 3 Detroit 0 Top of the 7th* and *Rubbers*, were produced at the American Place Theatre in New York in 1975, and on the basis of those two one-acts, Francis Coppola invited him to the Philippines to write the book about the making of *Apocalypse Now*. However, what was conceived as a three-month project soon threatened to be a life's work, and he left to write the play, *Geniuses*, based in part on the film, which was produced at Playwrights Horizons in 1981. Several years of movie work followed, and he returned to the New York stage with the controversial *Stonewall Jackson's House* in 1997.

While working on two additional plays and a musical, he currently writes a bi-monthly column about food for the New York Times and is the Treasurer of the Dramatists Guild, the organization of professional playwrights, composers, and lyricists. He lives in New York and has two distinguished sons, Frank and Eddie.

RUBBERS

RUBBERS was first presented by The American Place Theater, in New York City, on 16 May 1975. The cast and creative contributors were:

MR CLEGG	Charles Siebert
MR MUTRIX, ACTING SPEAKER	Lou Criscuolo
MR DAMIANO	Robert Lesser
MR TOMATO	Michael Prince
MR P VLITSIAK	Mitchell Jason
MR BAPP	William Bogert
MR FERMRLNR	Michael Prince
MRS BRIMMINS	Laura Esterman
MR PARD	MacIntyre Dixon
MR TOWNSEND	Albert Hall
MISS SINKK	Lane Binkley
PAGES	Warren Sweeney, Jaome Tirelli
Director	Alan Arkin
Scenery	Henry Millman
Lighting	Roger Morgan
Costume	Susan Denison

Place: The Assembly Chamber of the State Legislature, Albany

(The lights come up on a scrim on which is depicted the New York State Capitol Building in Albany. Then the lights bleed through, revealing the assembly chamber, a handsome neo-Gothic room. MR MUTRIX, ACTING SPEAKER of the Assembly, sits behind an elevated wooden desk up center, surrounded by officers and a CLERK on a lower level. The other desks fan out below him on the floor level, Republicans to his left, Democrats to his right. MRS BRIMMINS sits downstage just right of center, MR CLEGG is across from her just left of center, MR DAMIANO, MR VLITSIAK, MR BAPP, and MR TOMATO all sit up left of MR CLEGG. MR PARD sits up center of MRS BRIMMINS, MR TOWNSEND sits up right of her. Other chairs are filled with very lifelike dummies. Above and around the chamber—but never seen—is the Visitors Gallery. The floor itself is filled with constant motion—legislators popping up and down to speak, visiting with each other, coming and going. The pages, too, exit and enter frequently. The background is never quiet. Each legislator stands whenever he talks and speaks through a microphone attached to a box in his desk by a coiled wire long enough to allow two or three steps' movement in each direction. The volume of the mikes is the same as the volume of each speaker's normal voice—the mikes are not used for volume but for vocal quality. As the lights come up, there is a loud grumbling from everyone.)

MR DAMIANO: On the bill, Mister Speaker.

ACTING SPEAKER: On the bill, Mister Damiano.

MR DAMIANO: ...ladies and gentleman, in conjuction with my wildlife legislation, I would like to illustrate the desperate need my constituents up in beautiful Schroon River feel for a bounty on the rattlesnakes that are biting them so recklessly by introducing Mister Dick Bleak, the reptile executive of the Nosewater Game Preserve, who has something scary named Briget the Rattler to show you—

(DICK BLEAK enters carrying a reptile case marked with a skull and crossbones.)

MR CLEGG: Wait a minute, Vic, you got a snake in there? You can't do that, this is the New York State Assembly, we're not in Georgia, ya know.

MR DAMIANO: C'mon Willie, I brought this snake all the way down here, I put her up in my hotel for two days, I had to buy her a mouse to eat. It's for my bill.

MR CLEGG: All right, but make it snappy!

MR VLITSIAK: Has he got a snake in there?

MR DAMIANO: Presenting: Bridget the Rattler!

(DICK BLEAK produces the snake, everyone reacts unhappily.)

MR DAMIANO: How'd you like that to bite through your boots, Mrs Brimmins! How'd you like little children and babies torn to pieces by that oily creeper!

MR BAPP: Look at those fangs! They'd cut through bone!

MR TOWNSEND: Look at those fangs? Look at that face!

MR TOMATO: Atlantic Ocean!

MRS BRIMMINS: Mister Speaker! Mister Speaker!

ACTING SPEAKER: *(Banging gavel)* Just a moment, Mrs Brimmins, everybody'll get a chance. This is your state government in action. Let's settle down now, settle on down.

(The noise gradually subsides.)

MR TOWNSEND: Mister Speaker!

ACTING SPEAKER: Mister Townsend!

MR TOWNSEND: How on God's green earth does Mister Damiano think he has the right to bring a deadly poisonous, furiously writhing timber rattler from the Schroon River area into this hallowed chamber, its body held and fumbled by a gamekeeper clearly inept at snakehandling!

MR DAMIANO: Dick Bleak is head of the snakepit at Nosewater! The finest gamekeeping snakehandler in or out of my district, and I apologize to no man for his presence!

MR TOWNSEND: Some of us have children at home, homes themselves, outside concerns that depend on us for guidance! How could you! And how do we know that your so-called snakehandling gamekeeper will be able to control Bridget the Rattler? What about the visiting schoolchildren in the halls? They're wearing shorts!

MR BAPP: What on God's green earth was the purpose of bringing Bridget the rattler in here in the first place, Mister Damiano!

MR DAMIANO: Audio-visual, audio-visual! Children up in beautiful Essex County are being snakebitten by Bridget the Rattler and her friends, and there's gotta be a bounty on them!

MR TOWNSEND: Couldn't you have gotten that across without terrifying all the people in this room?

MRS BRIMMINS: Never mind terrifying the people—what about the snake!

MR CLEGG: Oh, please.

MRS BRIMMINS: It was the height of inhumanity to bring Bridget the rattler in here, Damiano! I cannot bear to see a frightened, defenseless creature, particularly a female, tortured and plied thusly for purely political reasons!

MR CLEGG: Hey, whatta ya talkin' about, whatta ya talking about—it's a snake! He'll bite ya and kill ya! I know according to *The New York Times* compassion is supposed to be your middle name, Mrs Brimmins—

MRS BRIMMINS: For whom do I have insufficient compassion in your view, Mister Clegg?

MR CLEGG: Victims of violent crimes insteada their perpetrators, that's who for one thing.

MRS BRIMMINS: Can I believe I once went to bed with this man for five months?

ACTING SPEAKER: Mister Clegg, Mrs Brimmins...

MRS BRIMMINS: Children starving in India, eight to ten percent unemployment...!

MR CLEGG: Not now, Marge.

MR PARD: Snakes frightened Melissa once.

(*Everyone freezes and listens to this old sage.*)

MR CLEGG: Who's Melissa?

MR PARD: One of my hundreds and hundreds of grandchildren. Little girl blondie wears taffeta sometimes...looks so cute when she eats a burger. Well sir, some kind of snake or a duck come over and just frightened her all up. So I say kill the buggerer!

ACTING SPEAKER: Thank you Mister Pard, as always.

MRS BRIMMINS: What I'm looking forward to is 6843-D—*my* bill.

MR DAMIANO: Mister Speaker, I have a great and sincere caring for all of God's living things—

MRS BRIMMINS: Who are you fronting for, Damiano, who's slipping you the greenbacks on this one! You don't care about Essex County snakebite! Who is it, Damiano?

MR DAMIANO: Listen to this, listen to this! I don't have to pay attention to bilge and garbage from a toxic Brooklyn shrew! You're here on charity, little lady, and don't you forget it. Victory by plurality is charity, Mrs Brimmins, if that is really your name!

MRS BRIMMINS: He's hiding something, Mister Speaker, putting up the old Nixonian offense as the world's most transparent defense—trying to distract our attention from Nam, as it were, with a trip to China!

ACTING SPEAKER: Mrs Brimmins, you are out of order.

MR DAMIANO: Pluralities are for sissies, lady, and dried up brown bags!

ACTING SPEAKER: Mister Townsend.

MR TOWNSEND: Mister Speaker, either this body should institute a limited bounty on timber rattlers, or it should not. We have much work to get to in the morning of this long winter light and I suggest we call for a vote and move onward.

MRS BRIMMINS: At last, the voice of reason.

MR CLEGG: *(Disparagingly)* Reason, reason.

ACTING SPEAKER: Mister Vlitsiak.

MR VLITSIAK: Mister Speaker, I would like to call your attention to the arrival of Joe Paella and his little league football team the Paella Marvels who have just entered the gallery above. The Paella Marvels have compiled an admirable eight-and-one record last year behind the standout quarterbacking of Pieter Carvalho, the thirteen-year-old Dutch whiz. Would you kindly extend the usual greetings?

ACTING SPEAKER: On behalf of the Speaker of this Assembly who is otherwise engaged, I, the Acting Speaker, cordially extend a warm state welcome to Mister Paella, the Paella Marvels, and Dutchman Pieter Carvalho, whom we have all heard so much about. We hope they enjoy the deliberations.

(The Assembly applauds.)

MR DAMIANO: I now move the bill.

MRS BRIMMINS: I demand a slow roll call.

ACTING SPEAKER: Willie?

MR CLEGG: No.

ACTING SPEAKER: Request for a slow roll call is denied.

MRS BRIMMINS: It's always turned down. But I can't let up; someone has to keep these moral surrealists clipped and shorn.

MR DAMIANO: I could really use this bill, Willie.

MR CLEGG: It ain't gonna come back to embarrass me, is it, Vic?

MR DAMIANO: Oh no! On my mother's fingers, Willie—it's for a friend of mine in the cement business. It's legit.

(MR CLEGG nods, waves his finger almost unnoticeably.)

ACTING SPEAKER: Mister Clegg.

MR CLEGG: Mister Speaker, after a thoughtful perusal of Mister Damiano's bill, it is my firm conviction that this legislation would enormously benefit the people of this great state as well as the good people of Schroon River, and I am proud to endorse its passage. As is customary, of course, each member is free to vote his own convictions.

MRS BRIMMINS: Free to vote his own convictions; in the first place, no one in this room is free; and second, no one in this room has any convictions.

ACTING SPEAKER: Read the last section.

CLERK: This act shall take effect immediately.

ACTING SPEAKER: The clerk will call the roll.

CLERK: Aabey, Gwathmey, Dallenbach, Zyzzeroso.

ACTING SPEAKER: The bill is passed.

MR DAMIANO: *(Giving him a wrapped present or some hot jewelry)* Thank you Willie. From the bottom of my heart.

MR CLEGG: Anytime, Vic. But dispense with the soipents, from now on, huh?

ACTING SPEAKER: Calendar of the day. The clerk will read.

MR CLEGG: Joey...get me a container of cottage cheese and some prunes, will you? My duodenum is giving me torment.

CLERK: Assembly number 10501, Mister Tomato. An act to amend the alcoholic beverage law allowing beer wholesalers to also merchandise syrup-based soda pop.

MRS BRIMMINS: Syrup-based soda pop. I came here to argue in the Socratic-Platonic tradition, to ease suffering in cold water flats, and syrup-based soda pop is my just desserts. I demand a slow roll call.

ACTING SPEAKER: Willie?

MR CLEGG: Nope.

ACTING SPEAKER: Request denied.

MRS BRIMMINS: Every day, questions of syrup-based soda pop. Oh, I cared about the Bridget the rattler bill—I'm a humanitarian after all. In fact, if I had to be categorized, I'm sure everyone here would concede with open arms that I'm a professional caring-sharing-nurturer—with discerning, unflinching stances on all issues of the day. I was, of course, against the war, that goes without saying; I brought local opposition to its uncaring knees during the lettuce strike; I initiated the bill prohibiting insults of all kinds.

MR TOMATO: *(Approaching MR CLEGG)* I hate to ask you, Willie...

MR CLEGG: Don't be shy, Augie, I'm very accessible. Who's it for?

MR TOMATO: My step-nephew. He's in the brewery business and he's very unhappy with his lot. It'd mean so much to the family.

(MR CLEGG waves his finger again.)

ACTING SPEAKER: Mister Clegg.

MR CLEGG: Mister Speaker, after a thoughtful perusal of Mister Tomato's bill, it is my firm conviction that this legislation would enormously benefit the people of this great state as well as the good people of Mister Tomato's constituency, and I am proud to endorse its passage. As is customary, of course, each member is free to vote his own convictions.

ACTING SPEAKER: Read the last section.

CLERK: This act shall take effect immediately.

ACTING SPEAKER: The clerk will call the roll.

CLERK: Aabey, Gwathmey, Dallenbach, Zyzzeroso.

ACTING SPEAKER: The bill is passed.

MRS BRIMMINS: All he has to do is wave that index finger, and the bill is passed; I can't even get the floor.

MR TOMATO: God love you and yours, Willie.

MR CLEGG: How's Joleen?

MR TOMATO: Fine, Willie, fine. She asks after you every day.

MR CLEGG: Give her my hellos.

MR TOMATO: Oh, I sure will, Willie.

MRS BRIMMINS: That fat, balding Republican over there with the stranglehold on all who enter is the one I earlier intimated lay with me for five months two years ago. He confuses me lately. I think he hates me, but I can't be sure. In a way I hope he does—it can be kind of exciting when someone hates you. I thought he would tie me to the four corners of the room and lasciviate me like a two hundred and twenty-pound flesh jockey, my truckdriver fantasy. But he never did. He's an ex-cop, and he can be so mean and thrilling in here—he broke one Assemblyman's left elbow over the milk dispute last year—but at home he just never came alive. Shame is what drive most men away, and he was out the door from the very first.

MR BAPP: Willie, could I ask a favor? I know you don't like me particularly, but—

MR CLEGG: In a minute, Dick, when your bill comes up. And cut out this "don't like me" stuff. You're one of my all-time greats.

(He squeezes MR BAPP's neck hard in a friendly gesture.)

ACTING SPEAKER: Calendar of the day. The clerk will read.

CLERK: Bill 6843-D, Calendar number 660, Mrs Brimmins.

MRS BRIMMINS: At last. My bill. The fearful slumber hath an end. The giant awakes.

CLERK: An act to amend the education law in relation to the display of—yicchh—contraceptives in pharmacies.

MR CLEGG: Oh, no, not this again.

(*There is general angry consternation.*)

MR DAMIANO: On the bill, Mister Speaker!

ACTING SPEAKER: On the bill, Mister Damiano.

MR DAMIANO: Mister Speaker, this bill had been introduced four times in the last three weeks! Surely we don't have to suffer another one of these schoolteaching, moralistic explanations—particularly from a woman who's up here only on a plurality. I have an extremely important license plate bill to get to, Mister Speaker...

MRS BRIMMINS: This is the purpose of my bill. The law currently states that a pharmacist must keep all prescription and non-prescription contraceptive items hidden behind his counter and that customers must ask often embarrassing and inhibiting questions just to see them, let alone buy them. My bill changes that to allow non-prescription contraceptives and their advertising literature to be displayed *openly*—so customers may examine their prices and ingredients comparatively, just as they do now with toothpaste and shampoo. This is all the bill intends—nothing subversive. As for the number of times this bill has been brought to the floor—

MR DAMIANO: Uh-oh, here comes the moral—I can see the glint from here—

MRS BRIMMINS: Such continual amendment wouldn't be necessary, Mister Damiano, if it weren't for the repressive, nineteenth- century blindness of my tightly corseted opponents, many of whom, I might add, voted for restoration of the death penalty with glazed eyes bordering on the sexual...

MR CLEGG: All right, all right...

MR PARD: No advertising in the window this time, is there?

MRS BRIMMINS: No advertising in the window, Mister Pard.

MR PARD: You know what this legislature thinks of making sport of natural bodily functions, don't you?

MRS BRIMMINS: I was made painfully aware of that last week, Mister Pard.

MR PARD: (*Furiously*) Good. Stool is not funny, lady.

MRS BRIMMINS: Mister Speaker, this is an important, humanitarian bill. It may help prevent a few unwanted pregnancies, stop even a fraction of venereal disease. Not like Damiano's self-serving, back-scratching Bridget the Rattler bill.

MR DAMIANO: Watch it lady, I'm a lawyer.

MRS BRIMMINS: A lawyer.

MR DAMIANO: I am!

MRS BRIMMINS: If it wasn't for no-fault, you'd still be chasing ambulances, you sleaze.

MR DAMIANO: Listen to this! Listen to this!

MRS BRIMMINS: You couldn't stop no-fault, no matter who you bribed, could you? Marrying the Speaker's daughter didn't help you on that one, did it? So now he's Mister Medical Malpractice Suit, driving all our doctors into Pennsylvania. Ho, I'd never even *listen* to a bribe from you!

MR DAMIANO: Who'd ever offer you one? Pluralities don't get offered bribes, lady, pluralities just fill up a chair!

MR CLEGG: All right, all right, Mrs Brimmins, Mister Damiano, let's just try to stick to the contraceptive bill, okay? *The New York Times*'ll be keenly disappointed if you keep wandering around like that.

MRS BRIMMINS: This plurality business will drive me screaming into the cold. Is it my fault I come from the most conservative district in Brooklyn and possibly the world? My fault two Viet vets split the vote and I sailed through the middle—not once but twice?

MR DAMIANO: What about my license plates bill, Willie! Tell her to hurry up.

MRS BRIMMINS: Your license plates bill—you know what that is? His daughter's name is Gussie Ogilvie Damiano, her initials boil down to G-O-D, God, and G-O-D isn't allowed on license plates in New York State, so he wants to pass a law—A LAW!—allowing the initials, G-O-D God, on license plates in New York State. Over my livid body!

MR VLITSIAK: Oh, come on, it's for his daughter—we're allowed to do that up here. I think it's kind of sweet.

MR CLEGG: Will you get back to the contraceptive bill, Marge!

MRS BRIMMINS: Open display of contraceptives and their advertising literature. Period.

MR PARD: You mean according to this bill little children can sell these things?

MRS BRIMMINS: No, Mister Pard, little children can't sell these things— no one who isn't at least sixteen and who doesn't have working papers can be employed in a pharmacy in the first place.

MR PARD: Haw, kids can get around *that*.

MRS BRIMMINS: Mister Pard, I doubt seriously boys and girls under sixteen are going to lie about their ages and forge working papers just to be in close proximity to boxes of contraceptives.

MR PARD: Then you don't know kids—which you don't, by the way. Cross-eyed Sephardic!

MRS BRIMMINS: Mister Speaker...

MR PARD: She doesn't know kids. *I* know kids. I'm the oldest man in the world! Goodtime Larry Pard! Chairman of the Way and Means, a hammerlock on the Rules Committee, for years before that a harsh and unbending judge! The very best friend Franklin Eleanor Roosevelt ever had!

MRS BRIMMINS: On the bill, Mister Speaker.

MR VLITSIAK: Mister Speaker.

MR DAMIANO: C'mon Willie, I got my license plates to get to!

ACTING SPEAKER: Mister Vlitsiak.

MR VLLITSIAK: Mister Speaker, I would like to introduce several of my constituents who have just arrived here to watch these proceedings— the Nina Rohan Five, a singing group of elderly widows from Conewango Valley over in beautiful Cattaraugus County, and the Douzy Saints Gang, a rehabilitated street mob gradually integrating into the wonderful community of Skaneateles in the great county of Onondaga. They are here with their faculty advisor, Monsignor Honest Nick O'Cake.

ACTING SPEAKER: On behalf of the Speaker of this Assembly who is otherwise engaged, I as Acting Speaker welcome the Nina Rohan Five, the Douzy Saints Gang and Monsignor Honest Nick O'Cake to this hallowed chamber and hope you will all enjoy the deliberations, so help me God.

MRS BRIMMINS: My childhood wasn't easy. Only Jewess of a middle-class Central Park West family, I was forced into a life of competitive and aggressive art early on—mastering the flute, failing terribly with the cello, a puberty jam-crammed with the Brontes and Virginia Woolf. Music and Art, Radcliffe, nominee for a Woodrow Wilson, honors at Harvard Law. Politics I learned in the hot and salty crucible of '68— '68, when protest was an art form!

MR PARD: I hate her!

MR CLEGG: Easy, Mister Pard.

MRS BRIMMINS: Children starving in India! Rising cost of the defense budget!

MR CLEGG: Mister Speaker, will Mrs Brimmins yield for a question?

MRS BRIMMINS: Yes, if it's relevant to my contraceptive bill, Mister Speaker.

MR CLEGG: If it's relevant to your contraceptive bill, eh? Always the little barb, always the niggling eye gouge. Well, you're gonna see some blood flow like wine in a minute. Here's the question, Mrs Brimmins, and it's relevant all right: you finished?

MRS BRIMMINS: Yes.

MR CLEGG: Good. I'm sick of this bill. Let's get this debate movin', Terry. *Him* first.

ACTING SPEAKER: Right. Mister Tomato.

MR TOMATO: Thank you, Mister Speaker. I have mail from all over the state on this bill, Mister Speaker. The people are aroused, and I don't mean maybe. I have letters from Schaghticoke, Schenevus, and Schodack Landing; Sagaponack, Oriskany Falls, and Kenoza Lake. I have mail from Sodus and Shandaken, even some from Scipio Center in the great county of Cayuga. Everyone—concerned mothers in Felts Mills, common laborers in East Pharsalia, two shut-ins from Cropseyville; good Lord, even the people of Claverack just down in Columbai County send mail—and Claverack doesn't really write as a rule. Pifford; Nedrow; Hoosick Falls six letters. I have a small *drawerful* from Beemus Point! I don't think you're all aware how much commotion this woman's bill has stirred up. Ho, they're dancin' mad over in Arkport, furious in Bible School Park, drained of all hope in Blodget Mills. That ain't all, Mister Speaker—oh, no you bet your socks. It just doesn't stop—I got mail from the likes of Sparrow Bush, Tupper Lake, Waccabuc, Wappingers Falls, and West Coxsackie. Even Chenango Forks in the usually happy county of Broome. And you know something? Every piece of mail except one from a family named Wormser in Ballston Spa urged me to vote against this wretched bill. Some even threatened my family with physical violence if I didn't. The people in this state are stirred up by this bill, Mister Speaker, up to the throat. I tell you, once you get outta your big cities—particularly that one Big City down there which I don't need to mention by name, everybody knows what I'm talkin' about—once you get outta there, I'm proud to say this state's filled with decent, God-striving families who decry hookers on every corner and one-on-one skin flicks where they're always showin' penetration. Down to a man—except this one Wormser family in Ballston Spa—everybody I've heard from believes open display of rubbers—for that's all they are, rubbers! Rubbers! —and their advertising'll lead to more and more porn and more porn and more and more and more porn more. No sir, I'd never vote for this bill, hand on the Bible! I thank you.

(He sits to applause. The PAGE delivers MR CLEGG's lunch.)

MR CLEGG: Thanks, Joey. That was quick.

MRS BRIMMINS: I can answer that, and with celerity.

ACTING SPEAKER: Mister Vlitsiak.

MR VLITSIAK: What about little children, Mrs Brimmins—what if these things become popular with little children, Mrs Brimmins? Start catching on in stores, establishin' themselves in kiddie buying habits, becomin' fads like

Pez machines and silly putty, Mrs Brimmins? What if kids start tradin' 'em like ball cards, flashin' 'em around near urinals, wearin' 'em in their lapels—

MR PARD: Blowin' 'em up in public places!

MR VLITSIAK: Blowin' 'em up in public places, Mrs Brimmins, thank you, Mister Pard. Ladies and gentlemen, this mass of brazen wants to destroy our children with this bill, to make public jokes of their private parts, to force aimless, wandering permissiveness on them though they clearly long for heavy and corrective spanking. You boys know what I've always said: if the Lord above had wanted a permissive society, he would have given Moses ten suggestions, not ten commandments. I ask you. And what of those poor little kids who will choose *not* to play with rubbers, Mrs Brimmins? Do you know how venomous and ratlike little children can be, Mrs Brimmins? "Aram doesn't want to play with rubbers! Dooley's affray-ayd! Let's make everyone hate them!" Lord, this is a disgusting, dirty bill. For remember: every freedom *of* is a freedom *from*. I wouldn't vote for this bill if you attached an anti-abortion amendment and reneged on open housing. Not now, not later, not never!

(He sits down to thunderous applause.)

MR BAPP: Vote it down!

MR TOMATO: Clear the floor!

MR DAMIANO: Go home and polish the silver!

MRS BRIMMINS: Willie, I want to talk.

MR CLEGG: Sure. Hold it, Terry.

(They huddle down center. A pool table wheels on. MR CLEGG plays.)

MR CLEGG: Shoot.

MRS BRIMMINS: Is this sort of argument going to continue for the life of the debate, Willie?

MR CLEGG: I don't know what's on their minds, Marge.

MRS BRIMMINS: Oh, yes you do. Mister Majority Leader, you put them up to all this. Whose knuckles did you have to break this time?

MR CLEGG: Ball in the pocket with my own brand of English.

MRS BRIMMINS: But why not, Willie? It's a good bill, a decent bill. Even the pharmacists are in favor of it. You know how much work I've put into it, Willie—three months of research, hundreds of interviews, endless midnight committee meetings with the likes of goodtime Larry Pard—

MR CLEGG: Yeah, but in all that time you never changed one provision of that bill, Marge, not one provision, not one paragraph.

MRS BRIMMINS: Of course I haven't! This bill shouldn't be changed one comma!

MR CLEGG: Know what your problem is, Marge? You got no political savvy. On every issue you always got all your As, Bs and Cs in the right order, all your ones, twos and threes, but you know something? In the three years you been up here you ain't once changed one person's mind about anything. You gotta bend up here, Marge, you gotta flex. You shouldda learned that with all your summa cum laude phi beta kappa.

MRS BRIMMINS: I am not up here for bending and flexing! I am up here because I believe in things!

MR CLEGG: That's it, bring out the sanctimony. That ball in that pocket with my own brand of English. Look, Marge, your bill ain't a bad bill. In fact it's a pretty good bill—I'd probably vote for it myself if I was my own man. But you know who runs things in here—the Speaker. And the Speaker says bury it. So I'm buryin' it. Period. End of caucus.

MRS BRIMMINS: Oh, yes, the silver-haired, golden-tongued Speaker we never see, the Byzantine, celestial Speaker who's always off in the halls somewhere making deals! Why is he never here!

MR CLEGG: The Speaker is a very busy man, Marge. He comes when he's needed. You shouldn't get so emotionally involved with these things.

MRS BRIMMINS: I get emotionally involved with everything I do, Willie Clegg. You know that! Have you forgotten nineteen-hundred and sixty-eight so soon?

MR CLEGG: Yeah, yeah, everybody knows about you and nineteen-hundred and sixty-eight, Marge, but those traitors you played around with in sixty-eight ain't been seen too much lately.

MRS BRIMMINS: Do you know what the happiest day of my life was, Willie?

MR CLEGG: Of course I do, Marge. When you and that dyke named Heather exposed the capitalist system for the sham it really is by dropping those hundred one-dollar bills on the floor of the New York Stock Exchange and causing all the brokers to panic for twenty entire seconds. You only told me that twice a day for five months.

MRS BRIMMINS: Heather was not a dike, Willie! She was a saint! She had a stridency that was the envy of us all, ideals that cut through the fog like a laser.

MR CLEGG: Lest we forget, Marge, ya mind tellin' me once more what it was became of Miss Heather with the ideals that cut through the fog like a laser?

MRS BRIMMINS: Oh, she moved out west....

MR CLEGG: And what does she do for a living, this wonderful woman who dropped the hundred one-dollar bills on the floor of the New York Stock Exchange?

MRS BRIMMINS: She works for a Hollywood game show.

MR CLEGG: She works for a Hollywood game show. So much for nineteen-hundred and sixty-eight. *I* know what the happiest day of *your* life was, Marge, now let me ask you somethin': what was the happiest day of *my* life? *(A pause)* You don't know do you? That was what our relationship was all about.

MRS BRIMMINS: Who cares about the happiest day of your life, Willie! The people need this bill—!

MR CLEGG: Want me to be frank with you, Marge? *(He feels her rear end.)*

MRS BRIMMINS: You get your dampened hands off me, Willie Clegg— I'm not one of your fifteen-dollar Hoboken tootsies!

MR CLEGG: You got a real bad mouth on you, ya know that, Marge? I can get angry at you just sittin' around watchin' television. Everybody up here feels that way—you make us furious just sittin' around! Just because the first day you came up here, somebody whistled at you—

MRS BRIMMINS: Damiano!

MR CLEGG: —and you turned on him with your eyes all crazy and hollered "I will not be whistled at! I am an Assemblyperson!"

MRS BRIMMINS: I will not be whistled at! I *am* an Assemblyperson! What's the matter with that?

MR CLEGG: Bad legislative style, Marge. Ball over there, this time with Swedish.

MRS BRIMMINS: Bad legislative style!—I suppose yours is good legislative style? Pouring dark beer over your head on New Year's, sleeping with a gun under your pillow, and cowering in front of a mysterious Speaker who's never here—that's good legislative style? You're just his patsy, Willie Clegg, his spineless, quivering patsy!

MR CLEGG: I am the Speaker's man! I have more raw power than any man in this Chamber! I control every man on my side of the aisle like a martinet and damn near everybody on yours! And those I can't handle with my jaws, I treat like pool cues! *(He smashes the pool cue into bits, possibly over his head.)* If you was a man, which you may well be despite my experience, I'd make *you* into a pool cue! Now, you wanna know the real reason you ain't gonna get your bill through?

MRS BRIMMINS: *(Thrilled at his display)* How come you were never like that at home?

MR CLEGG: *(Furious, in one breath)* I ain't gonna vote for your bill 'cause the Speaker, wherever he is, wants it killed once and for all and even though I'd probably vote for it if I was my own man 'cause it ain't such a bad bill, ya know why I couldn't use my considerable influence and occasional violence to get anyone else to vote for your bill? *(Another breath)* 'CAUSE EVERYBODY HATES YOU, THAT'S WHY!

MRS BRIMMINS: *(After a pause)* Oh, they don't hate me, Willie. They don't understand me, true—I'm not the usual politician. I'm consistently right on the issues. I'm supported by *The New York Times*, which infuriates everyone. I'm an idealist, a pragmatic realist—

MR CLEGG: You know what ya ain't, though, Mrs Brimmins? You ain't married.

MRS BRIMMINS: Who needs to be married!

MR CLEGG: Ya wanna be a political success up here, Marge, ya gotta be married. Nobody wants to vote for somebody nobody wants. Look at Bella, look at Shirley the Chiz, look at Mary Ann Krupsack—they're all married. I don't know to what, but they're all married.

MRS BRIMMINS: Married! I don't need to be married! No man can hold me down—you saw that! I made your life a living hell, and don't you forget it! I turned you into a waffle!

MR CLEGG: *(Furious)* Ya know if you were funny, I'd start laughin' but you ain't funny, anymore, Marge!

MRS BRIMMINS: I am too funny! I am very funny! In fact, one of my strongest electoral traits is my sense of humor.

MR CLEGG: Oh, yeah, many's the time you'd break me up with one of your snappy oneliners from *The New York Review of Books*. Whadda ya gonna do—get this bill through with jokes?

MRS BRIMMINS: I do have some jokes, yes, now that you mention it, Willie.

MR CLEGG: Oh yeah? This is gonna be good. Get this table outta here! Let's hear one.

(The pool table exits.)

MRS BRIMMINS: What, now? I'm not really prepared.

MR CLEGG: C'mon, ya gotta try 'em out sometime.

MRS BRIMMINS: Uh...well, once upon a time there was this...

MR CLEGG: No, no, not to me, I'm no audience. Tell it to them. C'mon, c'mon. Mister Speaker, the sensual version of Ralph Nader here has something to say on the bill.

ACTING SPEAKER: On the bill, Mrs Brimmins.

MRS BRIMMINS: Thank you, Mister Speaker. Oh, hiya fellas, what's new? What'cha up to? Jets won Sunday, didya see that? Hey, whadda ya say! By the way, got a good joke for you, you know, just to loosen up the air a little. You know me! Well, once upon a time there was a kindly old white-haired couple who lived together in a big white house. One day they decided to adopt a pet to take the place of the children they never had. But they wanted something really special, and after weeks of looking at dogs and cats and boring tropical fish they finally found the perfect thing: a baby octopus. They took him home, gave him his own room, and, because he was such a smart baby octopus, even sent him off to school, because they loved the baby octopus and he loved them. A year passed, and it became time for the baby octopus's birthday. Naturally the old couple wanted to get him something wonderful. And after weeks of looking they found it: a beautiful grand piano. So on the night before his birthday, when the baby octopus was asleep, they snuck the grand piano home, wrapped it up with beautiful ribbons and tags and went to bed too excited to sleep. The next morning they brought the baby octopus sleepily downstairs. He tore off the ribbons and tags gleefully, stepped back, and suddenly a large tear slowly formed in one eye. "Baby octopus, baby octopus, what's the matter?" said the woman, "don't you like your grand piano?" "Yes," said the baby octopus, "but I thought you were going to get me something I could fuck."

(The assemblymen are stunned. They make no reaction.)

MRS BRIMMINS: Think I'm daunted by this? I'm not daunted by this! Can't stand subtlety, can they? Makes them squirm. This room is where elephants go to die! And I don't mean just Republicans. You knew they wouldn't laugh, Willie Clegg, you little sneak, you humpy little gargoyle!

MR CLEGG: That's all you ever do—talk, talk, talk, shake that index finger and talk!

MRS BRIMMINS: You second-rate boss! Third-rate hack!

MR CLEGG: I ain't no boss! I ain't no hack!

MRS BRIMMINS: Boss boss boss! Hack hack hack!

MR CLEGG: This bill's a dead duck and so's anything you ever touch up here again—ever, ever, ever!

MRS BRIMMINS: No you don't, smoke-filled Boss! Oh, I know, you think you've got all the numbers, don't you—Vlitsiak and the West, Damiano the sleaze, Goodtime Larry Pard—but I'll show you! All of you! Nobody's ever seen me with my righteous indignation all a-pump!

MR CLEGG: That's the only way anybody's ever seen you—with your righteous indignation all a-pump! You and that wagging index finger!

MRS BRIMMINS: I'm going to the mat with this one, Willie! I'm going to mash your face in it, you skunky little weasel! See this smile? This smile can melt hearts of the purest gold!

MR CLEGG: I won't even have to lift a finger!!!

(They return to their desks, both smoking with fury. The floor action continues as if uninterrupted.)

MR PARD: Mister Chairman, Mister Chairman!

ACTING SPEAKER: I'm not the Chairman, Mister Pard, I'm the Speaker. The Acting Speaker.

MR PARD: Oh, that's right. Forgive me, Terry, I was lost back there in the Army-McCarthy hearings. Oh, those were grand days, weren't they? Such substance. I want to go back there so much, see those guys again. And Franklin! He ran this state with a glove of iron! Better than the sanctified Herbert Lehman or the Beloved Rocky, stronger than grand old Averell, who's gone deaf now and let his eyebrows grow. *(He speaks in tongues for a moment.)* Ah. Now. Hey! Hey, you, will you yield for a question?

MRS BRIMMINS: You were talking to me, Mister Pard?

MR PARD: Who you think I'm talking to—Harold Ickes? Lord, how I hate you woman. If you only knew. Answer me this question. Does this bill of yours mean that little children can buy these things?

MRS BRIMMINS: No, unfortunately.

MR PARD: Oh, you'd like little children to be able to fool with these things, wouldn't you, Madame Porno! Little children not even old enough yet to shave!

MRS BRIMMINS: I'd like everyone to be able to buy contraceptives if they need to, Mister Pard.

MR PARD: Lord! Little children just buy 'em and blow 'em up anywhere they like?

MRS BRIMMINS: Or not, Mister Pard.

MR PARD: Oh, the hate that's in the air! This is all such a disgrace, like not being able to control your bladder.

MRS BRIMMINS: On the bill, Mister Speaker.

ACTING SPEAKER: It's not your turn, Mrs Brimmins. Mister Bapp.

MR BAPP: Mrs Brimmins, do you have any idea what you're letting loose when you allow advertising free license in a pharmacy? Do you have any idea of the average ad man's mentality?

MRS BRIMMINS: Well...

MR BAPP: Well, I do, Mrs Brimmins, because I'm in advertising myself. Oh, not one of your big Park Avenue firms down in the Big City—I had my chance with those bozos years ago, turned 'em down flat. Oh, they may have all those thousand-dollar-a-day copywriters, all those picture-windows overlooking Saint Patrick's, but I've got something far more valuable than that, Mrs Brimmins! I've got my freedom!

MRS BRIMMINS: Mister Bapp...

MR BAPP: I'm not tied down to big corporations who won't even let you look at the Volkswagen *proofs*! They make me come back six days running, waiting in their reception rooms with a frizzy blonde temp who didn't even know where the men's john was! And me with my portfolio between my legs like a beaten dog! A *dog*! Those people, that city... Just let them try to get their mass transit through up here, by God! I'll show them "Hold please, he's in a meeting, can we get back to you!"

MR PARD: The last man to say "You're welcome" in New York City died in 1925!

MRS BRIMMINS: On the bill, Mister Speaker.

MR BAPP: That woman is out of order, Mister Speaker! No long French lunches for me, no bombed in the middle of the day and having to think up golf jokes or keep up with the fashions all the time, growing moustaches one year, shavin' 'em off the next. No sir, I'm my own boss, I can wear plaid to work if I want; and whenever I want, I can just take the week off in the R V with Dodi and little Dick Junior, free, free as the breeze. Got my own company up in Au Sable Forks. Oh, not a biggie, not a lotta clients, no pretentious initials either, just direct and straight: DICK BAPP ADS. That's all.

MRS BRIMMINS: Mister Speaker, please...!

MR BAPP: You open the door to public advertising, you open the door to public smut! Before you know it, fourteen by thirty-six wallposters, three-dimensional fold-out displays, two-for-one specials on Four Exx lamb membranes, penny sales at Christmas on Trojans and contoured reservoir ends in all the colors of the T V networks. Worst of all—and I know my field—French ticklers with tiny rubber protrusions that can drive a woman or a little child hysterical with pleasure, screaming and banging on the walls...I know all this stuff, Willie. That woman knows it, too. She comes from the Big City.

MRS BRIMMINS: Well, Brooklyn.

MR BAPP: Don't you try to get applause on me! Not while I have the floor! Miss Big City where everything happens first! These Big City admen know all the tricks. Which rubbers make you look younger, which one'll get you into the country club? I mean a little innocent girl like Mister Pard's Melissa!

Entrapped in drugstore ablaze with neon—her nightmare'd never end!
I'm voting my absolute conviction on this one! I'll never change to the end!

MRS BRIMMINS: Mister Speaker, will the gentleman yield?

MR BAPP: No, I will not yield!

MR PARD: Atta boy!

MR BAPP: But I have finished.

MRS BRIMMINS: I'm going under, I'm suffocating.

MR DAMIANO: That woman is out of order, Mister Speaker!

ACTING SPEAKER: I'm afraid you're out of order, Mrs Brimmins. Mister
Damiano.

MR DAMIANO: Thank you, thank you, Mister Speaker. You're very kind. It's
great to be here, just great. And that's why I always say... (Singing a few lines
of a popular "Italian-style" song like Lady of Spain or That's Amore. He breaks
himself up and laughs horribly.) Thank you...thank you...you're beautiful.

MRS BRIMMINS: This isn't happening.

MR DAMIANO: Ha ha ha. Ladies and gentleman, it was so cold today—how
cold was it, Vic? It was so cold today, Ed, that the drunks on the Bowery
were actually lighting their Sterno instead of drinking it! Now that's cold!
Ha ha ha! May the clangbird of paradise put camel chips in your fruit loops!

MR CLEGG: Let's get goin', Damiano.

ACTING SPEAKER: On the bill, Mister Damiano.

MR DAMIANO: Right, ha, ha, right. The tears come to my eyes. Whew. Uh,
as you know, I've given this legislation a great deal of thought, and I think
we're wasting valuable time with all this palaver. The good little people
who are my constituents don't really need any more info about
contraceiving in their pharmacies. They won't read it if it's there, they won't
like it if they do read it, and on the off-chance they do read it and they do
like it, they won't listen. Look to me now, I know—reading about rubbers
just gets people mad. And that's why I always say.... (Singing a few bars of a
romantic latinate ballad) Ha ha ha. You're too kind. But let's get down to the
real reasons for this bill, shall we? Mrs Brimmins, was not this legislation
introduced solely to boost sales of contraceptives in this state? Be honest
now!

MRS BRIMMINS: Of course not.

MR DAMIANO: I submit it is entirely possible that this woman—yes this
woman!—is a bag person for the entire prophylactic scumbag lobby in this
great and revered state! Passage of this bill would increase sales of these
awful things by the millions. This great land would be inundated with
rubbers and their facsimiles within minutes. This woman!

MRS BRIMMINS: Sit down, Damiano! No one listens to you, no one trusts you, you're a fraud, a gamecock!

MR DAMIANO: What do you mean no one trusts me! I'm a lawyer!

MR TOWNSEND: Mister Speaker, I cannot believe what I have seen and heard this morning. The discussion presented here today makes an absolute mockery of the legistative procedure and the concept of democratic representation.

MR PARD: You're the only person here wearing a suit!

MR TOWNSEND: I cannot for the life of me see the logic of any of the arguments against this tiny bill. Furthermore, parenthetically, I lament the absence of wit in this Chamber. You should read the Gladstone-Disraeli debates—now there was wit! Why, on one occasion, my fellow colleagues, Gladstone—six-foot-three, who used to split logs to relieve tension, addressed Disraeli on the Commons floor: "Sir, you will die, I pray either on the gallows or by a terrible disease." To which Disraeli replied, "That depends entirely on whether I embrace your politics or your mistress." That was wit, my friends, and spontaneity!

MR CLEGG: Wit? That wasn't funny. First reason, now wit.

MR TOWNSEND: As to the treatment this fine lady has thus far received—

MR CLEGG: Hey Townsend, c'mere.

MR TOWNSEND: (Crossing to MR CLEGG) This august body claims it realizes there is an epidemic of venereal disease, a critical birth rate, and yet when presented with two viable methods which might relieve these problems— abortion and contraception—most of you are aghast at the former and hysterical at the latter. Yes?

(MR CLEGG suddenly bops MR TOWNSEND on the head with his black jack, then bops him again on his way down. MR TOWNSEND recovers slowly.)

MR TOWNSEND: You really hate this bill, don't you?

MR CLEGG: Yeah, what about you?

MR TOWNSEND: Oh, I don't care so much about it one way or the other.

MR CLEGG: Good. Let me help you up.

MRS BRIMMINS: My brains are fogged with the heat. Platitudes usually on the tip of my tongue have dried up, my paradigms've vanished. I can't talk. I can't think. The only argument that comes to mind is the one about children starving in India, and I'm not sure that's relevant here. I hate to admit it, but I need a gimmick desperately.

MR VLITSIAK: Why is it no one's brought up house and home yet? What about parents? I'm a parent. We all know how embarrassing little kids can be in public, always askin' stupid questions in real loud voices. I mean suppose these things *are* lyin' around and advertised everywhere like he says, and my wife and me and my kid go in, and my kid says to me, real loud, "Hey Dad, hey, Mom, what are those funny lookin' things over there? I think I'll put one on my head"? See how embarrassing that could be? You should think about the plight of the parent for a second. Go ahead. Let's just have thirty seconds of silence while we think about the parents for a minute.

MRS BRIMMINS: Mister Speaker...

MR VLITSIAK: Sshhh!

MRS BRIMMINS: Mister Speaker, will Mister Vlitsiak yield?

MR VLITSIAK: Shh! No!

ACTING SPEAKER: No, he won't. And you're a prune, by the way, woman. I've been meaning to tell you that. Only thirty-eight and already a prune!

CLERK: Y'oughtta gussy yourself up, buy a corsage or something, get a new perm—then maybe somebody'd listen to you in here!

MRS BRIMMINS: But you two are supposed to be neutral.

ACTING SPEAKER: Not when it's a matter of taste.

(MR DAMIANO *whistles at her, but she doesn't see him.*)

MRS BRIMMINS: Who did that! Huh? I will not be whistled at! I am an Assemblyperson!

MR VLITSIAK: You're just making it longer, Mrs Brimmins! I have the floor! It's thirty seconds from the last word that's spoken. Now.

MRS BRIMMINS: I'm rabid! I want to eat my desk!

MR VLITSIAK: Ah ah! Begin again.

(*There is silence for thirty seconds.*)

MR VLITSIAK: Okay.

MRS BRIMMINS: Mister Speaker, I demand to be heard!

ACTING SPEAKER: All right.

MRS BRIMMINS: (*Surprised*) What?

ACTING SPEAKER: You've been asking for the floor, lady, now you got it.

MRS BRIMMINS: Children starving in India! Eight to ten percent unemployment!

MR CLEGG: Oh, please!

MRS BRIMMINS: I hardly know where to begin. But I doubt that anything in history can rival the vapidity of this morning's floor debate...

MR PARD: Don't you quote history to me. I *am* history! I've been a legislator in this Chamber nigh on to seventy years. Some say more. Chairman of Ways and Means, a hammerlock on Rules, and for years before that a harsh and unbending judge. And don't forget—F D R's very best friend.

MRS BRIMMINS: On the bill, Mister Speaker.

ACTING SPEAKER: You're out of order, Mrs Brimmins.

MRS BRIMMINS: But I just got started!

ACTING SPEAKER: That's not my fault, Mrs Brimmins. Mister Damiano.

MR DAMIANO: Mister Speaker. I hardly think this woman's in a position to legislate anything regarding children. She's never had any of her own, never adopted any, to the best of my knowledge she's never even had a miscarriage! And no one knows *what* the story on this *Mister* Brimmins is—nobody's ever seen him, nobody's even ever heard of him. It's only your word, lady, there's no records anywhere.

MRS BRIMMINS: If the hair I'm wearing was a wig, I'd tear it off and throw it on the table, that's how mad I am! This bill isn't for children, it's for adults!

MR PARD: What about my little Melissa?

MRS BRIMMINS: It's to avoid bringing morons like your little Melissa into the world in the first place. This is a bill to help prevent venereal disease and unwanted pregnancies among adults! And it isn't just about contraceptives for men. It isn't even *mainly* about contraceptives for men!

MR DAMIANO: Oh yeah! What's it about then?

MRS BRIMMINS: Contraceptives for women! *(There is a pause.)*

MR DAMIANO: Contraceptives for women? Such as what?

MRS BRIMMINS: Such as what? You can't be serious.

MR DAMIANO: Never mind heaping on the scorn, just such as what.

MRS BRIMMINS: *(Slowly, with passion)* Foams...jellies...pills...suppositories... diaphraghms...

MR PARD: Suppositories?

MRS BRIMMINS: Intra-uterine devices...even voluntary sterilization...

MR PARD: Suppositories...

MRS BRIMMINS: You all think it's about penises! What's complicated about a penis! Nothing! They're either hard or soft, some bend a little to the left, they shrivel up after swimming! That's it! *We* have tubes, valleys, nooks and crannies, hair pin turns...

MR DAMIANO: Mister Speaker! Stop this!

MRS BRIMMINS: *(Her eyes closed, oblivious to everything)* Grand adventure, high dark places...

MR PARD: Suppositories?

MRS BRIMMINS: Roadways, channels, sacks, fluids...

MR VLITSIAK: Mister Speaker! Where is this woman's sense of propriety!

MRS BRIMMINS: Delicious secretions...

MR PARD: Go on, lady, go on!

MRS BRIMMINS: *(Still enraptured)* Cushy softnesses you wouldn't understand...dreams, desires, flights of fancy...

MR BAPP: There is such a thing as legislative good taste!

MRS BRIMMINS: Pockets for our secrets...a pinwheel of lights...

MR TOWNSEND: Never heard such in all my born days!

MR PARD: Shut up, you nick-nack!

MRS BRIMMINS: Canals, poetry, street festivals, grassy knolls...pudendum, pudenda...a good brioche...

MR PARD: Mister Speaker.

ACTING SPEAKER: Mister Pard.

MR PARD: *(Salaciously, his voice low in his throat)* Can I ask you a question witout interruptin' your rhythm?

MRS BRIMMINS: Mmmmmmmmmm.

MR PARD: Are these things...you...put right inside you?

MRS BRIMMINS: Yes, Mister Pard.

MR PARD: Do they give you pleasure?

MRS BRIMMINS: What?

MR PARD: Do they feel good? Y'know, d'you get off on them?

MRS BRIMMINS: No, they don't feel good! They're boring! Sometimes they hurt!

MR PARD: *(Chuckling to himself)* They hurt? Oh, Franklin! Where...could I see this?

MR CLEGG: No you don't, don't fall for it! She's always like that! Brings you to the peak of sexual frenzy and then cuts you short! For five months she tantalized me with sexual imagery and the moment I caved in, she'd start lecturing!

MRS BRIMMINS: What!

MR CLEGG: All that finger-shaking, all that moralizing—you don't know what's in store for you! And all those organ meats! A woman like you's supposed to be a vegetarian, everybody knows that! But not you! All that liver and kidneys, sweetbreads, all those brains, Marge!

MRS BRIMMINS: Brains aren't organs!

MR CLEGG: They are when they're on a plate!

MRS BRIMMINS: This is absurd! I'd never even go out with a man like him! He's too fat for me!

MR CLEGG: Always making me exercise for my heart! My heart's strong as an ox! You just couldn't stand to be seen with a fat man! Well, I'll tell you something—Damiano was right! This woman never had a husband!

MRS BRIMMINS: What!

MR CLEGG: She's never been married or anywhere near it!

MRS BRIMMINS: MISTER SPEAKER! MISTER SPEAKER! POINT OF HIGH PERSONAL PRIVILEGE! I DEMAND THAT MAN'S MICROPHONE BE TURNED OFF! *(She runs to* MR CLEGG, *kicking him and hitting him with her purse.)* How dare you say that, Willie! This is the floor of the New York State Assembly—you're not at home taking a crap with a cigar in your mouth! Take that back, Willie, and on the floor of this Chamber or I'll tell them you were impotent for a hundred fifty days running! And then I'll kill you!

MR CLEGG: But it's true, Marge—you never were married, you did make me exercise though my heart's strong as an ox, and you did lecture all the time!

MRS BRIMMINS: I don't care if it's true or not, Willie, we had a deal! I'm going to find the Speaker wherever he is and tell him you're impotent! Impotent, Willie! Think you'll be the Majority Leader after that, Little Willie Clegg?

MR CLEGG: You got a point.

MRS BRIMMINS: I want this bill, Willie!

MR CLEGG: Your bill's dead, Marge—ya need a gimmick, and you haven't got one! You won't bend, ya won't flex!

MRS BRIMMINS: I do not need a gimmick and I wouldn't resort to one if I did. Now take back this not married stuff, Willie, or I'll shake the rafters and rattle your eyes! Mister Acting Speaker! Him!

MR CLEGG: *(Meekly)* I was only kidding. She was married.

MR DAMIANO: *(Holding up a jar)* Who cares! No one was listening! See this? This is the fetus of an unborn child—a murdered unborn child! Mutilated, chopped up, death by anguish! That's what passage of her contraceptive bill'll do!

MRS BRIMMINS: Put that away, Damiano, you used that in the abortion debate. It's not the same thing. Mister Speaker, I should like to quote Statute 34, Section 8 from *McKinney's Statutes*...

MR PARD: Don't you quote things at me, little sister! I knew the greatest quotemaker ever to stalk this fearful and abundant land! Ladies and gentlemen, our great Governor, Hyde Park's own, I give you Franklin Eleanor Roosevelt! I was with him in Warm Springs, Georgia—oh how those waters loved his legs—his cigarette a-cock, irrepressive grin slapped a-jaunt on his face when he said to me, "Larry, my grand old and probably best friend, the buck stops here. If you don't like the heat stay out of the kitchen." I was with him when—

MRS BRIMMINS: Just a minute, Mister Pard, Franklin Roosevelt didn't say those things—Harry Truman did!

MR PARD: Harry Truman! Harry Truman was a breadstick. I suppose Franklin didn't say "I shall go to Korea" either! O, he was the greatest of men—but not without his enemies. People thought he was stupid. When he first arrived in Washington, know what they said about him? "That man's so dumb he can't wheel and chew gum at the same time." But he showed 'em. "54-40 or fight," "Win with Willkie," "I love a parade"—F D R said 'em all. A dynamo in a rolling box, a razzle-dazzle stand-up comic with an eye to the international, re-elected nine or ten times and still going strong. So don't you ballyhoo me, you little whiner, fine-looking and sizeable-breasted as you may be, hot and juicy as I got when you said "suppository" to me. I'd give half-a-hundred in meaningful money for a quick look at you naked, lambie. I'd suck on you 'til my bugle playing days're numbered. Fine as your secretions may be—

MRS BRIMMINS: Is that really what you think of me, Mister Pard?

MR PARD: Suck, suck.

(She crosses to him, looks down on him.)

MR PARD: What're you doing here?

MRS BRIMMINS: I've come for your vote, Mister Pard.

MR PARD: Come for my vote? You're sure daffy, even for a woman.

*(She rips her blouse open, popping the buttons all over the floor.
Everyone gasps and freezes.)*

MR PARD: Oh my, oh my. *(For a moment, he is paralyzed, then he touches one breast with one hand, then the other breast with the other hand, slowly, and finally, all the fight gone out of him, lays his head on her breasts.)*

MRS BRIMMINS: May I have your vote, Mister Pard?

MR PARD: Yes my dear...if I live to cast it.

MRS BRIMMINS: Mister Damiano? For a touch and a fondle?

MR DAMIANO: I can get this for free, you know!

MRS BRIMMINS: I'm sure you can. But not from me. And not now.

MR DAMIANO: Okay.

MRS BRIMMINS: I've got your word? In front of everybody?

MR DAMIANO: Uh-huh.

MRS BRIMMINS: Upstate and Onondaga?

MR DAMIANO: This better be good.

MRS BRIMMINS: The best.

(He goes to her, touches her breast, and groans.)

MR CLEGG: Jesus, Marjorie!

MRS BRIMMINS: Mister Vlitsiak?

MR VLITSIAK: Yes, yes, and the West, too, just for the asking.

MRS BRIMMINS: Here you go.

(They bury their faces in her breasts.)

MRS BRIMMINS: Boys?

(Everyone onstage except MR CLEGG runs to her and fondles her.)

MRS BRIMMINS: You're the only one left, Willie.

(MR CLEGG starts to rise, but he is interrupted by an amazing burst of lightning and thunder. The SPEAKER appears and mounts the rostrum.)

MR VLITSIAK: Oh my God, it's Mister Fermrlnr—the Speaker!

MR CLEGG: It's the Speaker!

A PAGE: Good Lord, the Speaker!

MRS BRIMMINS: Is that what he looks like?

SPEAKER: *(Calmly)* What's going on, Willie? I trusted you to look after things.

MR CLEGG: *(Nervously)* Oh, it's nothing I can't handle, Mister Speaker. Just the boys having a little go-round. Okay, fellas, Vic, Dickie, knock it off, we got some legislatin' to do.

MR BAPP: But this is such good stuff, Willie!

MR DAMIANO: Y'oughtta see what's under here, Willie!

MR CLEGG: C'mon fellas, knock it off—you're makin' everything look outta hand.

MR DAMIANO: Get outta here!

MR BAPP: Go soak your face!

MR TOWNSEND: Leave us alone!

SPEAKER: I'm very disappointed in you, son. Leave you by yourself a few minutes and the sky rains chaos. Where's the old legislative loyalty?

MR CLEGG: Just a minute, Mister Speaker, I can do it! Remember me and the milk dispute?

SPEAKER: It's too late, Willie.

MRS BRIMMINS: You're dealing with the wrong man, Mister Speaker. I hold sway over the caucus. See?

SPEAKER: Don't be silly. Which do you want, boys—that with her shirt open there, or...THIS! *(He points his finger at* MR CLEGG *and sparks fly out.)*

MR CLEGG: AAAARRRRRGGGGGGHHHHHH! My shoulder!

MR VLITSIAK: Mister Speaker, Mister Speaker, what'd you do?

SPEAKER: I gave him arthritis.

MR VLITSIAK: Now that's what I call clout.

MR BAPP: Talk about your political muscle.

SPEAKER: And THIS! *(He points his fingers at* MR CLEGG *again, and an explosion occurs.)*

MR VLITSIAK: What'd you do this time?

SPEAKER: I took away his newspaper support, indicted his chief fund-raiser for fraud, and re-districted him right out of the ballpark. His next election will be won by a Democrat.

MR CLEGG: No, Mister Speaker!

SPEAKER: Not only that—I also know the secret of fire!

(He either lights a Zippo or strikes a match. A moderate flame shoots up. All the Assemblymen cower and mutter "Ooooo.")

SPEAKER: Well, boys, the choice is simple—me or that raven-haired vixen over there.

(There is a pause. MR DAMIANO *suddenly breaks for his desk.)*

MR DAMIANO: I didn't have nothin' to do with this, Mister Speaker! I was lured over there by Mister Clegg and his honeyed bimbo here under the misnomahension we were going to dole out a little patronage!

MR BAPP: *(Crossing to his desk)* I was on my way to the library for some billboard research! My hands are clean!

MR TOWNSEND: *(Returning to his seat)* I was just looking for my afternoon milk!

MRS BRIMMINS: What about your promises to me?

MR VLITSIAK: *(Moving away from her)* Mister Speaker, Mister Speaker!

SPEAKER: Mister Vlitsiak.

MR VLITSIAK: Mister Speaker, Rabbi Wonderling from West Chazy in beautiful Clinton County has just arrived in the gallery above with remnants of his beatific congregation. Would you be so kind as to extend your customary salutation?

SPEAKER: On behalf of the people of this great state, I welcome Rabbi Wonderling and the remnants of his beatific congregation to this hallowed chamber and hope they enjoy the deliberations.

(Applause)

SPEAKER: See how magnanimous I can be?

(Everyone returns to his desk except MRS BRIMMINS and MR CLEGG.)

SPEAKER: And now the contraceptive vote. The Clerk will call the roll.

CLERK: Aaeby, Gwathmey, Dallenbach, Zysseroso.

SPEAKER: The contraceptive bill is defeated.

MRS BRIMMINS: *(Collapsing at her desk)* No-o-o-o-o-o-o-o-o!

(MR CLEGG sits at his desk.)

SPEAKER: Ah-ah. That's not your seat anymore, Willie. Mister Damiano.

MR DAMIANO: *(Moving right in with his supplies and his fetus and his gifts, sweeping MR CLEGG's onto the floor)* Oh, Mister Speaker, I don't know how to begin my thank-yous.

SPEAKER: It's all right, son. You'll find a way. I've got work to do now boys, and I'd like to vanish as quick as I came.

MRS BRIMMINS: Just a minute, Mister Speaker! What about me? I've done everything I've been told to, I've even learned how to bend up here, how to flex! And the answer is, I just don't get it! What am I doing wrong?

SPEAKER: Why nothing, dear. In fact, I think you're doing rather well, considering. It's just that it's not that kind of club. Right, boys?

(They applaud and laugh. He exits accompanied by mammoth lighting and thunder.)

ACTING SPEAKER: *(Crossing back to his desk)* The calendar of the day. The Clerk will read.

CLERK: Bill 7883, Calendar Number 584, Mister Damiano. An act to legalize the letters G-O-D, God, for imprint on state motor vehicle license plates.

(March music begins quietly here.)

MR DAMIANO: On the bill, Mister Speaker.

ACTING SPEAKER: On the bill, Mister Damiano.

(Loud march music)

END OF PLAY

YANKS 3 DETROIT 0
TOP OF THE
SEVENTH

YANKS 3 DETROIT 0 TOP OF THE SEVENTH was first presented by The American Place Theater, in New York City, on 16 May 1975. The cast and creative contributors were:

EMIL "DUKE" BRONKOWKSI ....Tony Lo Bianco
LAWRENCE "BEANIE" MALIGMA ....Lou Criscuolo
OLD SALT ....Mitchell Jason
LUCKY JOHNSON ....John Horn
DONNA LUNA DONNA ....Lane Binkley
LINCOLN LEWIS III ....Albert Hall
GUIDO MOROSINI ....Robert Lesser
BRICK BROCK ....William Bogert
BASEBALL PLAYERS ....Warren Sweeney, Jaime Tirelli

Director .... Alan Arkin
Scenery ....Henry Millman
Lighting ....Roger Morgan
Costumes .... Susan Denison

CHARACTERS

EMIL "DUKE" BRONKOWKSI
LAWRENCE "BEANIE" MALIGMA
OLD SALT
LUCKY JOHNSON
DONNA LUNA DONNA
LINCOLN LEWIS III
GUIDO MOROSINI
BRICK BROCK
BASEBALL PLAYERS

(EMIL "DUKE" BRONKOWKSI, *dressed in the uniform of the New York Yankees, is in the middle of his windup on the pitcher's mound at Yankee Stadium, right of stage center. He is thirty-six years old and husky. His teammates are all offstage. An electronic score board would be helpful to keep the audience informed of balls and strikes, but it isn't essential. The bases are located either in the audience or on a platform suspended above the stage or on the stage itself. The noise of the crowd is constant (silent only once during the play), reacting wildly when the Yankees do well and silently or unfavorably when they do poorly. When DUKE is not addressing the other characters in the play, he is speaking to himself, and the effect should be one of the audience overhearing him—the actor playing DUKE should not speak directly to the audience, and he should not perform any activity which a real ballplayer would not perform on a real mound, except in his scene with DONNA LUNA DONNA. The ball is real. So is the rubber. So are the bases. DUKE pitches to his catcher BEANIE offstage left. Miming the ball and pitching into the audience have proved unsuccessful.)*

UMPIRE: *(Offstage)* STEE-RYE!

(The crowd approves enthusiastically. The ball comes back to him and he rubs it up, digs into the mound, and otherwise makes himself at home. He steps on the rubber and winds up and pitches again.)

UMPIRE: STEE-RYE!

(The crowd approves and the ball comes back to him once more.)

DUKE: Well, it's goin' pretty good now.

(He winds up and fires another pitch and the crowd applauds wildly again.)

UMPIRE: *(Hoarsely)* STEE-RYE!

(The ball comes back from first base side.)

DUKE: One down. Slider's workin' good. Lookin' good. Always could get 'em by Carvalho. Who's this?

P A SYSTEM: Number 23, the third baseman, Butch Dietrich.

DUKE: Oh, yeah, Dietrich. Bounced to short in the first, popped up to Bubba in the fourth. Inside and high fast one or he'll go for a good curve, or go ahead and scroojie him. If I had a scroojie. *(Looking offstage at his catcher, he shakes off two signs, then winds up and throws.)*

UMPIRE: STEE-RYE!

(The crowd approves.)

DUKE: God am I on. I can't wait! (*Ball comes back. He fiddles with the rubber,
the rosin bag, and so on. He shakes off a sign, then steps off the rubber.*) That's the
one thing Beanie's never learned—how to call 'em for me. He can call 'em
for everybody else on the staff but he can't call 'em for me. When m'slider's
hot, it can't be hit. He should know that after all these years we been
together, but he don't. Aaron couldn't hit my slider when it's hot.
Carew couldn't bit my slider when it's hot. But Beanie don't know that yet.
(*He shakes off two more signs.*) C'mon Beanie, c'mon, the slider, the slider.
I don't care if he is looking for it, no one's gonna hit this Polack's slider
today, particularly no German. Atta boy.

(DUKE *pitches. The crowd doesn't react. The ball comes back.*)

DUKE: Well, it's okay, it's okay, it's only one and two, one and two, I'm way
ahead of him. Just missed with it. He was goin' for it, he was gonna bite,
checked it just in time. It's goin' okay now. Don't wanna talk about the
whole season, of course, but right now it's goin' okay. Somehow I knew it,
too. This morning I got up and told Jeannie, "My arm feels like a cannon
today, hon, it's my day in the slot, and I'm gonna clock 'em." And here I am,
top of the seventh, a perfect game under m'belt, a real return to m'form of
sixty-five-sixty-six, a complete reversal of what was destined to be m'swan
song to the big time. I'm so happy I can hardly keep myself together. Just
two innings to go after this one-eight lousy outs—and I can write my own
ticket. One or two games like this one, I can write my own ticket. And so far,
no pangs of fear. Usually 'bout this time little terrors confront me, little
doubts gnaw at my neck. But not today. Coupla pangs of hunger, maybe,
but no pangs of fear. And I'm okay at home, too. As the late, great Ed
Sullivan used to say, "Are you all right at home? Then you're all right."
I got a wonderful wife named Jeannie watching me on the tube, two fine
boys named Mitch, seven, and Eric, six, one good with puzzles, the other of
a more artistic bent, strong and loyal friends, a rambling, two-story white
Victorian house in Roslyn that's almost paid for, I got three new Buicks,
m'sixty-nine Jag, a Black and Decker Self-Starting Roto 380, two good trees
planted outside, plenty of electrical appliances, ham radio band W2-LEO,
barbecue aprons with funny slogans on 'em, lotsa hobbies, and just today,
everything's startin' to look up like a bandit. Triumph's in m'blood. I'm
financially secure (it looks like), I'm puttin' in my sixth year doin' P R in
the off-season for Connecticut Federal and my roast beef franchise's doin'
beautiful. Some people might even consider me a pillar of society—Roslyn
society, whatever that means. Yessir, startin' today, after five years in the
sewer, life's lookin' grand. I'm comin' back—all the way back. This keeps
up, m'free agency next year'll be a bonanza!
  Back to business, now, back to business. Can't wander around like that,
no goin' back to bad habits. Let's see: Beanie's gonna ask me for the curve;
Dietrich's gonna expect the curve; he knows Beanie won't ask for the
fastball so that means the change-up's out. Sinker's murder, and I haven't

got a scroojie, so I say, guess what, the slider. Won't be ready for it four times in a row. The curve. I haven't had a grip on the curve since Norm Cash on this very same Detroit Tiger baseball team six years ago. *Then* I had a grip on the curve. But that was some year all around. Awright, awright, concentrate, concentrate. *(He looks offstage at the catcher.)* The curve. *(He shakes it off, looks again.)* Not again! *(He shakes it off again.)* C'mon, c'mon, Beanie. *(He nods, winds up and pitches. The crowd makes no reaction.)* Okay, okay, okay, boy, okay, okay, okay, okay, it's all right, all right, waste a few, waste a few, all right. Wind wasn't right on it. Remember: top of the seventh, nobody's even reached base yet, you're pitchin' better than *any time* any year, better'n *any pitcher* on *any team* this whole year! The fire's back, too, the perfect eye, the control, the confidence; knock this one off, you'll be right back in the Razor Blade League—six hundred-and-fifty thousand dollar buy-out from Rheingold or Gillette's New Foamy. Just don't lose your grip and you're in.

(The ball comes back.)

DUKE: Know what I like about baseball? Part of it's that it's calm, it's dependable, it isn't scary. It's got good, simple, faithful structure, a structure you can't count on. But most of all I like it 'cause it's a game of individuals. One against one. Hitter against pitcher; fielder against ball; runner against time. Oh, you can have teamwork in baseball, but you don't have to depend so much on blocks and tackles from guys who don't care; in baseball you always know just who's at fault. Like now...it's just me against this one guy, a former Nazi, Butch Dietrich. I love baseball. Okay, okay, now just concentrate on this boy. High and inside with the slider, or try the scroojie, which I don't have, Goddamnit. He's a little nothing, doesn't know his bat from a bratwurst, battin' .207, something like that, a little lampshade-making Kraut. It's all he can do to pick up the occasional gounder at third. He couldn't hit me today if I was throwin' tomatoes. ZA CHANCELLOR OF EIGHTY-SIXTH STREET! YOU ARE NUSSING! He's nothin'. Okay, Beanie, breeze me in there, boy, make his little Deutsch balls sing in the wind at my smoke. I'l do whatever you want Beanie boy, whatever you want. You call it, I'll throw it. Whatever you want. *(He gets the signal.)* Jesus Christ, the curve. Can't you have a little faith in my slider, for Chrissake? I don't know who's more against me, you know that, Beanie—you or the Bader-Meinhof! The slider, Beanie, call for the slider, just this once more, he'll never know it's comin'. Atta boy.

(He winds up and pitches. The crowd murmurs.)

DUKE: Goddamn son of a fuckin' bitch and a cunt and an oozing thigh and a fart, shit, piss, and a split beavoon, what the hell's happenin' to my slider?

(The ball comes back to him. He throws his rosin bag down.)

DUKE: Jesus, Jesus, Jesus. Can't lose m'slider. There goes my comeback, there goes m'no-hitter, the free agency'll be humiliating! All I've got's m'slider. If I lose that...I don't get Donna Luna Donna if my slider goes. Rizzuto's up there, jackin' up enthusiasm, puttin' me down like a bandit. "Holy cow, Duke Bronkowski's got himself in a little Polack jam here, folks! He's pitched five straight sliders and it looks like he just lost his toehold! The string's run out!" Lost his toehold. The string's run out. Baseball talk'll turn your brain to meatloaf. I mean "bunt"—what the hell does "bunt" mean? How d'ya like this, Des Moines? *(Blatantly scratches his testicles)* T V executives go crazy when balls are scratched on the tube. They don't acknowledge them. For all they know, I got a mixed floral arrangement down here. Once more, Des Moines. Or Queens, I guess, I know this ain't goin' any farther'n Queens. Jesus, I don't know. It's happened so often like this before. Goes real good for a while, then my slider goes, and I lose it. All right, all right, come on, easy...you're a seasoned ballplayer, fourteen years' experience under your belt, you're a *veteran*. Just breathe in...slowly. Quit talkin' to yourself. That's it. Hooo. That was a little glimpse of the fear I mentioned earlier. I get frightened pretty easy these days.

(He steps on the rubber, shakes off a sign, then steps off the rubber and rubs up the ball. BEANIE, *the catcher, enters.)*

BEANIE: Hey, whadda ya doin'? Why ya keep shakin' me off?

DUKE: Beanie, you gotta ask for my slider.

BEANIE: Oh, yeah? Why?

DUKE: *(Quickly)* 'Cause I wanna set a record for the most sliders ever pitched at four-o-five on a sunny afternoon to a Nazi third baseman from Detroit! I don't know, I wanna pitch it 'cause it's goin' good!

BEANIE: You missed with it three times, Duke. Hey, you're not getting crutty on me are you?

DUKE: No, no, I'm feeling great!

BEANIE: 'Cause sometimes from a certain angle you're looking sorta fragged, and I don't got time for no problems today, Duke.

DUKE: There are no problems—I'm pitching great, Beanie!

BEANIE: 'Cause I mean, listen to this. My twelve-year-old wants a snowmobile—a snowmobile! He's tired of his Honda—his gang says bikes are out—now he announces he wants a snowmobile.

DUKE: Your boy's got a motorcycle? He's only twelve!

BEANIE: Sure, all the kids got 'em. That's only openers. Try this. Ya know that children's therapist from Toledo I been doin'? Bobbi? Suddenly she wants a *pied-a-terre* to keep it outta the papers. A *pied-a-terre!* An' yesterday, Rowena tells me she wants custody of the kids, the house, and the legal right to tell me when I can quit playin' ball. To tell me when I can quit playin' ball!

DUKE: You getting a divorce?

BEANIE: No.

DUKE: Then why'd she say all that?

BEANIE: Just feeling her oats.

DUKE: But *you're* supposed to be takin' care of *me*, Beanie, you're supposed to be listenin' to *my* problems, but fortunately I don't have any today....

BEANIE: Whatever they are, you'd better get over 'em, fella, or Old Salt'll be out here like the Fordham Flash.

DUKE: Old Salt.

BEANIE: Yup. An' quit shakin' me off, or Old Salt'll be out here for that, too.

DUKE: Can I throw m'slider?

BEANIE: Think I care? Sure. Throw it all afternoon. I don't care.

(BEANIE *trots off.* DUKE *steps back on the rubber, shakes off two signs.* BEANIE *runs out again.*)

BEANIE: What's goin' on? Quit shakin' me off! You're makin' me look bad!

DUKE: How can I quit shakin' you off unless you ask for my slider? We had a deal.

BEANIE: All right, all right, I'll ask for your goddamn slider.

DUKE: How come you didn't ask for it just now?

BEANIE: I wasn't sure you meant it. (*Starts to trot off*)

DUKE: Hey, Beanie.

BEANIE: Yeah?

DUKE: I always wanted to know—how come you call yourself Beanie?

BEANIE: Oh, well, a ballplayer's gotta have a nickname, you know that. Just like yours, "Duke." Otherwise you don't fit in, people forget you. Announcers never mention you if your name is John. You know, something like Boog or Yogi or The Babe, something that's fun to say over and over again. Or, 'course, a good way is to be born with a good name—like Mickey or Bebo. Bebo's a great name for a jock—people think of you as a kid all the time, a son. Y'know, Hey, Bebo, Hey, Bebo, Bebo baby.

DUKE: Yeah, Bebo is great name for a jock. Jimmy and Rickey are okay, too.

BEANIE: That's right, Jimmy's real good. Even Jim ain't bad. Chico's real good if you're a Spic. There are just some names that can really increase your earning potential.

DUKE: But why'd you choose Beanie?

BEANIE: Why not?

DUKE: Beanie's so...coy.

BEANIE: Beanie ain't coy.

DUKE: Sure it is. You could just as easily have called yourself Pretty Boy or Cutie Pie or...Judith-Marie. Really, what's the matter with Cutie Pie? Cutie Pie Maligma. Gets the same idea across.

BEANIE: All right, look: I won't ask for nothin' but your Goddamn slider. Just don't shake me off, got it?

DUKE: Right.

(BEANIE *trots off, fuming.*)

DUKE: Cutie Pie Maligma. If anything, he should change his last name. Okay, let's see. Dietrich the Nazi. Slider high and inside or the nonexistent scroojie.

(DUKE *winds up and pitches. The ball is hit a few feet upstage of him. He dives after it acrobatically, retrieves it and fires it offstage to first base. The crowd goes wild, indicating the runner is out.* DUKE *picks himself up and heads back to the mound. In an instant, two players, a trainer,* BEANIE *and* OLD SALT *run out to him, all yelling and carrying on.*)

VARIOUS AD LIBS: Hey, hey, hey ya Duke. Hey ya, hey ya, how ya doin'? Great play, Duke-o!

(*The trainer rubs* DUKE's *shoulders avidly, then dusts off his uniform, offers him a drink, and combs his hair. Finally, he splashes talcum on his face.* OLD SALT *and* DUKE *walk around the mound as the* TRAINER *massages* DUKE.)

OLD SALT: A great play, son. How's the shoulder?

DUKE: Fine, fine. But I gotta tell you, every time Beanie comes out here, I feel worse, Old Salt.

OLD SALT: Walk it off, boy, walk it off.

DUKE: Sometimes, he makes me think about problems, and I can't walk 'em off.

OLD SALT: Do as I tell ya, boy, I know what I'm talkin' about. Walk 'em off, boy, walk 'em off.

DUKE: I don't know if I can.

OLD SALT: You goddamn college kids! Can't get anything straight! Can't just get on with it! You never shouldda gone there. College is the source of all your troubles.

DUKE: I know, I know. But I soon saw the error of my ways; I left after two years.

OLD SALT: Makes no difference. Two months is enough to catch the taint. What good d'it do you? *(Quickly)* Can you tell me for sure that it was the decline of the Baltic herring industry at the end of the fifteenth century that led to the dissolution of the Hanseatic League? No. D'ya know the chemical formula for common table salt or the subtrahend if the remainder is factorial three and the minuend factorial seventeen? No. Can you explain fully the symbolism of the bar of soap in Bloom's pocket in *Ulysses*? *(Pause)* Well, can ya?

DUKE: No.

OLD SALT: There y'are—what good d'it do ya? Ya didn't learn nothin', you don't remember nothin'—all it did was make it impossible for you to come to any conclusions, am I right? There's nothin' worse than an indecisive jock.

DUKE: I know, I know, but I've always been like this, even before college. I was like this in high school.

OLD SALT: High school? That's another thing!

DUKE: I know I did wrong, I know I did, but that's all in the past. I may have some troubles pretty soon, sir.

OLD SALT: Remember, my boy: Only fools and chickens scratch at yesterday's feed. From now on, Goddamnit, you remember: Too much bookin', not much cookin'.

DUKE: Yes, sir. But what about the trouble I may be about to be in?

OLD SALT: You're not gonna be in any trouble, son. You got two down, top of the seventh, you're seven outs away from a perfect game! That's not trouble! Beanie's in trouble! Don't look a gift horse in the mouth, boy. Remember: He who plants sproutlings before breakfast will reap mung beans by noon. Your slider's in there tight, your form's good, what more could you ask?

DUKE: I don't know exactly where I'm headed, Old Salt. I had two good years for you in sixty-four, and sixty-five, and sixty-six I led the majors with an E R A of one-point-four-one and won twenty-four games. I got married in sixty-six, confident of my future, ready to raise a family and settle down. Sixty-seven was okay but not great—a big disappointment according to the Associated Press. Then I started to crumble. My fastball lost its zip, I couldn't get the rotation on my curve, I never learned a scroojie—and it's too late to start now. All I've got left is my slider and maybe a knuckleball somewhere by the fireplace in my future.

OLD SALT: See how I'm listenin' to ya? Watch. Can ya see it?

DUKE: Yeah.

OLD SALT: Remember: The best talker is a good listener.

DUKE: Yeah, but ya see—

OLD SALT: Cross at the green, not in-between. Now what's botherin' you, boy? See me listenin'?

DUKE: I don't think I can do it, Old Salt.

OLD SALT: You'll see—the eagle that flies lowest flies longest.

DUKE: I never had any luck. I never had the charisma like Namath or the press like Mantle, or even the arrest record like Lance Rentzel. That can mean an awful lot to a fella. I never made the big money in my prime and now I'm past my prime and what if I can't get back on the track? I know I woulda been shipped back to the minors if this team weren't so rotten.

OLD SALT: It's that goddamn college shit! All this crap's in your head, boy!

DUKE: I know it is! That's the problem!

OLD SALT: Pshaw, boy, pish-shaw, pis-haw, washpi. You got a perfect game goin', son, a no-hitter, a shutout, what else could you want?

DUKE: I just feel it inside—my game's goin' into the toilet. I don't get it— I'm almost thirty-seven years old and the person I admire most is still Holden Caulfield.

OLD SALT: Who the hell is that? Now don't be crazy. Just pitch good. Now let me pat you on the ass and let's get on with it. I'm sick of this.

DUKE: Can't you tell me anything? I'm so confused.

OLD SALT: Why, sure, son, I wouldn't let you down. I have been waitin' for this the whole game! Ready? Ready. I HAVE CONFIDENCE IN YOU, SON. I'M THE MANAGER OF THE NEW YORK YANKEES, AND I HAVE CONFIDENCE IN YOU! That's all you need, boy. Repeat after me: CONFIDENCE. I HAVE OLD SALT'S CONFIDENCE, AND THAT MEANS THE WORLD TO ME.

DUKE: *(Depressed)* Confidence, right. Thank you, sir.

OLD SALT: Come on, boy, let's hear the old pep—I HAVE OLD SALT'S CONFIDENCE! HEY HEY!

DUKE: *(Embarrassed)* Okay, I have Old Salt's confidence. Whadda ya think, I'll stick to the slider...

OLD SALT: Louder! More gusto! HEY HEY! I HAVE OLD SALT'S CONFIDENCE!

DUKE: I HAVE OLD SALT'S CONFIDENCE.

OLD SALT: AGAIN! AGAIN! I HAVE OLD SALT'S CONFIDENCE! HEY HEY!

DUKE: I HAVE OLD SALT'S CONFIDENCE!!

OLD SALT: ATTABABY POOCHIE! LET'S HEAR IT JES' ONE MORE TIME FOR THOSE COMMIES IN HAVANA. I HAVE OLD SALT'S CONFIDENCE!

DUKE: I HAVE OLD SALT'S CONFIDENCE!

OLD SALT: All right, then. New lemme pat you on the ass and let's get on with it.

(They all leave, patting DUKE *on the ass and making additional cheerleading noises.)*

DUKE: I don't believe it. Old Salt? Old Saltine. That man lives for one thing: his obituary. Just keeps pumpin' out those quotes. Sooner or later he's bound to hit the right one—and then there'll be nobody around to take it down. Boy, was he furious when Vince Lombardi died first. Now he's just staying alive to put some distance between the two legends. If he was smart, he'd kick off this afternoon before anyone finds out what a goon he is. YANKEE MANAGER DIES AT SIXTY-FIVE OF EXCESS WISDOM. NATION MOURNS LOSS. PRESIDENT EXTOLLS VIRTUES: "TO THE BEST OF MY KNOWLEDGE, OLD SALT NEVER URINATED IN HIS ENTIRE LIFE—AN EXAMPLE, ONE OF MANY GOOD ONES, FOR THE YOUTH OF AMERICA."*(He yells to the umpire offstage.)* Hey, can I throw a couple? *(He quickly throws two pitches, each time limbering up his bruised shoulder. The ball doesn't return after the second pitch.)* I know this sounds silly, but whenever he does that "I have confidence" routine, I actually feel a lot better. Some of the brambles get cleared away. But it doesn't last. Lookit this team. I never felt so insecure in my life. If it hadn't been for those back-to-back homers by Popeye and Bruno in the second, I'd be in the toilet already. They came through. Not like my coconut buddy at third. Lookit him. All he does is flash his gums and say, "I'ng no Paneech, I'ng Coob'n." Lookit him? Lookit me—I just dove after that Nazi's grounder like a bus was after my boy Mitch. I could've dislocated my shoulder! Oh, this is a dopey game.

(The ball comes back.)

DUKE: There's no strategy in baseball. You know what the strategy is in baseball? When you got a right-handed pitcher, you put up a left-handed batter; when you got a left-handed pitcher, you put up a right-handed batter. That's it. That's all the strategy there is. I used to be so excited with all this, but I'm not anymore. I'm excited...but I'm also bored. I'm bored with the excitement. When I first came up, whew, when I was doin' good, this game meant everything to me. I could lick anyone. Now it's just bases...changin' clothes...fake dirt...sixty thousand paid and furious fans dyin' for me to fail. Well, I'll show them! Breathe. Oh, where's Donna Luna Donna, when I need her? She's outside guardin' m'sixty-nine Jag right now, listenin' to the game on the radio and protectin' my hubcaps from the Cuban's cousins. She's my Texas groupie, and I think about her all the time. What I like best about her is her body. What she likes best about me is that

I'm famous. C'mon, c'mon back to business, back to business. Let's see, who's this?

P A SYSTEM: Number forty-one, the second baseman, Lucky Johnson.

DUKE: How d'ya like that—a WASP. What can you say bad about a WASP—they're all perfect. They have so many advantages. They own all the banks; they don't have to take life seriously; they can be dull and nobody cares. They're so much better than other folks—leaner; tighter; sharper round the edges. I'm not a WASP. I'm a Polack. Not a Pole; not Polish—Polack. I get very suspicious of people who call me "Polish." Y'know inside they're all thinking "starched bowling shirt, six to turn the ladder, count the basement windows and multiply by nine..." The main advantage WASPs got is that there's so many of 'em. All those governors! *(Suddenly dejected)* I can't fight that. It's all out of my hands anyway, I'm fed up with this. I wanna take a shower. I'm gonna let him hit. I'm gonna give up my perfect game and my no-hitter and just get the hell outta here. It's all outta my hands anyway. I'm gonna give up my razor blade commercials and my whole economic future and I'm just gonna let Lucky Johnson hit this next one as far as he can make it go. WASPs are the chosen people and they should be allowed certain graces in times of stress. Let's see...Lucky baby: switch-hitter, popped to Bruno in the first, bounced to Popeye whenever it was the last time he was up. Can't hit it low and away 'cause he steps into the bucket, so we'll put it right across his letters where he can't miss it, and we'll make it a medium fast one—which is the only kind of fast one I can throw anyway. *(He shakes off a sign.)* He'll never ask for the right one. Gimme another sign, Cutie Pie. The hell with it. Here comes Sunday, Lucky Boy.

(He winds up and throws. The crowd cheers. DUKE is amazed.)

DUKE: He missed! That was the fattest pitch I ever threw anyone! Right down the alley! Helen Keller coulda hit that one with a fishing rod! An' he missed it! Boy, Old Salt is a Goddamn genius. If I can get by with that sort of stuff, I got it knocked. I could put a wing on the house, I could keep a little apartment in the Village for snatch, I could even give Jeannie a bauble of some kind from Bulgari. Let's go, baby. He's no better'n me. That's all the charity you get, you pasty-faced bigot. Hoo, I'm hot today. C'MON, CUTIE PIE, THROW THE BALL BACK. *(The ball comes back.)* Old Lucky Boy, the golden WASP must have been droolin' for my slider. Well, this time he's gonna get it. All right, here we go, Lucky Johnson, outside and low. *(He pitches. The ball is hit to third. DUKE follows the ball along the ground, then the throw to first, narrating the play all the time.)* 'At's it, little bingle along the ground, scoop it up, baby, fire it right on target, a perfect strike, easy out...SAFE?!

(The crowd boos loudly. To Camacho:)

DUKE: You stupid Camacho, you pulled him off the bag! You blew my perfect game! I don't believe it! I just don't believe it! Goddamit, you come over here, you make us advertise our beer in Spanish, you paint all your walls green, you get us all addicted to plantains—and now you and your neon gums ruin my perfect game! I'll get you for this, Gummo!

(The ball comes back to him from the first base side.)

DUKE: All right, all right, who cares, who cares? It's my old buddy, the self-fulfilling prophecy...although if I'm gonna be self-destructive, you stupid banana, lemme do it on my own! Who cares, still a no-hitter, still a shutout, still a big, big victory. This ain't even a jam. Who's this?

P A SYSTEM: Number twenty-two, the left fielder, Lincoln Lewis.

DUKE: Ah, one of our dusky brethren, da highly mo-bile Lincoln Lewis Da Third. He get mah singin', dancin', watermelon pitch, right down the alley. How did I get to be such a bigot? I mean I should be watchin' his hands, figurin' out what he can hit, where the sun is in his eyes, but I'm doin' a riff on handkerchief heads. It's this game—makes you do it. No it isn't. It's because I don't know what to throw him, and I'm scared. Is that all racism? Just don't know what to throw people? I gotta focus on the other stuff. It's just self-defense. Concentrate, concentrate. Still got a no-hitter, still got a shutout, still a big win for ya. Lincoln Lewis...popped to Felez in the second...hey! He's one of my strikeouts! That's right! Don't pitch him low and outside...don't pitch him high and inside. Where the hell did I pitch this guy? On the hands? Across the letters? With my eyes closed? I forget. A slider, I guess. Or a scroojie, which I don't have. Ask for my slider, Cutie Pie, ask for my slider. *(He shakes off two pitches.)* ASK FOR MY SLIDER, CUTIE PIE!

(BEANIE marches out.)

BEANIE: All right, that's it, knock it off, cut out this Cutie Pie shit. My name's Lawrence or Larry. My friends call me Beanie. You can call me Mister Maligma. Mister Maligma.

DUKE: Gee, I'm sorry. I didn't know it meant so much to you.

BEANIE: All right, then. From now on, Mister Maligma.

DUKE: But I can't do that. Who ever heard of a pitcher calling his catcher "Mister"? I can't go around calling you "Mister Maligma."

(BEANIE takes the ball.)

BEANIE: If you don't, the next time I throw this back, there's gonna be a grenade in it. And don't think I ain't man enough to do it.

DUKE: Gee. Okay.

(BEANIE leaves. DUKE realizes he doesn't have the ball.)

DUKE: Uh...Mister Maligma? Could I have the ball please?

(The ball comes back to him.)

DUKE: I wonder if the President has to put up with stuff like this? Command is sure lonely. Okay, one more for Des Moines, and we're off.

(DUKE scratches his testicles, winds up and goes into the stretch. LUCKY JOHNSON is on first base.)

LUCKY: You've haven't got it anymore! You're finished! Finished!

DUKE: Whew, I forgot how rattled I get with someone on base. Concentrate now.

LUCKY: You're a failure as a man, a failure as a husband, a lousy father, and you can't mambo!

DUKE: My whole life's been like this. Just as I start goin' up the corporate ladder, wham, the pressure gets me. Rizzuto starts watchin' me up there, I can feel his eyes on the front of my face. I can feel that camera cutting to my right cheek, then my left cheek, then a close-up of the sweat on my forehead. I can't get away from it—that damn camera sees everything: my arm, my lack of concentration, I'm always on the spot. I freeze at the pinnacle. I'm afraid of success, that's it.

LUCKY: Mambo! Mambo!

DUKE: *(Dreamily)* Sixty-seven was sure a good year. The curve had rotation, the fastball had zip...I got the loan for the fast food franchise, Jeannie's breasts didn't sag. Everyone knew my name, even at away games. I could've been dating Julie Christie in sixty-seven. All right, all right, concentrate, concentrate.

LUCKY: Mambo! Mambo!

(DUKE winds up and throws a wild pitch. The crowd groans and LUCKY trots down to second base.)

DUKE: Oh, no. A wild pitch. Nothin' looks as bad as a wild pitch. Jesus. Okay, okay, no problem. You're a *veteran*, a fourteen-year veteran, you've been through situations like this dozens of times. Dozens. Yeah, but what did I do to get out of them?

LUCKY: You're through! You're too old, Bronkowski! Can't even find the box! You're undisciplined, scatterbrained, inarticulate!

DUKE: Jesus, what's he sayin'? YOU GOT ON BASE ON A GIFT, YOU KNOW! That son-of-a-bitch don't bother me. To think I almost gave him a hit. Sure wish I could think of something mean to say to a WASP. All you can do is insult their taste and hope for the best. THE KINGSTON TRIO'S NEVER GETTING BACK TOGETHER AGAIN! THANKSGIVING IS

BO-RING! JEWS ARE SMARTER! Oooo, that'll get 'em. JEWS ARE SMARTER! MORE CREATIVE! They don't like *that*.

LUCKY: Don't try to get out of it! You just can't throw anymore! You can't even pay for the furniture! What about that couch, huh? Poor Jeanie was in tears! You're a washout, a wet rag, a failure!

DUKE: Gee, these insults are awfully personal. Whatever happened to "Hey, pitch, hey pitcher"? Ah, forget it. Two down, you still got your no-hitter. *(He goes into the stretch, looks at second.)*

LUCKY: Failure! Fraud! *(He steps off the rubber.)*

DUKE: In sixty-seven I made two *Rapid Shave* commercials and a public service spot against T B. I barely lost out on an Oldsmobile radio spot to Sandy Koufax which grossed him thousands. I had an agent and a lawyer and broads with thighs of honey all year long, whenever I wanted, way before groupies. I started to hang out with Billy and The Mick, did a spot on the Carson Show, almost got invited to the White House. I should've known it wouldn't last. C'mon, c'mon, concentrate, concentrate, no more talkin'. You're behind on him two and oh. I'll throw whatever you want, Mister Maligma. Boy, the first six innings were fantastic, weren't they? Got 'em down one-two-three in the first, one-two-three in the second, one-two-three in the third, and so on. Christ, I not only live in the past, I live in the past few minutes.

(He goes into the stretch. LUCKY *dances off second.* DUKE *pitches and the crowd groans again.* BEANIE *comes trotting out.)*

BEANIE: What's happenin' to you?

DUKE: I threw what you wanted, didn't I? You asked for the curve and I threw it, didn't I?

BEANIE: You asked for the curve and I threw it, didn't I, what?

DUKE: What? What what?

BEANIE: You asked for the curve and I threw it, didn't I, Mister Maligma?

DUKE: Oh, Christ.

BEANIE: You asked for the curve and I threw it, didn't I, Mister Maligma? Say it.

DUKE: You asked for the curve and I threw it, didn't I, Mister Maligma...this is stupid! I feel stupid.

BEANIE: Well, you should. It's your own fault, you know.

DUKE: Look, Beanie, Mister Maligma, I'm sorry, I didn't mean to make fun of your name—but I got problems.

BEANIE: Everybody's got problems. You'll just have to walk 'em off, just like Old Salt says. Did I ever tell you about my boy? He's twelve and he wants a snowmobile.

DUKE: Yeah, you told me.

BEANIE: And Rowena wants custody of the house, our children, and my career.

DUKE: I know, I know.

BEANIE: And Bobbi, the children's therapist, wants a *pied-a-terre* to keep it outta the papers.

DUKE: I know all this!

BEANIE: Well, those are problems! Those are real problems!

DUKE: But they're the only ones you got! Anybody can solve those problems!

BEANIE: Oh, yeah, Mister Dear Abby? How?

DUKE: Don't buy your son a snowmobile, you're bigger than he is and you can beat him up; don't worry about Rowena, you're not gonna get a divorce; and get dopey Bobbi a *pied-a-terre*. What could that cost in Dayton? Okay?

BEANIE: Not bad.

DUKE: Now your problems are solved.

BEANIE: Not so fast—what about my slump?

DUKE: Keep your eye on the ball.

BEANIE: Okay. Now what's the matter with you?

DUKE: I'm suffering from malaise, I feel downtrodden. I have problems of the spirit. Ya see what's weird—I know what the problems are...I even know what's causin' 'em. I just don't know what to do about them.

BEANIE: Aww, it's all in your head.

DUKE: I know that! That's the problem!

BEANIE:Well, you better do somethin' about 'em or Old Salt'll be out here faster'n the Fordham Flash.

(BEANIE *pats* DUKE *on the ass and starts to leave.*)

DUKE: Hey, Mister Maligma!

BEANIE: You can call me Beanie—you've learned your lesson.

DUKE: Whatta we do about Lincoln Lewis Da Third?

BEANIE: Wanna try your slider?

DUKE: Okay. Good idea.

(BEANIE *leaves.*)

DUKE: I had a therapist once, out of Detroit, too, in sixty-eight, my first bad year. I would've left home for her. She was the beginning of the end for me. I fell in love with the insides of her thighs, too, but she got tired of me when I didn't pan out professionally. I knew it was all over the last road trip of the season; I kissed her at the ballpark and her lips turned to ashes. (*He goes into the stretch.*)

LUCKY: You don't finish with a better won-lost record or E R A than last year, you ain't gonna be back! Connecticut Federal ain't interested in a P R man with no P R!

(DUKE *pitches and the crowd groans again. The ball comes back.*)

DUKE: Jesus—another ball. Well, the rest is history. It's out of my control completely. I can't keep anything on my mind for longer than a single second—except Donna Luna Donna, and I can't keep her *off* my mind. I think of her and her honey skin constantly. They're overpowering; they make me lose my balance. And she's always so *bronzed,* I can't stand it. She loves to lie in the sun—it's the only thing she cares about. I met her six months ago in Texas, and...and, why, here she is now, just as you like her...

(DONNA LUNA DONNA *enters, singing quietly, dressed briefly and very sexily.*)

DUKE: Hi, Donna Luna Donna. Your tan sure looks great.

DONNA: If I could spend my whole life lying on sand in the sun, I would. I mean it, sugar. I love it, I love it, I love it. I used to love other thing— fleshy things in my mouth, whispering sex word in your ear, but now I only love the sun.

DUKE: I understand. I used to love big breasts. When I married Jeannie, her breasts were firm, but not any more. Big breasts used to be very popular— but the times have changed and I've changed with them. See the breasted Donna Luna Donna. Small. Compact. Barely noticeable. Just a hint of mammary. (*He moves behind her, pressing against her and rotating her breasts with his palms. They both moan quietly.*) Mmmm, these are so good. I love your honey thighs, how they come together like this.

DONNA: Duke first came to my attention a year ago. He looks like my father, and there's this essence of failure about him which is very attractive to me. Besides, there's hardly any competition for baseball players anymore, and none at all for unsuccessful ones, so I've got nothing to lose. All my friends were after rock stars or else just busy going down on their boyfriends in parked cars—that still happens, you know, very few parents actually allow their kids to fuck right in the house, despite all the talk. Duke always provides a good, clean HoJo's. Also, there's some nice peer notoriety in going with a middle-aged ballplayer. And I wasn't otherwise engaged at the time, having just recovered in seclusion from some serious skin grafts necessitated by Duane the automobile mechanic's fondness for putting out cigarettes on me. So one night at the ballpark about six months ago, when Duke'd been taken out of the game in the bottom of the third—when I see him failin' like that, I just get hot as hell, even now—I approached him outside the locker room and put my hand right inside his pants. He's warmed to me ever since. He never says an unkind, restless word to me; he never treats me with anything but the kindest consideration. He's a true sweetie. I reckon I'll have to dump him if he can't stay on the team— I do have a failure threshold. San Antonio Normal is a very demanding institution in that regard. But right now, I still lather for him right off.

DUKE: No hair gluts these armpits!

DONNA: I know it's just a phase, but for what it is, it's a good relationship. I have to go now.

DUKE: Okay. Still want me?

DONNA: You know I do, shoog.

DUKE: How's m'Jag?

DONNA: Apple red and clearwater shiny.

DUKE: I'm doin' okay out here, ya know?

DONNA: I sure do, and I'm real proud and pouty. I better let you get on with it. Soon I believe I'd like to go to Baja where there's ocean and convertibles and money eighteen hours a day and a person can truly flourish. 'Bye now.

(She leaves. DUKE is ferocious with passion.)

DUKE: Where's the ball, where's the ball? *(He finds it in his glove. He yells to* BEANIE.*)* HEY, LINCOLN LEWIS—IT'S GONNA BE A FASTBALL!

(He winds up furiously and pitches. The crowd cheers.)

UMPIRE: *(Hoarsely)* STEE-RYE!

(The crowd cheers. The ball comes back.)

DUKE: ANOTHER ONE! *(He pitches fast.)*

UMPIRE: **STEE-RYE!**

DUKE: Okay, mama—I knew she'd get it back for me. She always does. I sure don't wanna lose her. Hey! What's the count?

LUCKY: Six outs! Three balls! Trouble comin' back!

*(*DUKE *waves to* BEANIE, *who runs out.)*

DUKE: What's the count?

BEANIE: Three and two. Christ, were those fastballs beauts! I haven't seen you pitch like that in years!

DUKE: Two down?

BEANIE: Yup. Smoke one more of 'em in, this boy'll be back in the minors by breakfast.

DUKE: Gotta do it with m'slider.

BEANIE: What?

DUKE: The fastballs were quirks of fate. I know my own arm. I gotta do the slider. I'd rather lose with my slider than win with my fastball.

BEANIE: Jesus, you're stupid.

DUKE: You're a real consolation, you know that? Mister Maligma?

BEANIE: Beanie's okay.

DUKE: Oh no, not after that. I like Mister Maligma.

BEANIE: Just get on with it. (*Trots off*)

DUKE: Three and two. The payoff pitch. Gotta do it with the slider. Low and outside, make him hit it on the ground, and let's end this goddamn inning. (*Goes into the stretch*)

LUCKY: Male chauvinist pig! Base Hungarian wight! Brazen hussy!

(DUKE *pitches and the crowd groans. The ball comes back and* LINCOLN *trots down to first base.*)

DUKE: Jesus, I walked him. Now it really starts to be my fault. Can't blame it on the Cuban anymore. (*To* LINCOLN) Welcome to first base, Colonel. That Donna Luna Donna inspiration stuff never lasts very long. I could be slipping. Hey, what's that?

(*In an aisle of the theater, a right-handed relief pitcher named* O'DONNELL *warms up with a* CATCHER. *Their throws rhythmically emphasize* DUKE's *action.*)

DUKE: For Chrissake! One walk and they bring out the fire truck! "I got confidence in you, son," says that fart Old Salt and then he starts warming up O'Donnell after one walk and an error that wasn't even my fault. He looks pretty sinister, doesn't he? All right, all right, who we got here?

P A SYSTEM: Number twelve, the third baseman, Guido Mancini.

DUKE: Ah, the clothing magnate. In seventy-one this sleaze-o batted three-twenty-one and then went out and started up a line of clothing. Now he sells his outfits everywhere—every time he gets up to bat, it's a network commercial. Let's see, bounced to the Cisco Kid in the second, lined one to Popeye in the fifth. Let's try the curve. (*Goes into the stretch*)

LUCKY: What about your poor Jeannie? You haven't snookered her in three months! Think she's not playin' around? She wears a mattress to work every morning! That's the trouble with you guys that cheat—so much guilt it never occurs to you she may be talking remedial pelvic action of her own! With a guy built like a swimmer!

DUKE: Jesus.

LINCOLN: Unctuous suburbanite! Ivory tower thinker!

DUKE: Christ, there's two of them now.

LINCOLN: I'ze frightenin'! I'ze frightenin'!

DUKE: Oh...drop dead! How lame was that?

LINCOLN: Movin' in! Movin' in! What I'm gonna do to you! What I haven't done already!

DUKE: Don't answer him. Don't dignify with a reply. Oh yeah? What?

LINCOLN: Maximize your terror! Play upon your fears! Plunge headfirst into little Mitchie's nightmares! Oooo, you should see me when I wear a hat!

DUKE: I'm starting to shiver. I feel acrophobic all the time. I can't remember what I was gonna pitch.

(Pitches and the ball is hit to deep left. Follows it foul)

DUKE: Aaaaaaggghh. Foul. Jesus, was that long. No more curves for lilla brother Guido. I'VE SEEN YOUR CLOTHES, YOU KNOW! You should see some of his stuff. Hang a Mancini sportjacket in the bedroom, you don't need a night light. Hang one in the bathroom, you don't need a mirror. This is it. The beginning of the end. I'm crumbling fast. I'm no fatalist, but this is it. *(He looks at* O'DONNELL *warming up.)* He looks happy. IT WAS FOUL, YA KNOW! But hoo, was it long.

LUCKY: Hey, man, whadda you make of this guy?

LINCOLN: You kidding? He extinct!

DUKE: Quit talking about me like I wasn't here! I can hear it all! All!

(Pitches. The crowd groans.)

DUKE: Ball one.

(As the ball comes back to DUKE, O'DONNELL *throws one at him that narrowly misses.)*

DUKE: Hey! Hey, what the hell is that? You threw a baseball at me! I'm havin' a hard enough time up here—knock it off!

LUCKY: Freemason! Homesteader!

LINCOLN: Opponent of the Patrolman's Benevolent Association!

DUKE: I never heard such insults. The curve or the slider—I'll throw anything you want. Just tell me what to do.

(Goes into the stretch as DOC MATTHEWS, *a left-handed relief pitcher, warms up in another aisle.)*

DUKE: Hey, what's this? Another reliever? Doc Matthews, too? All my fair-weather friends.

LINCOLN: Fantasy monger! Prince of Daydreams! This is what you get for watchin' your momma in the shower at thirteen!

*(*DUKE *pitches, the crowd groans. The ball comes back.)*

DUKE: Two and one. There are times when a fella really needs a rosin bag.

(As he plays with a rosin bag, O'DONNELL *and* MATTHEWS *throw baseballs at him, and one of them hits him.)*

DUKE: Hey! Knock it off—what's goin' on here? Since when do relief pitchers throw baseballs at the guy in a jam? Jesus. It's getting awfully lonely out here. Here's the part of the game where inevitability asserts itself. I don't like this part, but I'm sure familiar with it. Hope m'Jag's okay. Such a nice reminder. Two and one. Ask for the slider, Beanie boy. *(Shakes off a sign)* You can always count on Lawrence Larry Beanie Maligma to be in your corner on the night of the big fight.

LINCOLN: Neighbors hate you—even friends! Mainly friends! Now you know why Brademas wouldn't lend you that mower! Not 'cause it didn't work!

*(*DUKE *goes into the stretch, pitches, and the crowd groans. The ball comes back.)*

LUCKY: I told ya! I told ya!

DUKE: Christ, I feel like I'm falling off the side of the earth. Let's approach this logically. Suppose my career in the majors is over, A; B, suppose the roast beef franchise has one more bad year like last year when McDonald's moved in two blocks away; C, suppose the Golden Wasp there is right, suppose Connecticut Federal doesn't want a public relations man with no public relations. *(Pause)* I've got no answers! Grab the ball! Tighter! Whew. That was close. I was fucking scared.

*(*O'DONNELL *and* MATTHEWS *unleash balls at once.)*

DUKE: Hey! Cut it out! Jesus! How come you guys are throwin' baseballs at me! Huh? Now where the hell's the ball? I'm being bruised black and blue by these two so-called friendly teammates of mine, and now I can't even find the ball. *(Motions to* BEANIE *to throw the ball back. Nothing happens.)* THROW ME THE BALL!

(A basketball bounces out from left.)

DUKE: This is a basketball. Hey, c'mere! GET YOUR ASS OUT HERE!

*(*BEANIE *jogs in.)*

DUKE: What's the wise idea?

BEANIE: Whadda ya mean?

DUKE: What's the idea of throwin' out this basketball?

BEANIE: Just pitch the ball. I'm tired of your problems.

DUKE: This is a *basketball*. This is the *wrong ball* for this game.

BEANIE: C'mon, c'mon, you gonna let a little ball get the better of you?
I'll ask for the slider if that'll make you happy. *(Trots off)*

DUKE: I don't believe it. Not only do I have to put up with these clowns out
here—not to mention a third baseman wearing mittens—now this. What if
I make it to the next inning? I have to pitch with a hockey puck?

*(DUKE goes into the stretch, pitches the basketball. Mancini singles to shallow left,
but it's too short to drive in a run. The bases are loaded.)*

DUKE: Jesus, a single. There goes my no-hitter. There goes everything. The
razor blades, Donna Luna Donna, everything, forever. I can't take it. Oh no.

(OLD SALT enters.)

OLD SALT: I mean business. Listen to me, son, and listen hard. The worst pig
gets the best pear.

DUKE: What?

OLD SALT: *(Singing)* Happy talk, keep talking happy talk!

DUKE: But wait a minute—

OLD SALT: Listen to me, son: A vision for the ages. I love you like you were
my own boy—that goes for all of you! Listen: Remember: Women, priests,
and poultry, are never satisfied.

DUKE: What?

OLD SALT: You've gotta do some of the work yourself, Dumbo Doody,
Jesus! Remember: Life is too short to waste time on truffles. He ain't heavy,
father, he's m'brother; never trouble til' trouble troubles you. Like a
snowflake, no two scrotums are identical; it's a blind goose that comes
to the fox's sermon. Huh? Huh? Here's Johnny. Peaches with honor.
No house without a mouse, no throne without a thorn. Get it?

DUKE: No...I...

OLD SALT: Jesus! Mail early in the day, it's the better way. Here's the kicker.
Listen: Morals are the core of culture, and therefore letters without virtue
are like pearls in a dunghill. Right, Beanie?

BEANIE: Damn right!

OLD SALT: Does that help you, son?

DUKE: They made me pitch with a basketball!

OLD SALT: DOES THAT HELP YOU, SON?

DUKE: Oh, yeah, yeah. There's much wisdom in what you say, much wisdom. But they made me pitch with a basketball!

OLD SALT: I know, son. I know. The swine! I'll see it doesn't happen again.

DUKE: Then Mancini's hit doesn't count?

OLD SALT: Of course it counts! Don't be a fart and a handjob! And I'm saying that for your own good.

DUKE: Even though I had to pitch with a basketball?

OLD SALT: Why you so upset about that?

DUKE: Because a basketball's harder to pitch than a baseball!

OLD SALT: True, but it's also harder to hit. Think about that for a second. You have to learn respect for your opponents when they do well, son, even if you don't like them personally. Remember: when the going gets tough, the fuffle gets sluddy. Now if there's anything else I can do for you, son, don't hesitate to let me know. I can't come out again in this inning, you know, except to replace you, but you can phone me. Now let me pat you on the ass and let's get going.

DUKE: Sure. Thanks.

(OLD SALT *runs off to wild crowd approval.*)

DUKE: At least I got a baseball back. I'm gonna have to do this all on my own. Two down, bases loaded, bottom of the ninth. No, it's the top of the seventh; it just seems like the bottom of the ninth.

P A SYSTEM: Number three, the center fielder, Brick Brock.

DUKE: Oh, Jesus, not Brick Brock. Bases loaded and I get Brick Brock, the home run king of America. He hit m'slider so hard in the second, Digiatelli damn near broke his hip diving into the stands to catch it. I whiffed him in the fifth, but only by not looking where I was throwing. Jesus. Brick Brock.

(*Takes a full wind-up and pitches as he finishes the last line of dialogue. The crowd groans. The ball comes back.*)

DUKE: Ball one. I know what's gonna happen. It's inevitable. First my perfect game, then my no-hitter, in a minute my shutout, then victory. Either this guy hits a home run, winning the game and ending my career, or I do something humiliating like hit him in the face with m'slider. Gotta be. Rizzuto must be goin' crazy up there in the booth. I wonder if the cameras are pickin' up my panic—Jeannie'll be able to see that, if she's watching. Get those cameras off me, Rizzuto!

GUIDO: You're doomed!

DUKE: Jesus, not another one. I can't take it!

GUIDO: Can't you see the handwriting on the wall? What'll you do when you're through here? Nobody'll want you, you won't be traded. Back to the minors!

DUKE: Oh, God, no, I couldn't stand that. Jeannie couldn't stand that. My boys'd be too ashamed to look me in the eye. Donna Luna Donna'd be gone for sure.

LUCKY: You're gonna lose her anyway, you know that. Your last chance to be young! Blow this and you'll be thirty-six goin' on seventy!

(DUKE *fires a strike.*)

UMPIRE: STEE-RYE!

(*And the crowd cheers. The ball comes back.*)

DUKE: Jesus, I made it! A Goddamn strike! (*To* LINCOLN) Did you see that? I'm gonna make it. Did you see that, honkie?

LINCOLN: One strike, one strike, that's all, you got two to go, you'll never get it by him! You could, but you'll talk yourself out of it!

DUKE: Jesus, you guys won't budge, will you? ALL RIGHT, FROM NOW ON, I'M NOT LISTENIN' TO YOU ANYMORE! YOUR WORDS MEAN NOTHING! THESE CANALS ARE CLOSED TO INSULTS!

GUIDO: (*Seductively*) Oh, Dukey...

DUKE: ...Yeah?

GUIDO: (*Harsh again*) The trick ain't to keep us out. It's to keep us in!

DUKE: (*Winding up and pitching*) Christ, Christ, throw the ball, throw the ball! (*Pitches. It's a ball.*)

LINCOLN: What'd I say? What'd I say?

LUCKY: Ball Two! Ball Two! Soon ball four or outta the park!

(*The ball comes back to* DUKE.)

GUIDO: Your future's blank! Lasts five minutes! No horizons, Bronkowski, no safe places!

DUKE: (*Whispering intensely*) I got a future! It's a secret! It's a knuckler! I ain't never pitched one before, but I know I can do it right now. I can feel the shaft. Tips of the fingers, right, Whitey? Tips of the fingers, right Old Salt? Tips of the fingers. Let's see a little forecast of what's comin' up.

LUCKY: (*As* DUKE *pitches*) This is the knuckler? This is your future!

(DUKE *pitches a wobbly knuckle ball and makes a terrible face.*)

DUKE: God. A crazy pitch. I hate to say it, but thank God for Mister Maligma.

(BEANIE *trots out, just barely onstage, and throws the ball back angrily.
Then he disappears.*)

BEANIE: You almost killed me!

DUKE: SERVES YOU RIGHT! What's the bad knuckler s'posed to mean—
I got no future?

LINCOLN: *(Falsetto)* Breee! Breee! Breee!

LUCKY: *(Pointing to* BRICK*)* He's got fourteen girls! You got one!

GUIDO: *(Overlapping)* Breee Breee Breee!

DUKE: They're whistling like cranes! The loons are closing in. I'm no closer
to an answer. CUT IT OUT! SETTLE DOWN!

(The yelling dies down.)

DUKE: I know what the solution is! God, why didn't I think of this before?
I've been pitching all these years—it's so simple, Jesus—with the *wrong arm*!
I'm a natural left-hander, momma knew that!

GUIDO: What about the kids? What if they find you wanting? They laugh at
your jokes now, but what about their adolescence? They'll see right through
you! You've got no flesh, no spunk, no saving grace!

DUKE: God. It's gonna be left-handed. It's my last hope. *(Winds up.
The insults come as he pitches.)*

LUCKY: Still can't dance! Still no savvy!

LINCOLN: Slapdash tramp! Got no flash! Got no verve!

*(*DUKE *pitches. The crowd cheers. He is amazed.)*

DUKE: Jesus, a strike! How ya like that? All well and good, but what do I do
now? Pitch again left-handed? Is that the answer? Arbitrarily change my
way of life in midstream?

LINCOLN: Left-handed's just a trick, just a gimmick!

LUCKY: Don't be stupid! You can't do it!

DUKE: Jesus.

P A SYSTEM: He's a better man than you are, plain and simple.

DUKE: Hey!

LINCOLN: He's a better man than you are, plain and simple.

ALL THREE: Plain and simple, plain and simple!

GUIDO: You're through! Your life is over and you're only thirty-six!
What're you gonna do? What *can* you do?

DUKE: Don't be stupid—I could always be a football coach, football coaches are very respected. Look at Woody Hayes, look at Bear Bryant...

LINCOLN: Woody Hayes! Bear Bryant!

DUKE: Look at Bud Wilkinson! He's in the President's cabinet, for Chrissake! Or he was, anyway. I could manage a movie theater or a bowling alley, be a dental assistant...I've got a nice sense of irony, I could be a newscaster. I could be a chauffer to someone famous, or a counselor...a bootblack...think up new names for automobiles or cigarettes...there's lots of things I could do! I'm not helpless, you know!

ALL THREE: Woody Hayes! Bear Bryant! Woody Hayes! Bear Bryant!

(DUKE *goes into the stretch.*)

DUKE: Three and two, the big one due. This is it—I got no place to hide. This is the final pitch, this is the end of my life. Okay. I'm ready, I'm prepared. Bases loaded, two down, the count's unavoidable—three and two. Gotta be the slider. And in the slider, he's getting' my best. This is it. Here it comes.

LINCOLN: This is it! Here it comes!

ALL THREE: This is it! Here it comes! This is it! Here it comes!

(*The base runners chant like maniacs until* DUKE *releases the ball, at which point everything—including the crowd—becomes silent for an exaggerated moment. Then the sound of bat hitting ball lifts the roof off the theater. It's a home run. The runners clear the bases.*)

LUCKY: Thanks, Duke.

LINCOLN: Thanks, Duke.

GUIDO: Thanks, Duke. Nothing personal.

BRICK: Thanks, guy. You're okay in my book.

(DUKE *walks off the mound into the audience.* BEANIE *and* OLD SALT *enter left.*)

DUKE: Well, that's it, folks. Maybe Old Salt's right—maybe it was those two years of college.

OLD SALT: Just where d'ya think you're going?

DUKE: Me? To the showers.

OLD SALT: Come back here.

DUKE: Why?

OLD SALT: Come back here!

DUKE: My life's fallin' down around me! My future's an empty barrel. My slider won't break, my fastball isn't fast, my catcher hates me, my teammates are throwin' things at me, three guys on the other team somehow found out all about my life and are torturing me with it, my house is infested with termites and was burgled early this morning. My wife's in bed with a swimmer's body, my two boys have become homos, my darling Donna Luna Donna's taken her thighs out of circulation, my ham radio's been dismantled and broken for good, the vote's been given to eighteen-year-olds, I'm thirty-six going on seventy, and I don't know what to do! Why should I come back?

OLD SALT: For the good of the game, son.

DUKE: For the good of the game.

OLD SALT: That's right, son, for the good of the game.

(DUKE *walks back to the mound.*)

DUKE: I don't believe this. Why'm I goin' back? You mean I'm not out of the game?

OLD SALT: Oh, you're out of the game. Whoo, are you out of the game!

DUKE: Then why'd you make me come back?

OLD SALT: So I could tell you that. My power must be absolute.

DUKE: Oh, no.

OLD SALT: You don't play the piano when the house is afire, boy. And thou hadst better eat salt with the philosophers of Greece than sugar with the courtiers of Italy. I'm a father figure to all of you, Goddammit, how come you never got that?

DUKE: You mean I have to walk back across the field in front of all the fans again?

OLD SALT: Of course.

DUKE: Why?

OLD SALT: Why? Why? Why? Why? 'Cause that's the way it's done. This is ball! This is organized ball!

DUKE: Oh. Yeah.

OLD SALT: With your head down, boy. You know. Or at least you should by now.

DUKE: Don't I get a pat on the ass this time?

OLD SALT: No, sir, bob-o-linky. You been a bad boy. No son o' mine.

(DUKE *walks into the audience.*)

DUKE: Well, that wasn't so bad. At least the uncertainty's over.

BEANIE: *(To* OLD SALT*)* You wanna go with the right-hander or the southpaw?

(OLD SALT *flips a coin.*)

OLD SALT: Uh...

(Blackout)

END OF PLAY

FIGHTING
INTERNATIONAL FAT

The play opened in May 1985 at Playwrights Horizons, in New York City, with the following cast and creative contributors:

ROSALIND .... Jessica Walter
SHEP .... John Gabriel
VI .... Ann McDonough
AUNTIE PRAM .... Constance Barry
LILLIAN .... Ruth Jaroslow
JACQUES .... Stephen Ahern
D'RALEIGH .... Lisa Banes

Director .... David Trainer
Sets .... Tony Straiges
Costumes .... Rita Ryack
Lighting .... Frances Aronson

CHARACTERS

ROSALIND GAMBOL, *thirty-nine to fifty; smart, chic, highly successful career woman and founder of International Fat Fighters. She both lives up to and defies the WASP stereotype, alternating between cool efficiency and a warm sensuality.*

SHEP BRADLEY DIEDRICKSEN, *forty to fifty, handsome and suave, the extremely popular host of* At Large in Depth, *a mid-morning T V talk show, he is the sex object of every red-blooded American woman.*

VI WICKERS, *mid-thirties to fifties, with a decidedly suburban air. She is invariably on the verge of tears, most of which she bravely holds back.*

AUNTIE PRAM, *mid-nineties and extremely feisty*

LILLIAN RAPKIN, *mid-fifties, comfort-conscious and often the life of the party. She will always be happy as long as she has plenty of money, and at the moment she has plenty of money.*

JACQUES LAFACE, *anywhere between thirty and fifty; earnest and well-meaning. A Canadian who has had very little success in any aspect of his life. It is essential his Quebec accent is intelligible and not distracting.*

D'RALEIGH BELL, *an absolutely gorgeous woman of twenty-seven, perfect summers, with a honey-voiced, low-pitched voice (Southern, if it doesn't define the character). Her hair is a different color from Roz's, as is her whole style.*

CISSY SNILLET, *twenty-five to thirty-five, shy to the point of near-muteness*

PRESIDENT WILLIAM HOWARD TAFT, *sixty-five, jolly, and still unelectable*

SETTING

The play takes place in and around a New York television studio: a white, sterilized barn of a room cluttered with cameras, mikes, lights, yards of cable, and other relevant broadcasting equipment.

To the right of center is the set for *At Large In Depth*, the popular daytime talk show. It contains a background of highly polished, obviously fake foliage in front of which is a semi-circle of Queen Anne-style, antique wing back chairs that miraculously swivel and tilt. The floor is brought to life by a carpet of garish brightness—preferably electric blue or nuclear orange, both popular choices at the moment.

The set-within-a-set takes up more than half the stage and ideally should be on casters,so it can be moved around; if it proves too cumbersome for casters, it should be placed far enough downstage so the actors don't get lost. To the right of the set-within-a-set are two doors for entrances and exits. Stage Left is another door through which six hundred screaming women will stream in high dudgeon later on; it should take on a trembling significance as the play progresses. Other locales are explained.

The times, Sir, are changed. —In such a day as this, an American kitchen used to be the palace of plenty, jollity, and good eating. —Every thing was plain, but plenty. —Here stood the large, plump, juicy buttocks of roast beef, and there smiled the frothy tankards of beer with a little good West-Indian Rum in them; here smoaked the solid sweet tasted mince pies; and there the curling fumes of plumb-pudding perfumed the sky with delicious fragrance. Humour and eating went hand in hand; the men caroused, and the women gave loose to gay but innocent amusement. —Now mark the picture of the present time; instead of that firm roast beef, that fragrant pudding, our tables groan with the luxuries of Pensioners...The solid meal gives way to the slight repast; and, forgetting that good eating and good beer with a little rum are the two great supports of the American Constitution, we open our hearts and our mouths to new fashions, &c which will one day lead us into ruin.
—*The Norwich Packet; or, The Chronicle of Freedom* (Connecticut), 1 January 1784.

I have eaten to my sanctification; anymore would be flippus-flappus.
—*Maternal grandfather of the Editor, A News Letter from the Institute of Early American History & Culture.*

for Lee Remick

ACT ONE

(At rise: lights discover ROSALIND GAMBOL *downstage center gnawing on a chicken wing. She weighs two hundred and fifty pounds, dresses like a hag, and looks seventy.)*

ROZ: The virtues of the American chicken wing. One, they're portable. Two, tasty. Three, they take forever to eat, and four they're only twenty-six calories once you take the skins off. Ohhhhhhh, I used to eat these forever! But then for many years I found intense pleasure in self-denial. There is enormous sensual satisfaction in refusal. Being offered whatever you crave most and then turning it down——mmm, the vulvic flush is awesome. It's why martyrs are so happy. And so stubborn.

I used to bite my fingernails down to the blood because it was so pleasurable; when I stopped, the power I felt almost made me faint. Used to smoke cigarettes and quit, used to drink more and now drink less, once lost seventy pounds in less than a year. I reversed my life—smoke, booze, flesh—through enlightened self-denial. It was the basis for my success. I helped—forced, really—more than three million North American men and women conquer their weight by just such spartanism. Spartanism and my near-religious belief in the strength of groups. Any number more than one is strong—at least that's what I thought in those heady, self-deluded days. And the mass marketing of that insight made me Den Mother to the National Overweight. As for self-denial, it never made me feel frigid, though others claimed it should. No, my self-denial made me feel...sexual. Until that one particular night awhile ago that changed my life forever. That night, sex made me feel sexual.

The unloved behemoth you see before you didn't always look like this. My current appearance has a direct and simple cause, a single event—which should please you Freudians and movie enthusiasts. I never thought life could be so easily explained, but mine can be. Perhaps I was just ready for it. I never wanted love, not since my marriage exploded, hadn't for years. Career and boy toys were my life's work. For a successful woman, hard bodies are the rule, if you want them, not the exception. But the real thing? Never. Visit with me that incident—that night, that morning—back X number of years, when narcissism was the nationally unifying ethos. Picture me, in mid-life, thrilled, successful, and best of all, envied. Picture me...perfect! *(She whirls around and magically becomes thirty-eight and stylish. Compared to the world-weary woman we've just seen, she is youthful and girlish. She throws the chicken wing and hag clothes away.)* Eh? Eh? Quite a difference. I wasn't expecting it. So when love—or what looked like love—broke down the door with a nightstick, a whistle, and some large dogs, who was I to say no?

(She pirouettes, runs S L into the studio. VI *holds forth as* SHEP *paces with a mike.)*

VI: I was at the zenith of my nadir. *(Stopping)* I don't know if I can.

ROZ: Yes you can; you know you can.

CISSY: Have a heart, Roz.

ROZ: You've done it before. Be strong!

LILLIAN: Don't choke now—

VI: All right. Six years ago, I weighed a blistering three hundred pounds. More!

ROZ: There you go, brave Vi, wasn't so hard...

VI: I was at the zenith of my nadir. Husband gone, children fled, one as far as the Dakotas! House was a shambles: Beds in turmoil, clothes a-cluster, dust in clumps like basketballs.

LILLIAN: God, everything everywhere!

ROZ: *(Rubbing her temples)* Let me rub your temples, Vi.

VI: All the furniture lay in shards and splinters, exploded by my massive tonnage. The fridge was filled and emptied twice a day and I was the only one eating!

LILLIAN: Good lord...

ROZ: That's it, that's it—

VI: Mouth never still, hands never empty—my gums'd become soft and my teeth infirm from the sweets, breads and coconut cakes. I lost two bicuspids in a week!

LILLIAN: Oh, this is too much folks!

VI: The veins in my legs had swollen to the size of dachsunds, grease hung from my chin like a beard. I was a gargoyle!

JACQUES: Doesn't look like a gargoyle—

CISSY: That was then, this is now—

ROZ: Oh, and mercy, the scales, Vi—

VI: Livestock scales were all that would hold me, Mrs Gambol, and two days after I bought them the springs boinged out all over the room, smashing my one remaining painting.

LILLIAN: I didn't know that.

VI: My body'd become too big for a mirror to contain no matter how far back I stood. I don't even know my exact poundage—nothing could measure me!

SHEP: (Pacing back and forth) You must have really hated yourself, Vi. I know I would have.

VI: Hate? I wanted me dead. But I knew no gravesite could hold me. Sometimes I wouldn't see anyone for months. Deliveries'd come, I'd hide in the chimney.

SHEP: The...chimney—?

VI: Wedged in there, squirming and panicking, ripping the blue pup tent I so laughingly called a nightgown, covering myself with fireplace soot and deep Ohio shame.

SHEP: All right. Relax now, Vi. (To crew, with impatience:) Could we have some Kleenex, please, the poor woman's in tears! (Nothing happens.) Oh, I forgot—they're on strike.

(He finds a roll of paper towel, gives her one.)

SHEP: We can all see that everything turned out all right. You're no longer overweight, a very attractive woman—

VI: (Recovering) Thank you, Shep.

JACQUES: She seem the very sincere.

AUNTIE PRAM: Hah!

SHEP: (Outraged for her) The misery others force us to lay on ourselves! How did you get to that point in your life? Was it your folks?

VI: (Hysterical again) My parents were tyrants!

SHEP: When will the American parent learn—

VI: I could have been one of the major beauties of North America if I'd of gotten off on the right foot. "You've got such a pretty face," everyone always said. Instead, I was just a helpless pawn in a seriously deranged household.

LILLIAN: I had an uncle like that once. Boy was he no fun.

SHEP: I know the feeling. My parents fought all the time, split up when I was ten.

VI: Oh, mine weren't like that—they were true dears most of the time. Why, when I think back on those cos-cozy family suppers in Ohio, I want to cry with a nostalgia that only the what-might-have-been could know. The whole family planted around the kitchen table: Momma and Poppa, Junior and Butch, Rickersnick and Bill with their trombones; Irish setters at our feet, warmed by the mid-winter cheer of the Franklin stove, our insides coddled by Momma's sugared sticky buns, bubbling stews filled with cubes of sheltering meat, and the indescribable security of hot...soft...carrots.

SHEP: The hidden American agony—

VI: Oh, there was no agony. Poppa with stories of the day's hard chores, Bill razzing Rickersnick, Rickersnick punching out Butch; serenades in brass. There was love all around in those golden Ohio days. Not like Wyoming...

SHEP: Everybody loving everybody doesn't exactly give you somebody to root for—

VI: Everybody loving everybody's just the point! Their evil was subtle. Everybody loved everybody too much—on purpose. Their too much love led me to expect the same too much love from everyone else, and when I didn't get it, I ate like a computer-animated movie monster. Rip, rip, tear, tear!

SHEP: Wait a minute—too *much* love? Where's the conflict in that? Who are we supposed to sympathize with? I mean it's all very moving—cut to a blonde woman nodding, cut to another, tears in her eyes—but look, what we need here are stories—vital, searing, that expose your degradation at its worst. You mustn't be afraid to wallow in your misery, Vi!

VI: Okay, listen to this. When none of us got that childhood love back, we'd go home, heads hanging in defeat, and eat. We all became addicted to whale suppers around the Franklin stove. And years later, before I married the first time, do you know what I'd sit down to by my miserable self in lonely city apartments with water spots on the wall? *(Suddenly ferocious:)* More sticky buns, dozens of them! Every night without fail, dozens of sticky buns, a soft meat roast, mashed potatoes thick with gravy and packets of frozen peas; a box of rice for garnish, bread and biscuits on the side, glasses of cream to wash it all down. This wasn't once, Mister Diedricksen, this was every night!

SHEP: Every night?

LILLIAN: You're out of your depth here, soldier boy!

JACQUES: What a tale!

VI: *(Pointing to hers and laughing)* What a tail is more like it!

(They all laugh.)

VI: I used to be able to tell jokes like that all the time—kept my husband and children in stitches. But once I really started chowing down, I lost my sense of humor. I think they left me as much for my loss of humor as for my inability to get through door jambs unaided.

SHEP: But just a minute, Vi—

AUNTIE PRAM: Vi Wickers!

VI: *(Very upset)* Isn't that what you want, Mister Diedricksen?

SHEP: I don't know, a victim of too much love—

VI: I've got more if that's not enough!

SHEP: *(Writing in a gradebook)* I hate to ask you after what you've been through, but was there one degradation above all others which was the worst?

LILLIAN: Oh, hasn't she suffered enough?

JACQUES: You television people are all the same—sensationalists!

LILLIAN: The only difference between *Time* magazine and *The National Enquirer* is the paper they use.

ROZ: Vi can do it.

VI: It's okay—I know what your talk show needs are. You need my grossest humiliation, the moment when you want to grab your uvula and wiggle it in pain *(She wiggles her uvula)*, the cruxis nub before the epiphany, am I right?

SHEP: As painful as it may be, that's what we need. Your maximum degradation. It's all that's missing, Vi, and I want you to know we're behind you all the way. Cut to a very fat woman wondering; cut to a grampa squinting his eyes.

ROZ: Deep breath...

VI: I...I...I haven't got one.

SHEP: Wasn't there at least one moment worse than all the others, one that led to your turning point?

VI: I...I...It's all just a blur of frenzy. A watercolor of despair.

(SHEP and ROZ huddle down left. JACQUES puts on a pair of Sony Walkman headphones.)

SHEP: *(Dismayed)* I can't use her either.

ROZ: I thought you liked her—

SHEP: A guest has got to have great degradation, Roz, and an epiphany, you know that.

ROZ: No, I don't. I'm learning, but—

SHEP: Christ, I saw thirty-five people yesterday, she makes thirty-six, and so far you're the only one that's bookable!

ROZ: I can't keep my hands off you.

SHEP: Me neither.

(They embrace passionately, unseen by the others.)

ROZ: Every nook and cranny.

SHEP: Skin like a mink...But I've got six hundred screaming women
streaming into this studio for a show in an hour, and I need guests!
If those six hundred banshee women don't get guests, they don't participate
from the floor, and if they don't participate from the floor, I've got a lousy
show going over the air to twenty million people. Maybe nobody cares
about International Fat Fighters after all. Maybe I should order up a tape
of a repeat show...we did an archive-quality forty-four minutes with the
hypnotherapist of an unborn fetus. We were saving it for the sweeps, but—

ROZ: No, no Shep, don't do that, we can pull it out! International Fat
Fighters has the best record of any weight-loss organization in the country—

SHEP: I'm not saying you're not remarkable, Roz, you are—

ROZ: It's not me I'm worried about—it's them. They've all worked so hard
together, helping each other...If you could just see the faces of those we've
put back together, the exploded relationships solidified. My members never
need be alone again—they have each other, to lean on and rely.

SHEP: You're too good to be true...I've never met anyone like you who
didn't work for the Christian Broadcasting Network.

ROZ: Besides, you told me yourself weight-loss was always a ratings
blockbuster. Weight-loss and sex changes. You said just as long as there
were no anorectics or bulimics—

SHEP: Well, the idea *is* good, Roz, but you can't televise ideas—they've got
to be made dramatic. What AT LARGE IN DEPTH needs are stories with a
beginning, middle and end. Like you! You've got a story!

ROZ: Oh, well, I —

SHEP: No, no, you were born for television. Self-made millionairess, former
fat victim, miserable for years who with her own hands forged the most
successful weight-losing organization in the country, Minnesota mother of
three, happily divorced. You're perfect!

ROZ: Oh, I have such flaws—

SHEP: But you're the only one! And now with my staff on strike—

ROZ: I thought it was just the stagehands who were on strike.

SHEP: Same difference. My staff's too chicken to cross the picket lines.
Afraid of severely broken bones, for which I don't exactly blame them.

ROZ: You're not afraid to cross the picket lines.

SHEP: But I'm management—I own the show. They can't break
management's bones, it's against union policy. But with no staff,
how am I supposed to get the show booked? That's why I'm doing
the pre-interviews—I don't normally do this, you know.

ROZ: Thank God for the strike! If you weren't doing the pre-interviews, we never would have met...

SHEP: I knew I should have stayed in the office last night...

ROZ: *(Dreamily)* Do you remember last night?

SHEP: I'm a self-admitted workaholic! I never play when there's work to be done!

ROZ: I remember last night.

SHEP: And once—just once—I let down my professional guard and look what happens. No staff and one guest.

ROZ: I had my legs locked around you like a vice. I could feel every twitch. Could you?

SHEP: Sure, sure, but...less than an hour to taping and only one bookable guest!

ROZ: *(Throwing her arms around him)* Most women just lightly loop their legs over the thighs. Very few lock the legs above the calf, then curl the toes back under the shins. They don't do that on the Christian Broadcasting Network. That's what I do. Remember?

SHEP: Yeah, but...

ROZ: And will do again! Oh, remember last night?

(She begins to undress him as the lights go out on the set-within-a-set and an Art Deco bed covered with satin sheets wheels on silently down left. ROZ and SHEP are transported to the previous night, but the action is continuous. They sip champagne and remove their clothing. Romantic music is heard softly.)

SHEP: *(Seductive but impatient)* You have such a sensual, sexual, shimmering body for a weight-loss magnate, Mrs Gambol.

ROZ: Call me Roz.

SHEP: I already have. Mrs Gambol is sexier. You have such wonderful arms, such a delicious mouth—

ROZ: Such an abnormally high sex drive—that's something you can't talk about on television.

SHEP: Are you kidding? That's *all* you can talk about on television.

ROZ: Mmmm, cheap physical contact...I love it...

(She kisses him passionately. They unbutton each other.)

SHEP: Have you always had such an astonishing sex drive?

ROZ: Just since my divorce. Have you?

SHEP: I don't have one now. I'm still married.

ROZ: Men usually find me glacial. I have trouble opening up, inevitably stiffen when required to confide. You should see my shoulders! But with you—my bones feel all rubber, my joints are lined with mush. I can't even stand up straight when you're in the room.

SHEP: You're such an incredible woman—beautiful, intelligent, witty.

ROZ: My fingers won't extend! That never happens!

SHEP: God a woman worth ten million bucks is sexy! You're not just *talking* equality—you *are* equality!

ROZ: Some say better....

SHEP: And you're not at all afraid to talk back to me.

ROZ: I don't want to talk back to you—I want to slide under you in one embarrassingly patriarchal maneuver.

SHEP: God you're sexy...sexy! Your skin glows with such...sex!

ROZ: You're sure fond of that word—weren't you allowed to say it as a child or something?

SHEP: I can't keep my hands off you!

ROZ: Then don't!

(By this time they are in their underwear. Both are very appealing. SHEP is unable to control himself and pins ROZ to the bed. She locks a leg around his as promised.)

SHEP: Oh Roz! Roz! Mrs Gambol!

(Blackout)

(Almost immediately, the lights come up on SHEP dressing. The music has stopped.)

ROZ: That was quick. What happened?

SHEP: Liberals are lousy lovers.

ROZ: How come?

SHEP: So much to do, so little time.

ROZ: We'll work it out. By force, if need be.

SHEP: By force? I don't like the sound of that. Goddam stagehands! Know who's on camera three? V P of Customer Relations. Today's entire show was out of frame. All you could see was everybody from the chin down. God, a whole show unbooked!

ROZ: *(Still seductive)* I know what you need...

SHEP: Three to five riveting guests a day, five shows a week, one thousand guests every fiscal year—that's what I need! Like a junkie. It's all I ever think about!

Roz: Oh, Shep, don't worry about the show—we'll pull it out. I had my secretary Cissy phone fifty members from all over the country, they're all flying in tomorrow—even some guy named Carvalho from Guam.

Shep: Maybe your secretary Cissy's got a story.

Roz: Too grisly. She wouldn't work out.

Shep: Well what will work out, Roz? And why do you need this show so much? I F F's huge, you've got three cookbooks on the best-seller list—

Roz: (Meaning it) I can help people, Shep. But I need help to do it—your help. They have incredible stories, you'll see.

(The bed wheels out. They have finished dressing, and we are back to the present. Lights come up on the I F F-ers. VI addresses CISSY.)

VI: Doesn't he understand? I'll do anything to get on a talk show. Anything!

CISSY: Roz said no lies this time, Vi.

VI: Yeah, yeah. Now you make sure he understands—I'll do anything.

Shep: Incredible stories, eh? Well, where are they, Roz? So far I'm not seeing them...

Roz: Well, I'm sorry, Sheppy, we aren't professional actors—

Shep: I'm attracted to you, Roz, but never call me "Sheppy."

VI: (To herself) More degradation, stupid, more, more more...oh no, and then there's an epiphany, too?

Roz: I thought we were at least intimate enough for me to call you Sheppy.

Shep: Nobody's that intimate.

Roz: Not even wifey?

Shep: Wifey yes, Rozzie no.

Roz: Cretin.

Shep: Mongoloid.

Roz: (Building) Yellow journalist muckraker...

Shep: Messianic entrepreneur tycoon...

Roz: Unctuous subservient!

Shep: Ice-cold Anglican!

Roz: God, I want you!

Shep: Your mouth, your sex!

(They embrace passionately.)

VI: I'm just so weepy—I no way understand what you want...

ROZ: Maybe you could help her, Shep—you have such a gift...

SHEP: No, no, there isn't time for a story tutorial! But ladies, gentleman, you've all got to realize in television, structure is what's important.

VI: Not content?

SHEP: Oh, yeah, sure, content, too. Just maybe not as. Look, I'll illustrate. Take yourself back forty years, the suburbs outside Chicago. Every night a small boy goes to sleep next to a photo of the first television image ever transmitted: a wobbly, distorted picture of Felix the Cat. The boy dreams of working in video and of making the new technology helpful to mankind. By ten he is a full-fledged news junkie, glued to Edward R Murrow weeknights, Lawrence Spivak and *Victory at Sea* in the Sunday morning ghetto.

Dissolve to twenty-seven years later. Wahoo, Texas. Although the boy, now a man, has achieved his dream and is a reporter for station W K K W K-TV—nicknamed "Wick-Wack," he lives in disillusion. Local politics are a quicksand of corruption, and his station is under their control. After years of holding back, he fantasizes what Murrow would have done and exposes the town's corruption on a Live at Five. Instead of the deserved Emmy, he is immediately fired from Wick-Wack and blackballed throughout the industry. Soon penniless, his wife is forced to eat fried dough instead of meat, his three sons steal the lunches of other schoolchildren. He despises himself for his failure and, guilt-ridden, takes to the bottle and drugs. Goes on a thirty-day bender culminating in a wild four hundred eighty-mile car chase into western Louisiana where he is sentenced to six months in jail, and he truly feels he is at the zenith of his nadir, Vi, with no hope in sight.

Then, the dawn. After five months of suffering, he happens to see on the prison television a local personality named Jonny LaRue interviewing a vengeful woman whose husband was alternately so abusive and boring that she locked him in a vertical smoker and turned on the mesquite. LaRue is an insensitive bully and accuses her of Murder One. The man with the dream is incensed. Each day he watches this talk show, his anger building at LaRue's lack of vulnerability. The night before he's to get out of prison, he looks at the now-yellowed, now-krinkly photo of Felix the Cat in his wallet and makes up his mind to act. His first day on parole, he marches down to the station, bursts in while the show is on the air and, risking re-arrest, humiliates Jonny LaRue with a tongue lashing so fierce that LaRue collapses to his knees, admits to three counts of child abuse and one of church embezzlement, and our ex-con is hired to replace him on the spot. He gives up drinking completely and reunites with his family. Today he is syndicated in one hundred and eighty-four markets—twice a day in seven—and has a following between eighteen and twenty-one million depending on local lead-ins. In case you're wondering, that boy with the dream was me.

VI: Wow.

LILLIAN: Sa-mooth.

(Everyone applauds.)

SHEP: *(Counting on his fingers)* But see, that's what you need: injustice, decline, degradation, epiphany, rising narrative, strong resolution. The only thing I'm missing from you, Vi, is that intense period of despair when you hit rock bottom, the epiphany that turned you around. Wasn't there a moment in your life—seeing the woman who barbecued her husband, for instance—that reversed your predicament, made you decide to join International Fat Fighters?

VI: *(Thinking hard)* Well, I remember I heard about the food smashing from DeeDee, I think I heard about the food governesses from Clydette Sidas.

SHEP: Food smashing? Food governesses? What's that?

ROZ: Food smashing is the first tenet of International Fat Fighters.

VI: Take everything in your house more than thirty calories and bash it to smithereens—throw it against the wall, hammer it, run over it with your car—

AUNTIE PRAM: —Jams and jellies in glass jars is best—c-r-r-u-u-n-ch!

SHEP: But isn't that kind of wasteful? And messy?

AUNTIE PRAM: Not as wasteful and messy as cellulite on the outer thigh!

LILLIAN: Damn right!

AUNTIE PRAM: I still carry a couple of jars of jams with me whenever I'm on the loose. Wanna see?

SHEP: No, that's not really necessary—

AUNTIE PRAM: Too bad!

(Before anyone can stop her, she whips out two jars of jam and fires them against the wall.)

ROZ: Auntie Pram, no!

JACQUES: Zut, sut, alors!

SHEP: What *is* this?

AUNTIE PRAM: Talk about catharsis!

ROZ: *(Comforting her)* All right, Auntie Pram.

AUNTIE PRAM: *(Calming down)* See why jams is best, Mister Television? *(Muttering:)* Don't need a rock or anything. Just wham! *(She sits.)*

SHEP: Roz, I got a show to do....

ROZ: She'll be quiet now, Shep. The point is, International Fat Fighters accepts bingeing as an essential facet of the Overeater Profile. By removing everything over thirty calories, when binges do occur, they're harmless.

SHEP: But why such violence?

ROZ: Breaking things is good for the soul. How much weight did you lose, Vi?

VI: Approximately one hundred eighty pounds in ten months. From a tent size three to a dress size six.

ROZ: *(Prompting her)* And...?

VI: Oh, *and* met a man, married same, met another better, married him, got a house, now there's kids. And I am generally just a very happy woman being. And I'm never going back to my fat-fat ways!

(They all applaud.)

VI: Is that what you want?

SHEP: It almost works—

VI: Because I'm not doing anything for the next couple of hours.

AUNTIE PRAM: Feck!—as the Irish say—

VI: I just want to be loved.

AUNTIE PRAM: *(Jumping up)* My name is Ochsen Pram, but you can call me Auntie; and I'm here to tell you, you don't want Vi Wickers!

VI: Auntie Pram!

AUNTIE PRAM: You don't! This scravawj will do anything to get on your show—lie, cheat, steal, make up a whole false bio, won't you, Blitzen!

VI: *(Hurt)* Auntie Pram!

ROZ: Now, Pram, bring up your nice colors—

AUNTIE PRAM: I know television and its crude demographic ways! You want women to watch women? You need someone to root for! You need D'Raleigh Bell!

ROZ: Who?

AUNTIE PRAM: Roz'd never let her on, but that's who you need!

ROZ: I don't even know who she is—

AUNTIE PRAM: You need people who are gonna get mad at each other! Only time these things work's when the air's filled with hate! I'm telling you, you need A: D'Raleigh Bell, you need B: Roz, and you need C: me.

VI: Why you?

AUNTIE PRAM: Because I know what to do on these shows. (*She becomes a game show contestant:*) "A new car!" (*She squeals.*) "The real price of the luggage is five hundred and ninety-five dollars!" "Rome, Italy! Paris, France!"(*She jumps up and down.*) I know what this country wants: female orgasms! "A complete patio barbeque set!"

(*They all squeal.*)

VI: That's game shows, Auntie.

AUNTIE PRAM: I know that, I just wanted to show you my range.
Talk shows? Confessors, preferably female, all willing to plunder their souls, demeaning self-degradation and crawling on the belly, incredible self-loathing and swinishness which in one mystical revelation transforms itself into a self- satisfaction so beatific it borders on the smug. And then everybody feels better about themselves. Am I right?

(*Much protest from everyone*)

SHEP: Well...yes, actually.

AUNTIE PRAM: Told you I'm a natural for your show. Here's why else:
A: I'm old and I'll get you the grey vote, B: I'm peppy and I'll get you the underdog vote, and C: and mainly, I've got a Nielsen box in my living room.

LILLIAN: Uh-oh.

JACQUES: Hold the phone!

SHEP: You do?

AUNTIE PRAM: See? He knows power when he sees it. With me you can beat the final episode of *Friends*, and all the Super Bowls put together! I'm telling you—me, her, and D'Raleigh Bell.

ROZ: Auntie, are you free for lunch Thursday?

SHEP: Roz—I've got twenty-eight minutes to taping! You're fine and Auntie with the Nielsen box is a stroke of luck, but I need more and that fast. I don't even know how your organization works.

LILLIAN: Uh-oh, Ace didn't do his homework!

SHEP: Who's this?

(LILLIAN *cockily strolls to the podium.*)

LILLIAN: Who's this? *This*, as you call it, is Lillian Rapkin, and I'm the fattest person I've ever known.

(*They all applaud.*)

LILLIAN: I am Chairhuman of the International Fat Fighters chapter on The Island, and I can tell you anything you want to know about I F F, backwards, up the downside, and from the middle out. As my father, God rest his psycho soul used to say with a wink, "The shmekarka of the fuhtictuh is meshgoiz!" *(This is meant to be a joke, but there's no respons*

LILLIAN: Hoboy, you don't get it, do you. WASPs never get it. You car the goy to Great Neck, but you can't make him drink.

ROZ: Lillian, Mister Diedricksen's got a time crunch.

LILLIAN: I hear you, Roz, and I'll tell you one thing, I didn't get fat like what's her name with the grease hanging from her chin like a beard ann all that golden Ohio stuff.

VI: Vi, Vi Wickers.

LILLIAN: Yeah, right, Judy, no offense, but with me it was just the reverse I *hated* my mother. Hey—and here I mean you—I hated her so much I used to dream of throwing darts at her eyes. So much you know what— I wouldn't eat her cooking! Just to get back at her. That's how I got fat.

SHEP: By *not* eating your mother's cooking?

LILLIAN: I'd sneak off to Babbleboinberg's Deli twice a day and shovel dow ice cream sundaes. Orange Fudge Ripple, Burpled Rumple, all ladled with Babbleboinberg's steamy hot butterscotch, which sizzled and stuck, half hard, half goo, then the whip cream, those nuts, that cancerous cherry. I ate so much ice cream it actually lowered my body temperature! Whoa, I would go home shivering. Mother would spend the whole day cooking up shmeckelah, roast goonus, gefetkukuh, and I wouldn't touch a bite! You know what that does to a Jewish mother her only daughter won't eat her cooking? Best revenge I ever had, and I'm a vindictive person!

SHEP: That *would* be painful. But how did you get to I F F?

LILLIAN: I'm getting to that. The years went by as they will, I married the Great Izzy, and at the rate of only three-and-a-half pounds per year for twenty-six years, I figured I better start losing some of this stuff or the Great Izzy's gonna start phoning up porn stars. So I tried all the diets and flesh beatings you could find. Finally, after six years of quacks and fads, Izzy says to me, he says, "Why not try this woman Rosalind Gambol out in Minnesota, I been reading she's having a lot of success," I bow to him, and because Izzy is who Izzy is, he gets her to fly in personally.

SHEP: Who is Izzy?

LILLIAN: Who is Izzy? What is Tiffany's.

SHEP: Izzy has something to do with Tiffany's?

LILLIAN: *(Contemptuously)* Yes, Izzy has something to do with Tiffany's. He sells them things. Diamonds.

SHEP: Oh.

LILLIAN: Emeralds.

SHEP: I see.

LILLIAN: Got Paloma Picasso right under his thumb—get the picture?

SHEP: Yes.

LILLIAN: Izzy can buy and sell your network *and* its missile production plant and still have money left over for a fleet of F-15s in case al Qaeda or however you spell his name gets out of line again. Get my meaning?

SHEP: Yes...

LILLIAN: So Izzy gets her to fly in, and I send Armand to pick her up, she didn't have her own limo in those days, did you, Roz, God love you, not like now. And in she swoops like a goddam wraith, a single strand of lapis at the throat, and the first thing she says to me is, "Oh my, Lillian, I just saw the most beautiful dress on page thirty-six of the Horchow Collection that would go wonderfully with your azure eyes." *(Pause)* Well, I gotta tell you, I never had an approach like that. And six months later, I was a hundred and twenty-one pounds lighter.

SHEP: Really. How come I F F worked and all the others didn't?

LILLIAN: There is only one thing that makes this work, and that is Rosalind Gambol, I don't care how bitter I get. Her and her divine concept of Obsessional Therapy.

SHEP: Obsessional Therapy?

LILLIAN: Don't come around looking for special food tricks and blitz gimmickry at IFF. We eat the same raw carrots and skinless chicken as everybody else, plus thank God for NutraSweet and Mean Cuisine, but the rest of it is her.

SHEP: But what does she do?

LILLIAN: What does she do? She sticks to you like a Siamese twin dipped in magnet oil. She was with me in the morning to make sure I had those boiled egg whites with no butter, one sliver of toast so thin you could only call it a slivette, coffee black, all the time telling me how beautiful I was going to be, how men found me witty and wonderful, constantly keeping my hands busy dialing telephones or flipping quarters. All day shopping, digital games, swimming, art galleries, strolls till dusk, then dinner without an ounce of fat, more activities, her more policework on me till my life was no longer my own; then before bedtime she'd force me to watch a graphic disgusting movie of how fat kills you. Half the time she'd sleep over in the den, ears perked for a midnight icebox raid. Never once got by her. It was like camp—camp with a very aggressive counselor.

SHEP: Really clung to you, huh?

LILLIAN: Clung? She was closer to me than you are to your mike! She was Wiesenthal to my Mengele! I was her ob-sess-ee-yon, get it?

SHEP: But wait a minute! I F F has thousands of members—Roz can't spend six months with each of them...

ROZ: Hundreds of thousands—

LILLIAN: Of course not! I was special. Once a regular member loses weight, she becomes an I F F food governess and gets to do with a buncha new members what Roz did with me—hound them, nag them like a Scientologist in pursuit of a confused movie star.

VI: Scientologists? I hear they're actually really happy.

AUNTIE PRAM: You muskrat!

LILLIAN: They lose their weight, and you're so busy obsessing about them, you don't regain yours.

SHEP: So that's Obsessional Therapy. The old members keep the new ones from eating....

LILLIAN: But what you may not get because you're with television and only interested in the superficials, is how pleasant it all is. I'm sorry Roz, but for me it was like a dream....

ROZ: Easy, Lillian...

LILLIAN: Soft summer nights, the sheerness of silk, skirts rustling in the breeze...

ROZ: Lillian...

SHEP: Go on—

LILLIAN: Our relationship grew and grew as the months went by—beautiful windings and spiralings up white stucco staircases of intrigue and delight, abandoned doorways in the Mediterranean, affection physical and rampant, a burnishing of angels...!

SHEP: What does that mean?

LILLIAN: We became lovers.

ROZ: Lillian!

VI: No!

JACQUES: You?

AUNTIE PRAM: *You* got *her*?

VI: What!

LILLIAN: Izzy sent us to Corfu for six weeks....

ROZ: Lillian, don't...

LILLIAN: Sun-bleached beaches, bright blue bungalows and white hotels, the best low-calorie food and champagne all the day long, whatever we wanted. I never knew if Izzy knew or not—still don't—but I was crazy for her, out of my mind. Still am, Roz!

ROZ: Don't torture yourself, Lillian.

LILLIAN: Oh, Roz, what a summer!

ROZ: *(Sternly)* Lillian!

LILLIAN: *(Pulling herself together)* Yes, of course. I know how much you hate public displays.

AUNTIE PRAM: All I ever got was Josette.

ROZ: Mister Diedricksen only wants to know about the diet.

SHEP: The hell he does.

LILLIAN: At that point I'd dropped seventy-seven pounds; in the six blissful weeks in Corfu, the greatest summer any woman ever had, I can tell you—I'd do anything Roz asked, and I dropped another forty-three. It was all that broiled butterfish and lobster, egged on by the embarrassment of appearing on the highly competitive beach. They say guns are the great equalizers—nunh unh. Bathing suits are. It was so easy with Roz! She molded me in the image of herself. Of course when I'd lost the hundred and twenty-one pounds and we were back in the city, she dropped me like a boiling bowling ball. Softly, but she dropped me.

SHEP: Now we've got a show!

ROZ: Come here, Shep.

(SHEP and ROZ cross down left.)

SHEP: This is amazing!

ROZ: Calm down.

SHEP: I thought International Fat Fighters was a legitimate weight-losing organization. Little did I know you were some sort of low-calorie dyke farm....

ROZ: It *is* a legitimate weight-losing organization!

SHEP: Do you sleep with all your members?

ROZ: Of course not!

SHEP: Just the women?

ROZ: No!

SHEP: Well, do all your whatever you call them—Food Governesses— do they all sleep with their Obsessees?

Roz: I F F forms relationships between the fat and the formerly fat; what happens next is up to the individual relationship. I think we need some levity here—

SHEP: But to have sex with someone just to get them to lose weight! You're running a bordello here!

Roz: Have you ever been fat, Shep?

SHEP: No, but—

Roz: Then you don't understand: If you've ever been fat, you will either be fat the rest of your life or you will worry about being fat the rest of your life.

SHEP: I'm sympathetic to the problem, Roz, but—

Roz: I've spent my entire waking life with these people! The fat obsess about food while eating, obsess about it while dieting, and continue to obsess about it when they're thin. What I do is channel their obsession. They still obsess about food, but now it's other people's food. All the psychobabble about poor self-image and male victimization may be right, but they don't help. I help.

SHEP: But Roz—Lillian Rapkin!

Roz: I get it—you're not morally outraged that some of our members wind up in bed together, you just can't believe I'd go to bed with both you and Lillian Rapkin!

SHEP: No, hey, I can understand it—you went to bed with her because Izzy the diamond merchant was paying you a fortune.

Roz: I went to bed with Lillian Rapkin because she needed my help!

SHEP: But you get paid for it!

Roz: And you get paid for this, but it's not the only reason you do it!

SHEP: Is that why you went to bed with me—to get I F F on the tube?

Roz: Shep, no! I love you!

SHEP: *(Terrified)* What?

Roz: *(Quickly)* Don't get frightened. Maybe it's just infatuation.

SHEP: Calm down. Remember, the camel crosses the desert one dune at a time.

Roz: Oh, Shep, Shep, let's not fight; I want to do amusing things with your mouth—not fight. Come on, I'm still so melting in your afterglow...

SHEP: We'll have dinner in front of the fireplace. I'll splay you like a crucifix.

(They embrace.)

Roz: Mmmmmm....

SHEP: But wait a minute—how come Lillian doesn't even look as though she's lost any weight?

ROZ: She lost a hundred and twenty-one pounds. She gained sixty back.

SHEP: Gained it back? Why?

ROZ: Can't you guess?

SHEP: *(Suddenly getting it)* Because she's heartsick over you? Boy, is this sick! Lillian, tell me, how much did all your dieting cost you?

LILLIAN: Izzy wouldn't tell me how much Roz cost. The other frauds cost a hundred thou.

SHEP: Good God, a hundred thousand dollars! Cut to a woman in awe, cut to another, eyes a-pop—

LILLIAN: No you don't cut to a woman in awe! You stick to me with your nonexistent attention span! You don't think I'm going on the air with this, do you?

SHEP: You've got to!

LILLIAN: I do not got to! You think I'm gonna ruin my life for eight minutes of quickly-forgotten mid-afternoon entertainment? Unh, in no uncertain terms, unh! Ho, find somebody else to exploit on your little tin show!

SHEP: No, no, Lillian, don't go! You're the first person I've wanted on the show all day!

VI: Don't say that, Shep!

LILLIAN: I'm not gonna play fish in the barrel for your fekoktah shotgun. Think you can supercilious it over me just 'cause you and Imus got your own jets?

SHEP: But why'd you come here if not to be on the show?

LILLIAN: Not because of you. *(To ROZ)* Do I have a prayer, Roz?

ROZ: We'll get that sixty pounds off, Lillian, you'll see.

LILLIAN: That's not what I meant and you know it.

SHEP: Lillian, won't you reconsider?

LILLIAN: You are talking to the Rock of Gibraltar.

VI: As it turns out, I'm hard to get but more or less available.

SHEP: No, no, I finally get a bombshell, and it dries up on me! Christ, twenty minutes to taping! What am I going to do, Roz?

JACQUES: *(Suddenly standing)* You don't want me.

SHEP: What? Who are you?

JACQUES: My name is Jacques LaFace, and I'm the fattest person I've ever known.

(They all applaud.)

SHEP: Why don't we want you?

JACQUES: I'm Canadian.

SHEP: What's that got to do with anything?

JACQUES: Oh, Canadians are way too dull for zippy American T V shows. Think I don't know that?

SHEP: What makes you so sure?

JACQUES: Thirty-two years of life, Mister Diedricksen! Nobody cares how we live or die or anything! In Canada they sink to their knees barking when they get an American on their talk shows! But is the reverse true? Of course not! Who'd want one of puny old us on the American tube? *(He sits.)*

SHEP: We'll take a Canadian—

JACQUES: *(Jumping up)* Look at us, twenty-two million people, twice the land mass as you, and we haven't even got our own car company! Twenty-two million Uriah Heeps toadying around in hand-me-down Fords and mini-vans! Of course you don't want us!

SHEP: There may be a show in this, but this isn't the one...

JACQUES: Do we have any famous actors? No! Is Sir Ian McKellen Canadian? No! Bobby DeNiro? The best we can do is Christopher Plummer, and he hasn't had a hit since *The Sound of Music* where he was sniffing around the toes of Julie Andrews, and she's from England! Were The Beatles or Elvis Presley Canadian? How 'bout Axl Rose? Of course not! The best we've got is Paul Anka, and he wrote "You're Having My Baby, What a wonderful way to say you love me!" We haven't got any car companies, we haven't got any actors or inventors, we don't even have any great explorers! We didn't even discover the North Pole, and that's right next door!

SHEP: Well, that may be, Mister LaFace—

JACQUES: May be? May be? It *is* be bub. But you can sit there and smirk, giggling at us singing "O, Canada" when we win our one weakling gold medal at the Olympics, and you can be proud of your national animal— the bald eagle is a soaring and imaginative symbol, like England's lion, courageous and romantic; but do you ever think what we've got? The beaver! A joke of a national animal! A joke for years, and now a porn joke! This is the only country in the free world where the Prime Minister's wife slept with Mickey Jagger!

AUNTIE PRAM: Paul Anka? The one who wrote "I ate it up and spit it out"?

LILLIAN: The same.

JACQUES: You even think our revolution's sissy because it's based on language—not earth-shaking like yours or the Russians. "Oh, I'd rather speak French, let's revolt," "No, I'd rather speak English, let's revolt." I can't stand it! We don't even have grown-up liquor! Everybody knows seven and seven's just a kid's drink after the prom!

SHEP: Please, Mister LaFace, this is supposed to be about losing weight—

JACQUES: Losing weight, losing weight! You don't care how Canadians lose weight! How could you—you never cared how we got fat!

SHEP: Roz—

ROZ: Jacques—

JACQUES: You just think we're all a bunch of lumberjacks with pencil-thin moustaches and red hats with ear flaps who say, "Oh, Pierre, you are dumb like zee fox" all the time. Well we're not!

SHEP: I don't think you are either—

JACQUES: And the big news is, the BIG news is, we aren't all trappers and mounties! Stupid word, mountie, mountie...somebody who mounts up is a mountie. Mountie, mountie...

SHEP: There *is* a show in this. There any other Canadians in this group?

ROZ: No.

SHEP: *(Musing)* "Overweight Canadians"...that does sound kind of dull....

JACQUES: Y'see! Y'see!

SHEP: Sorry, I didn't mean that.

JACQUES: Oh, yes you did, oh yes you did! You all do! I may have lived a wild life, how do you know? I may have eaten human flesh, shot men in cold blood, and fucked the moose! But oh, no, we're Canadians, and we're so dull we don't reflect light! I might be a really interesting human being! I'm not, but I might be! Not like you swashbuckling Americans cut a swath through the pride of our Canuck womanhood, all dying to make a V with their legs for you Uncle Sammers—and I'm not just talking about my wife, by the way, or even my girlfriend after my wife, I'm talking about 'em all! Can't get enough of your vigor and sass!

SHEP: Is that why you got fat? An American stole your wife?

JACQUES: Not just my wife! How about my second wife and two girlfriends, bub! My pets even liked Americans better, went away with them unasked! Why do you think I blew up like an indoor tennis court—four hundred, four-twenty? I don't even like food! Look, I don't care what you do in the Koreas or Grenada, your moment in the sun's about over, lasted a lot shorter than the Romans. Just keep your hands off our women! Now I am going to take what remains of my shredded dignity, go to the bathroom, and never come back. *(He exits.)*

SHEP: No way, Roz, no way. I can't put these people on the air. Every guest is a loon. I'm sorry. *(Calling to* MOROSINI*)* Morosini! Morosini! Order up a re-run!

VI: *(To herself)* Oh no...

MOROSINI: *(V O/O S)* Which one?

SHEP: What the hell, the Emmy winner. *(To* ROZ*)* That's the one in which I explore in depth the fad of interracial sodomy among missing children of alcoholic Afghan vets who were raised by paramilitary senior citizens and became promiscuous in backlash. Devastating.

ROZ: Shep, isn't there something I can do? It will mean so much to all of us, to the painfully overweight out there—

AUNTIE PRAM: He's right, Roz Gambol! You can't have paranoid Canadians and the bogus saint Vi Wickers over there! Even I wouldn't watch this trashheap! I'm telling you, the one thing you need to save your hide, and her initials are D'Raleigh Bell!

ROZ: Who *is* D'Raleigh Bell?

AUNTIE PRAM: I thought you'd ask that. *(She pulls a cord, unrolling an enromous poster of Amanda Blower, an unattractive three hundred-pound woman.)*

ROZ: Amanda Blower!

SHEP: My God...she's repulsive!

ROZ: My one failure. Six months with I F F, still weighed over three hundred. Extremely bitter woman.

AUNTIE PRAM: Boy are you in for a surprise! *(She exits.)*

VI: No, no, cancel that re-run, Shep, I've got it—I've suddenly got it!

SHEP: What?

VI: My epiphany.

SHEP: It's too late, Vi—

VI: Shep, for probably the only time in your life, you don't understand— I need this gig. I need to go on television. *Need.*

SHEP: No one *needs* to go on television—

VI: I do! It's my birthright! Just hear me out— *(Before anyone can stop her, she grabs the chair.)* It was Hallowe'en. I was living alone, about to head out for my daily midnight pizza run, when suddenly the car wouldn't start. I turned it and turned it, but no go. Called the Triple-A, they couldn't make it till twelve-fifteen, and Gwathmey's closed at midnight. I phoned them, they were busy—off the hook, the rats. In minutes withdrawal started: Sweat head to toe, the shakes—I counted on those midnight pies! Phoned former friends, but the second they heard who it was—the one-ton freak from Butte—they hung up and shooed their children out of the room. My house was on top of a hill less than half a mile from Gwathmey's. Walking it would kill me, I knew, even though downhill, literally, dead on the spot. Then, like a lightning vein, it came to me. I took an ambling start, tucked my fingers under my feet forming myself into a hoop, and rolled down the driveway. There I was, three hundred and fifty-plus pounds, cascading down Brainmount Drive, garbage cans banging in my windwake, cats screechclaw like the shrill cowards they are. I had such momentum I was down the hill in six-oh-three-point-four, leaned like a biker to make the right, and rolled into Gwathmey's parking lot at eleven fifty-nine.

LILLIAN: Pretty ingenious, considering...

VI: I brought both arms back at the last moment, breaking my terrible speed, and sideswiped the little bush in front, which saved the building.

SHEP: Good lord. Cut to a man adjusting his earring, cut to another mouthing the words.

ROZ: You poor thing! Tell Shep what you had to eat, Vi.

VI: Two large tomato pies, one with double sausage, double onion, double peppers and pep; the other with extra cheese, double butter, side of 'chovies and fudge parts. A glass of cream to wash it all down. The usual with variations. I remember it like yesterday.

LILLIAN: Talk about degrading...

SHEP: No, no—

CISSY: What're fudge parts?

SHEP: Nobody's gonna sympathize with anyone who rolls herself into a hoop to get pizza at midnight! Even if Vi could figure out the form, there aren't enough guests—just her, Roz, Auntie Pram. Unless you've got somebody else, Roz—

ROZ: No.

SHEP: *(Pointing to CISSY)* What about her? She's been awfully quiet.

ROZ: God no—it would kill her.

SHEP: Morosini! Sorry about the east coast.

(ROZ rushes to CISSY, and they mime argument. CISSY bursts into tears, finally crosses to chair.)

CISSY: My name is Cissy Snillet, and I'm the fattest person I've ever known.

(Applause)

SHEP: You? You're fat?

CISSY: It's just an expression.

SHEP: I'm sorry, Ms Snillet, we're going with the Emmy.

CISSY: *(Quietly)* I not only weighed over three hundred pounds, I was involved in an incest pentagon of Dad, Mom, and children.

SHEP: Incest *and* overweight?

LILLIAN: Oh, Cissy makes the rest of us look like A A Milne.

CISSY: Dad was a voracious lover—smooth and silky with a swarthy body that conjures up images of Edward James Olmos.

ROZ: This'll get you, Shep....

CISSY: He wanted every woman he saw—fat, thin, or what-have-you. For years he had affairs outside the family, two-timing Mom long before they were married. But when he tired of strangers, he turned to us. I have two sisters, each a prize-winner, and a mother who's a prize-winner, too. He used to boff Mom every night of the year for the long life of their marriage and still have enough vim left over for each of us; well, almost each of us. At first, when Dad used to watch Fawn and September change their bras, I wasn't alarmed; then once I found him with one of Fawn's breasts in his mouth, I knew something was up. Her smile was cherubic.

SHEP: Well, this is more like it....

LILLIAN: *(Admiringly)* God, this is worse than a soap!

CISSY: Soon Mom found out he was carrying on with Fawn, and she got crazy and made, screaming maniac insults at them whenever they performed their sex in the public rooms of our house. But that didn't stop Dad. Within weeks, he started two-timing Fawn with the frisky September, who was then 14. Dad was like a well-tuned Valvoline: he used to hummuz Fawn up in the second bedroom while September was at school and Mom was out shopping; then Mom at the proper time; then downstairs in the living room with September about three A M—which was dangerous because September always made a racket. Well, Mom found out September had joined the troika, but this time she didn't just get mad; instead, she turned the two girls against each other. When September'd come home from school, before she'd had her hummus 'n' cookies or anything, Mom'd just say, "Oh, September, your father's upstairs doing the woojy-woojy with Fawn, make sure to knock," and when Fawn'd turn on the tube after a very silent dinner—meals were pretty uncomfortable in those days—Mom'd say without being asked, "Don't you even know, you A D D, Fawn? Your father's upstairs playing The Elusive Cucumber with September" which would make poor Fawnie cry with rage and humiliation. Boy, Fawn and September got mad when Mom squealed, which was almost every day.

Those girls used to fight with each other and something fierce—real hitting and scratching battles. Mom'd get real upset at their skirmishes and call Dad to stop them, but he'd just tell them to fight again, only this time with their clothes off.

SHEP: And did they?

CISSY: Oh sure—right away! Nothing September and Fawn loved better than to strip down to their bikini underwear and wrassle each other hard, knowing Dad was watching.

LILLIAN: The woojy-woojy?

SHEP: What a story. Morosini—hold my calls! I mean, hold the tape! (*Back to* CISSY) No wonder you got so fat. Our hearts go out to you, Cissy, and so will the hearts of all who're watching. Notice the blonde boy, eighth row back, now an African-American, her bow is askew. Go on Cissy— when was it your father started in on you?

CISSY: Oh, he never started in with me.

SHEP: He didn't?

CISSY: (*Increasingly emotional*) No—that's how I got so fat. I was jealous out of my mind over Fawn and September! Nuts out of my mind! Daddy never wanted to watch me change bras, never asked me to wrassle a sister; never once when I'd sink into the carpet on my hands and knees begging for his beefy caress would he respond with anything but a grunt. Usually he'd be in his favorite overstuffed chair, I'd snivel around whimpering, and he'd just up and leave the room—or open a book he'd already read. Is it any wonder I ate in revenge?

SHEP: Because you felt rejected by your father who was sleeping with your sisters and mother?

CISSY: I know I shouldn't, but yeah. The place was a madhouse! Everyone competing for Dad's attention. I, by grovelling into the carpet; Fawn, who knew he liked 'em young, by dressing British grunge with blue coxcomb hair and articulated cheeks; September, always in blackface, had mastered the steel drums because Dad loved the Caribbean so; and Mom strutting around like a hooker saying, "You my pimp, man?" in a Moroccan accent no one knew where she picked up. She got so good, by the way, she actually *became* a hooker, made two hundred and fifty dollars an hour during afternoons while Dad was still at the factory before he came home to gonzago Fawn. Mom hoped to arouse him by jealousy. Cheapness and jealousy, those were her weapons.

SHEP: Did it work?

CISSY: Oh no—he didn't care what she did with her afternoons; but she made three hundred and thirty thousand dollars that first year which is why we all moved into the big house in Grosse Pointe.

SHEP: This is amazing. What happened next?

CISSY: Well, there we were, vying for Dad—I getting fatter by the minute, Fawn punking out, September on the steel drums, and Mom swinging her beads. Two of them were getting laid daily, one occasionally, and one— me—never. I'd come home from work evenings, seatbelt myself into a chair in front of the tube, and stretch my mouth so I could slip an entire Truncheonburger with the famous zephyr sauce right in there all at once. Like this. (She demonstrates.) It was great—the happiest time of my life many have said.

(She sits down to much applause.)

SHEP: Wait a minute! What happened?

CISSY: What happened? Oh, Fawn got mad and ratted, Dad went to jail, I joined International Fat Fighters, and the rest is history.

SHEP: But wait a minute! You've got brilliant degradation, but you need a turning point, an epiphany if you will—

VI: She doesn't have one either. That leaves me, Shep!

SHEP: You've got to have one, you've just got to!

CISSY: Oh, I do—I just thought you hated me and wanted me to sit down. I remember it was a tepid July afternoon. I took my emotional temperature and found I was miserable! Dad had a gun he used for rat shooting, and I got it and loaded it, and on that sticky July afternoon I decided to do myself in. Draw a permanent curtain over the musical comedy I called life. But my arms were too fat to get a clear shot at my head. This was as far as I could go in any direction. (She demonstrates the difficulties of shooting yourself with fat arms.) All I could do was wound myself, and that was no fun. So I decided I had to lose major poundage or I'd never make it.

SHEP: So suicide was your motivation for losing weight?

CISSY: Yup.

SHEP: But there are thousands of ways to kill yourself—you don't have to use a gun.

CISSY: I know, but I have a very limited imagination. Then, by accident, I picked up a copy of The National Star, and there was an ad for I F F right next to the story about the seven Hollywood stars who met in Barbra Streisand's living room with Warren Christopher to hammer out foreign policy? Remember that?

SHEP: Yes. I couldn't make it.

CISSY: Well, I saw the ad and I thought, what the hell. So I lost and lost until my arms were thin enough to get a clear shot; but once I'd lost that first hundred and fifty and could aim Daddy's rat-gun at my head, I no longer wanted to. I was having a wonderful relationship with the food governor I F F had set me up with—they have men, too, you know.

VI: Which one did you get?

CISSY: Skip Grazzuti.

VI: Ooooo, swoon!

SHEP: So I F F really saved you, eh?

CISSY: Oh yes. I quickly lost another seventy-five pounds, got a greater guy and his house, no longer crave my father—out now, by the way, stalking Mom like a beagle—and am generally just a very happy woman being.

LILLIAN: Good story, Shep, you gotta admit—

SHEP: Good? It's great! I mean that's the first story with a beginning, middle, and an end! It has the ring of truth, one can identify with it, it's great! You, Roz, Auntie Pram...I just may be able to squeak this one out....

ROZ: I wouldn't count on Pram.

SHEP: We have to count on Pram—she's got the Nielsen box!

ROZ: She'll be lost in traffic. I know her. Sometimes she can't even find her way out of the building.

SHEP: But then we've only got you and Cissy—

(The U S doors suddenly open. AUNTIE PRAM bursts in with D'RALEIGH BELL. Everyone is numbed by her beauty.)

D'RALEIGH: And one more.

AUNTIE PRAM: I got her! I got her!

(D'RALEIGH crosses to center chair.)

D'RALEIGH: My name is D'Raleigh Bell, and I am the fattest person I have ever known.

(A moment of silence; then applause, as PRAM, LILLIAN and VI rush toward her.)

AUNTIE PRAM: D'Raleigh!

VI: You're so different...transformed....

LILLIAN: My God, you're gorgeous—

CISSY: Gee.

D'RALEIGH: Hello Roz.

ROZ: Amanda Blower!

D'RALEIGH: I thought we could bury the hatchet—

ROZ: You did that long ago—in my neck. But you're not welcome here, Blower!

SHEP: Now hold on one second. We're talking about the right of the American people to know the truth! And the rights of this young, extraordinary-looking woman to tell it—agreeable to you or not, Roz.

ROZ: Rights, rights. Everybody's got rights all of a sudden—children, dogs, mass murderers. There are too many rights in this country. Too many rights and too many journals.

VI: I keep a journal.

CISSY: I keep two journals—one for my moods, one for my thoughts. Such as they are.

SHEP: There is no such thing as too many rights, Roz.

VI: I keep six journals! One for my every move!

SHEP: (Gesturing to podium) Please...Ms Blower-Bell...

(D'RALEIGH crosses to podium.)

D'RALEIGH: Thank you, Mister Diedricksen. It is most gratifying to see that your reputation for championing the underdog without an attendant loss of personal sensuality over the air hasn't been exaggerated. And may I say what an honor it is to be addressing the two-time Emmy-Award-winning star and executive producer of At Large In Depth Starring Shep Bradley Diedrecksen on such a fine autumn afternoon....

SHEP: I can't imagine—a beautiful woman like you—fat, ugly—

AUNTIE PRAM: She was so ugly, she couldn't get a date with the Elephant Man.

D'RALEIGH: Thank you, Prammie. So grotesque was I that only once in my first twenty-one years did a man make a move for me, and that was in the dark. In an elevator. But surely you don't want to hear sexually explicit material.

SHEP: (Quickly) No, no, maybe we do. The worst thing you can do is censor yourself.

D'RALEIGH: This is pretty hard core.

SHEP: We can take it.

D'RALEIGH: Well...

(D'RALEIGH seduces each of the members.)

D'RALEIGH: Summers get gummy in Saint Paul. One such dank night, I strode into the Bertholle Building elevator, blouse stuck and clingy from the thick and humid air. Between the third and fourth floors, the lights failed, the elevator stuck, a stranger's breath came hot. I never saw his face, but it was bearded; He caressed without force, entered quickly with my greased consent. My fingers clutched his hair, his hands my back and nether parts; we groaned and pushed, clumsy to a passerby but complex with nuance and heaven to my magenta soul. Quiet screams, pants at ankle height, wet images of fairy tales and buttered spikes. Bar none the most thrilling sexual *frisson* I've ever experienced. Dark, sudden, and anonymous, I throbbed and pulsated for days. Since my transformation, of course, I'm seldom alone, hardly ever stationary, and never unfulfilled. My new body requires almost constant rubbing, outside and in. *(Pause)* But I digress.

(There is a pause as they all imagine this, stunned. JACQUES *enters suddenly.)*

JACQUES: I forgot my hat! But why are you all so bizarre ? Did I miss something again? I am so stupid...

D'RALEIGH: Sit down, stranger.

SHEP: *(To* D'RALEIGH, *hoarse with passion)* Looking at you now...one would never think...you were once ugly...your honey voice, bronze thighs....

ROZ: My God, you're transfixed!

SHEP: How did you do it?

D'RALEIGH: I have touched the bowl's bottom, Mister Diedricksen. I have experienced the brown water.

LILLIAN: What brown water?

D'RALEIGH: I have endured the ultimate American bigotry and have thereby defined it.

LILLIAN: What bigotry?

D'RALEIGH: The hyper-bigotry which encompasses all other bigotries: The evil and insidious presence of internationally dehumanizing American Looksism.

JACQUES: Looksism?

AUNTIE PRAM: What's that?

D'RALEIGH: Ever-present and two-headed, the crypto-masculinist oppressionist pig brutality by which we are all enshackled.The fascist-elitist doctrine whereby what one looks like matters more than what's in one's soul.

SHEP: You mean obesity?

D'RALEIGH: No comforting euphemisms, Shep Bradley. Fat is only the tiniest subcompartment of Looksism. Texture of skin, size and shape of genitalia, preference for individual musical notes, deformities, warts, leaking orifices, inability of hair to curl naturally, simian postures, the ethnic schnozz, all fall totally under the Looksist-oriented outrage which drives us to our craven knees!

AUNTIE PRAM: This woman's on fire!

VI: Going like sixty!

ROZ: So far, you all might notice it's just rhetoric.

AUNTIE PRAM: Give her a chance, Roz!

D'RALEIGH: And there is only one way to reverse the historically suffocating trend of the Looksist mania; one simple, painless, inexpensive solution. I did it, the American people can do it.

VI: What is it, what is it!

JACQUES: Tell us before we go mad!

D'RALEIGH: *(A dramatic pause)* Surgery.

SHEP: Surgery?

JACQUES: Going under the knife?

VI: Incisions and sponges?

ROZ: Emotional salvation through surgery. Now you see why I kicked her out of I F F?

D'RALEIGH: Still bitter, aren't you, Roz. One stinging defeat for your Obsessional Therapy and still bitter. You all remember what I used to look like.

JACQUES: I don't. I never saw you before.

VI: This is genius!

JACQUES: But then, I don't get to New York too often.

D'RALEIGH: And, of course, the crowning achievement to insure my flab'd never return: the intestinal bypass.

JACQUES: The which?

D'RALEIGH: Top of the small intestine reconnected to the bottom, shortening it and bypassing miles of confusing obstruction. Absolutely foolproof. But to make sure, I also had the gastroplasty, which staples the stomach pouch so it is impossible for too much food to get in! Ho, I couldn't get fat now if I wanted to!

SHEP: You're amazing....

D'RALEIGH: And what took me eight years of trail-blazing operations can now be accomplished in one blissful, anesthetized afternoon. It's simple, painless, less expensive than International Fat Fighters—

VI: More genius!

D'RALEIGH: —there's none of the cheap smarminess of Food Governesses—

ROZ: Hyperbolist!

D'RALEIGH: —and best of all, it's forever!

ROZ: But why? Because you're too undisciplined to stay on a diet?

D'RALEIGH: Be generous to people, iron butterfly! Compassion is the word for our new decade—allow people their weaknesses. Encourage and subsidize them. Overeating simply isn't your fault!

ROZ: Oh, it's genetic, too, I suppose—

D'RALEIGH: Of course it's genetic! Everything's genetic! Plus indifferent society, cruel relatives, jealous peers. You're victims! You can't be blamed. And let me tell you, once you've had your surgery, you'll never have to endure fascist personality cults like this one again! Each and every one of you can have surgery tomorrow and in two weeks be eating beyond your wildest dreams! Wouldn't that be wonderful, Jacques?

JACQUES: I no longer have wild dreams about eating. Roz got me over that.

VI: Roz did the same for me....

D'RALEIGH: Roz. The precious Roz—

CISSY: We don't need surgery, D'Raleigh; maybe others do, but we don't.

AUNTIE PRAM: Sorry, D'; In I F F we never worry about overeating.

D'RALEIGH: Really. Really. (Suddenly ferocious:) Really??!!

(D'RALEIGH rushes to the S R door, wheels in an enormous table, groaning with beautiful food. A sexually plaintive moan rises from all.)

VI: What's all this?

(D'RALEIGH plunges her hands into grapes and mashed potatoes, rips off a prime rib and chomps on it like Henry VIII.)

D'RALEIGH: The potatoes and cream, the cheeses mixed in, the beauty of the pig! You haven't binged for months—years, some of you—and look at it all right now glistening before you!

ROZ: All right, listen up now, all of you! I am your Food Governess beginning right now! This is a trick!

D'RALEIGH: Can you fantasize the hollandaise on the sides of your tongues? The nutted crunch of the frozen mousses that glide down your gullet? Well, I can eat all of it! And never wince once!

ROZ: This is nothing! Remember our field trip to Western Steer? You snapped your fingers at that!

D'RALEIGH: Irresistible: frothy malteds, crisp, thinly sliced fries from Idaho, endless fruit pies and parfaits, refried beans for Jacques LaFace—

JACQUES: How'd she know about that?

D'RALEIGH: —slabs of white chocolate thick as gold bouillion, marbled with nuts. Zag-Nut, Bit O' Honey, and the long-thought-dead Clark Bar. Mmmmmm, who can resist? Who'll go first?

ROZ: Hold it!

JACQUES: This is a battle for the souls of the restless embodiment here!

ROZ: *(Confidently)* You've lost your craving for carbos and sugars, remember? Snap your fingers and walk away! Vi, come over here and let this Circe of Saliva tempt you all she wants. Just don't touch anything.

VI: Yes, Mrs Gambol.

(VI crosses to D'RALEIGH.)

ROZ: I'm sure the lady here with the face of an angel and the soul of a re-arranged bowel has made sure to bring all your former temptations. No quarter asked, D'Raleigh.

D'RALEIGH: None given, Roz.

(D'RALEIGH whips out a roast and a plateful of sticky buns.)

VI: Soft meat!

D'RALEIGH: And sticky buns, warm and bursting with butters, pecans crunched atop, sugars and caramels dribbling down the sides. And a glass of cream to wash it all down, if I'm not mistaken.

ROZ: Vi?

(VI stares at the buns, snaps her fingers, returns to her chair.)

VI: No, thank you.

ROZ: Jacques? Refried beans, all you want.

JACQUES: *(Afraid)* I have not had the refried bean in six years!

D'RALEIGH: And the creamy enchiladas—

(He goes to D'RALEIGH, she whips out a plate of steaming refried beans and enchiladas, grates cheese over them. JACQUES' mouth waters, then he snaps his fingers and returns to his chair.)

JACQUES: No, thank you.

D'RALEIGH: Why y'all're certainly proving me wrong! Jacques-y, why not go the whole way and really bury me—take a little bite.

ROZ: Oh no you don't!

D'RALEIGH: Shep Bradley, would you restrain her for just a second? You'll have a show if you will.

SHEP: Well, for a second, in the interest of entertainment.

(SHEP *holds her arms.*)

ROZ: What are you doing? Don't you dare, Jacques, be strong...

JACQUES: I am strong, Mrs Gambol. I am the Canadian.

(*He bites into the enchiladas, snaps his fingers, moves away from the table unseduced.*)

ROZ: No, no!

JACQUES: See? My first Tex-Mex in six years, and nothing...

D'RALEIGH: You come back, too, Vi. Nothing happened with Jacques.

ROZ: No, Vi, don't do this to yourself!

(*She lunges for* VI, *but* SHEP *restrains her.*)

SHEP: But nothing's happening, Roz—they're fine!

ROZ: Remember the tenets! One, food smashing, Two, don't take that first bite! I've got chicken wings in my purse—all you want!

CISSY: Excuse me, but I don't see—

D'RALEIGH: The Truncheonburger with the famous zephyr sauce? Right under the hog's head.

CISSY: (*Spotting it*) Oh, you did, you did....

ROZ: Just walk away, Cissy.

D'RALEIGH: (*To* VI) I'm sure Mister Diedricksen would consider you favorably for a slot on the show if you passed this test.

VI: Yeah?

SHEP: Well, sure, if—

ROZ: No, Vi, no!

LILLIAN: You are a swine, Bell-Blower!

SHEP: You said no quarter asked, Roz.

D'RALEIGH: Why thank you, Sheppette, you are fair-minded, indeed. Vi?

(VI *cautiously takes a bite, walks away.*)

D'RALEIGH: Cissy? The zephyr blows in your ear...?

CISSY: I have very little personality.

(CISSY *takes a bite of a gorgeous Truncheonburger, walks away.*)

D'RALEIGH: See? Nothing! I am certainly being proven wrong. Mrs Rapkin—

LILLIAN: Not on your insulated life! But...what have you got there?

(D'RALEIGH *opens a gallon of ice cream, dry ice emanating. She pours butterscotch over it, a bag of nuts, a dozen cherries. It is the world's largest portable sundae.*)

LILLIAN: *(Breathless)* Babbleboinberg's butterscotch-hardened Burpled Rumple!

ROZ: No, Lil, no!

(JACQUES *suddenly screams.*)

JACQUES: Aaah! I just had an erection—and it was in my mouth! Just one more bite, Roz, no problem.

(*Before anyone can do anything, he takes a fast bite of the enchiladas—much bigger this time, and as soon as he swallows it, he sinks to his knees and pours refried beans down his throat, moaning. VI suddenly charges back to the table, LILLIAN brandishes an ice cream scoop in each hand.*)

VI: My God—this is hog! Gimme, Gimmee!

CISSY: *(Panting)* The Truncheonburger...hollyhock bun...

SHEP: *(Shocked)* What happened? They were all doing so well....

ROZ: You fool, why didn't you listen to me!

LILLIAN: Two scoops, one for each hand like sixguns!

D'RALEIGH: Never fails—just wait thirty seconds for the juices to get going.

SHEP: They're like drug addicts...

ROZ: You've got to help each other, remember? Vi, Jacques—this'll take weeks to undo!

D'RALEIGH: No it won't! They can have surgery tomorrow!

(AUNTIE PRAM *has been sneaking for the door S R.*)

D'RALEIGH: Hold it, Pram!

AUNTIE PRAM: No, no, D'Raleigh, please, I'm an old woman....

D'RALEIGH: *(Increasingly nasty)* Come on, come on, it doesn't hurt, you know...here's your Ry-Krisp... (*She pulls out boxes of Ry-Krisp.*)

SHEP: Ry-Krisp? You can't get fat eating Ry-Krisp.

D'RALEIGH: You can if you eat it the way she did—by the carload and like lightning. Smeared with an inch-thick of cream cheese and fresh fruit jams from New England states.

AUNTIE PRAM: No, no, D'Raleigh, don't do this to me! I've always loved you, not Roz, who wouldn't even answer my phone calls, always treated you like a daughter! A daughter *and* a mother for the ones I never had! And a sister, D'Raleigh—a sister, a cousin, and a great-grandmother, don't do this to me, Raleigh-Raleigh!

D'RALEIGH: Why, Prammie, just come to mama...

(Not kindly, she jams Ry-Krisps into AUNTIE PRAM's *mouth.)*

LILLIAN: *(Eating wildly)* Do something, Roz, do something!

ROZ: Hold! Hold! For one split second! Jacques! Vi!

(She smacks the food out of their hands, slaps headlocks on them, whatever it takes to stop them from eating.)

ROZ: I will show you—be strong! Back in the dank dark days before I started I F F, I had a weakness, too, just like you. I had the chocolate bug—anything made of chocolate I couldn't resist. Pies, pastries, even chocolate sauce over steak and chicken like my friends the Mexicans, Jacques. I haven't had a grain of the stuff in nine years. But I will show you you *can* be strong. I will make the ultimate sacrifice. D'Raleigh, bring on your worst chocolate. Hold, hold! You, Vi, hold!

LILLIAN: Atta girl, Roz!

*(*D'RALEIGH *reveals a huge bowl of chocolate pudding.)*

SHEP: Chocolate pudding? That's the most tempting chocolate thing you've got?

ROZ: Of course it is, Shep—people don't get fat from *haute cuisine*—people get fat from junk food. D'Raleigh knows that.

AUNTIE PRAM: The last people got fat from haute cuisine were A J Liebling and Paul Prudhomme!

*(*ROZ *slurps some chocolate pudding.)*

LILLIAN: Good, Roz?

ROZ: Good ? It's delicious...everything I've ever wanted. Brings back families, childhood, learning bridge and tennis, the sororities I so wanted to join but was too fat to, love, hate, abandonment....

VI: Then you know what we're going through.

ROZ: Of course I do. I'm eating it; it's sliding down... resonating...I feel the tongue massage, the gullet entrancement...my knees are buckling...I can't do it! *(She staggers, grabs a table for support; she lets out a primordial scream, like a dinosaur.)* Muuuuuggwaaaahh! *(She collapses on the floor, buries her face in the pudding, gulping it down.)* More, more!

D'RALEIGH: Where's your group to back you up now, Roz—where're all your governesses and twaddle when you need them most?

(They are all aghast except D'RALEIGH. *But with superhuman effort,* ROZ *struggles to her feet.)*

ROZ: ...but...I don't want...any more...!

(She flings the bowl across the room. Her membership is stunned and impressed.)

VI: Good God, Roz, how can you do it?

ROZ: I'm strong, that's how! You can all do it, you don't need me—just be strong!

D'RALEIGH: But with me you don't have to be strong! Be weak! Be middling! You can eat forever, guilt-free and poundless!

ROZ: Graceless seducer!

JACQUES: Sacrifice isn't what we need, Mrs! Refried beans is—

LILLIAN: The sides of my tongue!

VI: The throat massage!

(They resume eating wildly. D'RALEIGH *crosses to* SHEP, *puts her hands down his trousers.)*

D'RALEIGH: And as for you...your needs lie somewhat below the stomach....

ROZ: No, D'Raleigh, no, have a heart!

D'RALEIGH: Come on, Shepard, while her world is falling apart...just come on upstairs where there's satin sheets. Or, if you like tramp stuff, in the hallway on the stairs.

SHEP: You mean it?

D'RALEIGH: I've got your erotic options covered luxest comfort to tenement sleaze....

(She leads him to the door. The I F F-ers continue to swill food.)

ROZ: No, Shep, no!

SHEP: I've got to, Roz—this is too much to turn down!

LILLIAN: *(Like a cheerleader)* Butter-scotch! Butter-cream! Butter butter butter-fat!

(The phone rings. ROZ *answers it.)*

D'RALEIGH: I'll let you wear my heels, big boy....

ROZ: It's Morosini, Shep—the banshee women are on the way!

SHEP: *(In a trance)* Cancel them. Rack up the tape...

ROZ: You can't just cancel six hundred women!

SHEP: They'll wait outside till tomorrow's show. Tell 'em it's the union's fault, not mine.

(Six hundred women scream and knock on the door left.)

ROZ: No, Shep, no!

SHEP: You've no idea the feeling, Roz!

D'RALEIGH: She's never known it, never will....

JACQUES: Dee beans, dee beans!

ROZ: But where's your group strength? You can lick this, just stick together!

LILLIAN: I love you, Izzy, I love you!

CISSY: Zephyr madness! Madness!

(CISSY swirls like a dervish, forcing the Truncheonburger into her mouth, shrieks, and collapses.)

ROZ: God in heaven! My flock!

(SHEP exits with D'RALEIGH; the screaming and knocking on the door increases. Food is everywhere.)

(Blackout)

END OF ACT ONE

ACT TWO

Scene One

(At rise: ROZ *enters U S, gnawing on a chicken wing and addresses the audience.)*

ROZ: They sent the banshee women away. And now America is enjoying Shep's Emmy winner exploring the new fad of the furniture-abusing, missing-children-of-alcoholic-Gulf-War-veterans-interracial-incest-practicing, promiscuously-raised-by-paramilitary-senior-citizens backlash. The whole array of human experience is on television, weekdays at three P M, twice a day in many markets. *(To* D'RALEIGH*)* I'll get you if it's the last thing I do!
   And now for a brief history of American fat.

(Lights change; a screen flies in behind her.)

ROZ: In the beginning, as everybody knows, there were only Indians—

(Slide of several seventeenth-century indians, muscles bulging)

ROZ: —or "Native Americans," as everyone except the indians themselves insists on calling them. You'd have to look very hard to find a pinch of fat on the indians of the seventeenth century. True, the Peroquods were sluggish and the Roggohonecks given to individual sloth at times, but by and large, these people were doing far too much running around to get fat.

(Slide of a sluggish Peroquod and a slothful Roggohoneck)

ROZ: At around that time, however, the double Pieters—Minuet and Stuyvesant—succeeded in bringing Dutch stuff to Nieuw Amsterdam—

(Slide of the double Pieters)

ROZ: —that's "New" spelled "N-i-e-u-w"—

(Slide: "Nieuw Amsterdam")

ROZ: And it's possible Dutch stuff may have started fat in America.

(Slide saying "Dutch stuff"; slide showing gouda cheese and Dutch chocolate)

ROZ: The first publicly accepted figure of fatness was when President and First Patriarch George Washington—himself lean as a sinew, six-three with auburn hair—appointed the spherulitic General Henry Knox Secretary of War. Knox weighed over three pounds, thus beginning the trend toward fat warmongers. For the next hundred years or so, Americans were led to believe that ponderous jowls and bellies shaped like a globus were signs of prosperity. And so the prosperous, who didn't mind eating till it hurt, sat behind desks and in lawn chairs and didn't move a muscle. Most popular public figures were Diamond Jim Brady, who basked in his fat, priding himself on stuffing till his tummy touched the table; Babe Ruth, of course; Henry Hobson Richardson, the architect; Roscoe "Fatty" Arbuckle; and, while not strictly American, Santa Claus. As for business folk, although Henry Ford was thin, J P Morgan was relatively fat, and the unsinkable Molly Brown was big as a house.

(Pictures of all the above beginning with Washington are projected.)

ROZ: But the greatest ambassador of American obesity ever was our twenty-seventh president, the inflatable William Howard Taft, who ranged between three hundred sixty-five and three hundred seventy-four pounds for most of his life.

(The screen flies out. PRESIDENT TAFT enters upstage left laughing quietly as if in a memory. His laughter is continuous but never competes with ROZ's narrative. He circles the U S L area.)

ROZ: Taft was the last president to keep a cow at the White House; also the only one who decorated the place with Filipino furniture, which gives you some idea of his taste. Everybody's friend, from Teddy Roosevelt right down to the common bank president.

(TAFT sits on a piece of furniture and breaks it. He gets, up, chortling, and heads for another.)

ROZ: His favorite food was tapioca, which he enjoyed at least four times a day in a large soup bowl. His breakfast always began with tapioca and was usually followed by spareribs or some large beeves. There isn't time to tell you what he had for lunch and dinner, but it was plenty.

(TAFT sits on another piece of furniture, breaking it. He laughs, rises, and heads for a third.)

ROZ: And he never lost his sense of fun—even when he was defeated after only one term by the extremely thin and soon-to-be-old Woodrow Wilson. Undaunted in public life as he was at the groaning board, William Howard Taft went on to become the only ex-President ever appointed to the Supreme Court—except for Hillary Clinton, of course. Heh heh—just kidding.

(TAFT knocks off one more piece of furniture, then exits, chortling. The screen returns.)

ROZ: It must be admitted, however, that while Mister Taft represented the pinnacle of America's love affair with human tonnage, today he wouldn't make it to the Iowa caucuses. For in Europe, a hotbed of revolutionary fervor was brewing, its ripples soon to be felt on all sides of the Atlantic.

First, the poor discovered cheap carbohydrates and promptly got fat, causing the enraged affluent to complain that you couldn't tell the bums from the swells anymore.

(Slide of a naked fat bum and a naked fat swell looking exactly alike. They are labelled "A bum" and "A swell" and a caption reads, "WHAT'S THE DIF?")

ROZ: And second, the heir to the British throne, for a few minutes to be Edward VIII then everafter the Duke of Windsor, torn between stewardship of the Greatest Empire the World Has Ever Known and cruising round the world inventing necktie knots with the bimbo he loved, stepped down from the throne, at which point he and his wife the Duchess coined the rallying cry for an angry generation: "You can never be too rich or too thin." Millions followed in half her footsteps. Such figures (or lack of them) as Audrey Hepburn, Hildegarde Knef, Gabby Hayes, and Ewell "The Whip" Blackwell of the Cincinnati Reds all became national idols. Today, only those working-class millionaires Charlie Durning and Jack Girmonde can get away with heft in public.

(Slides of those mentioned. She shouts to a stagehand. The screen flies out.)

ROZ: Okay! Does this sound glib? Flib? Gilp? Well, it should and it shouldn't. On the one hand, fat is trivial and ridiculous. It announces to the world that the owner of a fat body is wildly out of control—and in such a babyish, obvious, and embarrassing way, it can only be compared to bedwetting. And fat people look funny; should be made fun of—just the way a drunk stumbling down the stairs should be made fun of or a Quaalude freak driving his car into a telephone pole should be made fun of. Yes, just as funny as those. For like alcoholism and other drug addiction, overweight also destroys lives, ruins relationships, explodes self-esteem, and causes suicides and immeasurable suffering. Fat people are miserable, helpless, tragic, pathetic. Is International Fat Fighters immoral? Am I? The answer should be obvious. Would you befriend—and possibly sleep with— an alcoholic if it would help him give up alcohol? A heroin addict if he'd give up smack? Don't give me psychoanalytic theories about lack of love or feminist notions of male victimization; they may be right, but they don't work. *I* work.

The question is, why here? Why don't the Europeans care much about being fat? Why don't the Chinese? The answer is, fat is fashion—or right now, the lack of it is fashion. And we all know how much fashion matters. I happen to like fashion. It's nice to look nice; it's exciting for standards to change—maybe not quite so often, but often enough to keep you one step behind and guessing. We need the frivolous; it's what makes us different from other countries. And don't get self-righteous: Without fashion's frivolity there wouldn't be more food in Rwanda or justice in Bosnia—it doesn't work that way. There'd be more frivolity somewhere else, that's all—more professional athletes, or news commentators, or film directors.

Clearly, it is only a matter of time before the poor will get thin again, and the haves will need something to distinguish them from the have-nots. It's been proved by cigarette smoking and suntans that health is clearly no barrier to the dictates of vogue, and I fully expect by the end of the decade to be running a clinic for *gaining* weight, jamming funnels down the throats of idle Americans like geese whose livers are swollen for *foie gras* so they can fill out the new plump-line couture. But enough of this emotional cover-up. My real sub-text is, of course— *(Suddenly furious)* What's She Doing to Him!

(Blackout)

Scene Two

(Lights come up on D'RALEIGH and SHEP wrestling on a fire escape right. They are disheveled from arduous lovemaking. He is down to his shorts, she wears whatever undies make this particular actress look sensational. At the moment, she stands over him, the stiletto heel of her shoe in his furiously sucking mouth.)

SHEP: *(Breathing heavily)* Oh...oh...oh...

D'RALEIGH: *(Also breathing heavily)* Anything you want...anything!

(SHEP pulls her down next to him. They slam away at each other with their fists in ecstasy.)

SHEP: My god you're sexy...there's such sex in you! You are sex, pure SEX.

D'RALEIGH: Oh...I'm in the hands of a complete master...so knowing! Everything you touch turns to electric heat!

(They flail away at each other. Her wrist alarm goes off.)

D'RALEIGH: Hold it. *(She opens a vial, tosses pills down her throat.)*

SHEP: Hey, you okay?

D'RALEIGH: Oh sure. This surgery sometimes has a couple of little side effects. Nothing that can't be handled.

SHEP: Side effects? Like what?

D'RALEIGH: Oh, a little anemia. Now and then some esophagal inflammation...

SHEP: Esophagal inflammation?

D'RALEIGH: Oh, well, there's a lot of vomiting with the gastroplasty. When they staple the stomach pouch, nothing gets in that isn't supposed to; if it gets too full, why all the effluvia just comes back up. It's wonderful! *(He sucks on the back of her knee.)* My God you're a good lover, sugar. *Very* good.

SHEP: Very good but not excellent, right?

D'RALEIGH: Oh, certainly excellent. Excellent! I didn't realize we were using the high school grading system.

SHEP: Excellent, but not as excellent as the bearded guy in the elevator, right?

D'RALEIGH: Holy stars, Shep, that was five years ago! I was three hundred pounds. I didn't know any better.

SHEP: What was so wonderful about it?

D'RALEIGH: It was...religious...beyond words, you know? But oh my, you—you were terrific. And you can be again. Just one second. *(She reveals a syringe.)*

SHEP: *(Alarmed)* Hey, what are you doing!

D'RALEIGH: *(Matter-of-factly)* Sometimes you get a little liver problem with the bypass.

SHEP: A little liver problem? How often do you have to do that?

D'RALEIGH: You get used to it.

SHEP: How many operations did you actually have?

D'RALEIGH: Thirty-six in eight years. Oh, there is not an original bone in this body. I had to have *two* nose jobs—the first just so the doctors could get my proboscis into the O R.

SHEP: Thirty-six...that's a lot of...hard sewing....

D'RALEIGH: Ho, that was only the groundbreaker. I've had my nose done twice, my chin chiseled, double chins tucked; hair transplanted, eye pouches drained and patched, ears cracked and reshaped, my neck lengthened; I've had three-foot slits down my arms and the fat spooned out; the guy in Brazil did my saddlebags, the Armenian in Maryland vacuumed forty pounds from my knees by suction curettage, and where I used to have piano legs, silicone implants to round the calves.

SHEP: Boy, you're really committed to this, aren't you.

D'RALEIGH: Committed? It's my life. *(She gives herself an injection in the inner thigh.)* Aaaaahhhhh...Okay, ready, Slim Jim?

(She puts her equipment away, lies down next to him.)

SHEP: Wait a second, D'Raleigh, I'm a little dizzy. Hypodermics aren't exactly an aphrodisiac.

D'RALEIGH: Really? Most men find it arousing when I inject myself.

SHEP: Well, not me.

D'RALEIGH: Well, I don't exactly get off on you sucking my high heels either.

SHEP: You're kidding! That always works! How come?

D'RALEIGH: I guess I don't have too many nerve endings in my shoes.

SHEP: Well, how about when I nibbled the inside of the leg all the way down to the knee?

D'RALEIGH: Oh, yeah, that was great! Did you like it when I squeezed your nipples?

SHEP: Oh, yeah! Just a little pain—you know my woodie switch.

D'RALEIGH: Yeah, that one's pretty foolproof.

SHEP: What about when I got the inside of your elbow in my mouth? (*He goes down on the crook of his elbow.*)

D'RALEIGH: Oh, yeah, I've never had that done before! I've had my toes done, but not that. Fabulous. How 'bout when I squeezed the muscle in your thigh?

SHEP: Oh, man, I didn't even know that little muscle was in there! How'd you like it when I had you trapped up against the door, the knob digging into your back and pulled your hair back like this?

(*He demonstrates on her.*)

D'RALEIGH: *Very* exciting! Cold, but exciting. You pulled the hair just right—you meant business but it didn't hurt.

SHEP: Yeah, that's pretty effective generally. So the only thing I really did wrong was the shoe thing?

D'RALEIGH: Oh, Shep sugar, that wasn't wrong! You didn't do anything *wrong...*

SHEP: Then how come you liked the bearded guy in the elevator better? Damn!

D'RALEIGH: Forget about the guy in the elevator! That was five years ago!

SHEP: You never saw him again?

D'RALEIGH: Never. I searched high and low for forty-nine months; but it's hard to locate someone when all you've got to go on is sexual performance. "Excuse me, I'm looking for a single white male who is extremely good in bed."

SHEP: One thing I've never really understood—what makes a guy really a great lover? I mean what really, specifically made it impossible for a woman to turn down Errol Flynn or Michael Douglas or Emilio Estevez? What exactly do they...do?

D'RALEIGH: You don't need to ask me—I'm sure you have a very full sex life, Shep.

SHEP: *(Depressed)* Well...yes, it is very full. But it's not...one hundred percent, you know? I don't get everyone I go after. *(He picks up her pancake makeup.)* What kind do you use?

D'RALEIGH: T V twelve.

SHEP: Close enough. *(He applies the make-up to his face.)* I'm so depressed!

D'RALEIGH: No one gets everyone they go after, sugar.

SHEP: Charlie Chaplin did. Billy Idol does. I mean why is that?

D'RALEIGH: It's hard to explain...

SHEP: I'm attentive, considerate, generous. My only interest is in their complete physical gratification. Sometimes I don't even enjoy it. I watch my effect on women, they seem to be having a good time—

D'RALEIGH: Oh, I'm sure they are!

SHEP: Then how come I'm not, you know, one of the *great* lovers you read about all the time? Women don't *automatically* come after me. Oh, fans do, but I mean real women, you know? I mean, sometimes I really have to work at it.

D'RALEIGH: Uh-huh.

SHEP: How come?

D'RALEIGH: Well...first of all, you've got to really *love* sex. I don't mean the occasional obsessive fling in a hotel room for a weekend. I mean love it three and four times a day every day for years.

SHEP: That much?

D'RALEIGH: Uh-huh. If you really love sex, you'll be a famous lover.

SHEP: I've really got my work cut out for me. I suppose that guy in the elevator was like that.

D'RALEIGH: Will you please stop comparing yourself to the guy in the elevator? How would you like it if I kept asking you whether I was better in bed than Roz?

SHEP: Oh. Yeah.

D'RALEIGH: See? *(After a pause)* Am I?

SHEP: What?

D'RALEIGH: Better in bed than her.

SHEP: Oh, there's no comparison!

D'RALEIGH: Shep honey, that doesn't sound too awfully candid.

SHEP: Not candid? I'm always candid! I've made a study of candor! Candor and vulnerability are what I'm known for. I'm just not used to giving women compliments.

D'RALEIGH: Well, force yourself.

SHEP: Oh, well, she's much older than you are. More sensual than you'd think, maybe, but not like you!

D'RALEIGH: Well, now let me ask you, if you had to make a choice— who'd you rather be with, day in and day out?

SHEP: Oh, well, I, uh, oh, hey, I'm not really ready to settle down just yet. *(As an afterthought)* And, hey, I'm married!

D'RALEIGH: I don't want to marry you, Shep. I just want an off-the-cuff opinion: over the years, day to day, who would you rather be with? Her or me?

SHEP: Well, she's pretty difficult. I look at you, I see jungle—fruited and green, deep impenetrable forests, cutting a swath through the underbrush with my machete, and inside there's you—a lioness! With her, there'd be a lot more...talk. Responsibility. You, I don't think we'd ever get out of bed!

D'RALEIGH: I see.

SHEP: With you, I could become...I could become....

D'RALEIGH: One of the world's great lovers?

SHEP: Yes!

D'RALEIGH: *(Sarcastically)* I'll do what I can to spread the word.

SHEP: *(Deep in thought)* I need a biographer, you know? Someone to write about me. In depth.

D'RALEIGH: I could help you with that. I'm not a writer, but I could help.

SHEP: What are you, exactly?

D'RALEIGH: I? I'm a...public figure.

SHEP: You are? How come I've never heard of you?

D'RALEIGH: You will.

SHEP: How?

D'RALEIGH: I'm going to take over International Fat Fighters. The ugly and the fat are grossly underrepresented in Washington.

(Blackout)

Scene Three

(Lights up on ROZ. *She stands in front of the dying bodies of her charges which are displayed in the following ways:* VI *in a fetal position, rocking back and forth and moaning quietly;* JACQUES *sprawled on the floor, one arm outstretched toward a stack of enchiladas inches away, his head buried under a sombrero;* LILLIAN *out cold, surrounded by cherries;* AUNTIE PRAM *comatose, a sheet over her face as if dead, boxes of Ry-Krisp scattered around her.* CISSY *is dead, a trail of zephyr sauce leading from her mouth. A vulture perches on the table, waiting.)*

ROZ: Oh God, what am I to do here? They just couldn't hold out, and I couldn't help them. They're like lost sheep. They needed me, and I couldn't do a thing. For the first time in nine years, I couldn't control them. Everything I've stood for—discipline, democracy, the strength of the group—mowed down by Ry-Krisp, sticky buns, and refried beans.

And you, you cathode Casanova—what passion you gave me! And I don't even know why. Part of it's your celebrity, I guess—everything's so much faster-paced when you're with someone famous, as though all you do is on cocaine—all magnified, neon, more important. But it's more than just celebrity. After months of work-possessed celibacy, you opened windows in me I thought had been closed forever. You made me feel like a pre-feminist "girl"—empty and bubbleheaded, funny and pretty and even a little irrelevant. It was heaven! I was fifteen again, yearning to be a debutante again—only this time thin enough to pull it off. That's it, you made me feel thin. And now it's back to groceries, laundry, sorting through the junk mail. Oh, Shep, you could've wormed your prematurely ejaculating way permanently into my life if only you had an attention span not reared on television! But like a dog compelled to water every hydrant on the block, you have to leave a little of your juices with every woman whose hand you shake. *(She pulls herself together.)* All right, think corporately. It's why God invented work—to distract us from the pain others inflict on us. All right, ho up!

(Lights come up on The Wounded. ROZ *consoles* VI.*)*

ROZ: Vi? Are you all right?

VI: *(In agony)* I haven't felt like this since eighty-nine!

ROZ: Jacques, how are you doing?

JACQUES: I am the very sick person.

*(*ROZ *shakes* CISSY. *She's lifeless.)*

ROZ: Cissy? Cissy? Oh no, no...she's—

JACQUES: Dead? Let me see!

(JACQUES *rushes over, puts a mirror in front of her mouth, listens to her heart, pulls back an eyelid—recoils at what he sees.*)

JACQUES: Zut alors, what is in that zephyr sauce?

ROZ: She had almost no personality. Now that she's dead, she almost seems more alive. Lillian?

LILLIAN: I forgot how much it hurts to overeat. For the temporary satisfaction of the mouth, you trade back-breaking pains all up and down here and here for hours. What's worse is that even though I'm sick as a dog, I'd still eat another butterscotch sundae if they hadn't all decomposed.

ROZ: I'm so sorry, Lillian.

LILLIAN: Oh, Roz, it's I who's so sorry! About everything. How could I have told him about us?

ROZ: I don't know. How could you?

LILLIAN: You get up there, the lights, the drama, I'd have said anything! And I was furious at you for getting involved with him. Pram was too.

ROZ: I should pay more attention to her. But I can't be everywhere.

AUNTIE PRAM: *(Moaning)* Ohhhhhhh....ohhhhh....

ROZ: *(Rushing to* AUNTIE PRAM*)* I'm not going to lose you, too, am I, Pram?

AUNTIE PRAM: I just...need a pillow.

ROZ: Of course.

(ROZ *puts one under her head.*)

AUNTIE PRAM: Under my buttocks. Improves the tilt.

(ROZ *tries to adjust the pillow,* PRAM *takes over. She's in a strangely sexual position.* ROZ *returns to* LILLIAN*.*)

LILLIAN: Aww, she's just overall trouble.

ROZ: Cissy's dead, you know.

LILLIAN: Well, it's not much of a loss, but it is a loss.

ROZ: I've never had a casualty before. Jacques, would you carry her out, please?

JACQUES: But of course.

ROZ: And get rid of that vulture!

(JACQUES *and* LILLIAN *cart* CISSY *away.* D'RALEIGH *enters buttoning her dress and followed by* SHEP. JACQUES *and* LILLIAN *enter.*)

D'RALEIGH: Rise and shine, rise and shine! Your beds are all reserved: Vi, Lenox Hill, Room 319, check-in time oh-eight-hundred tomorrow morning.

Jacques, New York Hospital, east wing away from the construction. Pram, I can either put you in Saint Vincent's where the nurses are mostly men, or in the Freddy Girardet Pavilion in Tarrytown, on a quiet suburban street where there's no noise after the operation—

AUNTIE PRAM: I like noise after an operation. Keeps me from falling asleep and dying.

D'RALEIGH: All right, Saint Vincent's. Lillian, Mount Sinai, of course—

LILLIAN: I hate you like the bubonic plague.

SHEP: Let's not be rude—

LILLIAN: You, too, Captain Video.

D'RALEIGH: Forget her, sugar. Love is blind.

ROZ: That's cruel. Haven't you done enough damage?

(JACQUES *wrestles with the vulture. The vulture fights back, but* JACQUES *gets it offstage.*)

JACQUES: Get out of here, you! Birds are filthy, but you birds are the more filthy!

VI: How could you do this to us, D'Raleigh?

D'RALEIGH: Not *to* you, angel, *for* you!

VI: For us? Make us deathly sick, destroy our lives—

D'RALEIGH: Y'all's lives aren't destroyed—they're just beginning. I had to show you how you were choking your natural spontaneities!

JACQUES: What natural spontaneities?

D'RALEIGH: Food, joy, self-expression! You can't focus on it now because you're writhing in hangover agony; but if you could have seen your faces while you were eating—radiant, beatific!

AUNTIE PRAM: But none of that's worth the wretchedness we feel now...

VI: Or the fat we'll accumulate—

D'RALEIGH: My stars, of course it isn't. But that's what I've been trying to demonstrate. With my method, you'll be able to indulge all the sensualities you can fantasize without a shred of guilt. You call this suffering? Visionate the thirty-six operations I suffered for eight years so you all could change in one day. These simple surgeries could set Puritanism back a hundred years!

JACQUES: That couldn't be bad....

D'RALEIGH: Not bad? It's a moral imperative! I want to improve your lives, all of you—not only here in this room but in all the fine International Fat

Fighters chapters throughout these great United States, Puerto Rico, and Guam. Come with me, share my vision of America!

AUNTIE PRAM: But how?

LILLIAN: What's this new bilge?

SHEP: Let her speak.

JACQUES: Anything to get our minds off gastro-intestines!

D'RALEIGH: Shoulder upon shoulder, rank upon rank, I see the quickstep march of the physically dispossessed. I'm not referring here to serious handicap, though that might be a subsequent subdivision—but routine ugliness and overweight. Do you have any idea how many of you there are? And the rampant dissatisfaction within those ranks? I'm talking immense political muscle!

ROZ: Haven't we had enough tabloid rhetoric for one day?

VI: Shhh! What do you plan to do?

D'RALEIGH: Mobilize International Fat Fighters as an instrument for social and political good.

JACQUES: Wow. You mean like, become the Senator?

D'RALEIGH: No, no. I'm talking real power. I wish to be the lobby for the physically vain.

LILLIAN: Megalomaniac.

D'RALEIGH: But altruistic megalomania, Lillian!

VI: But I F F belongs to Roz! Won't she mind?

ROZ: I think she might.

D'RALEIGH: I'll call it something else then—the Heft Lobby or the Full-Figured Political Action Committee—but same organization. If the other hundreds of thousands of desperate members decide Obsessional Therapy is a wash-out morally and pragmatically—as y'all have today—perhaps The D'Raleigh Bell Ugly Surgical Tax Relief Bill will convince them. Because it can be legislated.

ROZ: The what?

SHEP: See the planning, the foresight?

D'RALEIGH: The D'Raleigh Bell Ugly Surgical Tax Relief Bill will grant the savaged victims of American Looksism the longed-for equality they deserve. Its primary provision states that every man, woman, and American child must be given a minimum of six thousand dollars specifically for and limited to the plastic surgery of his/her/its choice.

LILLIAN: You think you can get that through Congress or something?

D'RALEIGH: Don't underestimate the unhappiness out there, Mrs Rapkin. If my polls are correct, the new I F F will make the National Rifle Association look like the arts lobby! People are mad other people look better!

ROZ: I know what you want to become—The National Scold. You're just going to equalize everything, is that it?

SHEP: Sort of aesthetic busing, eh?

D'RALEIGH: Exactly! *(Dreamily)* Oh, see? You know what my fantasy for America is? The ideal encounter: two strangers. Bags over their heads so you can't see their faces or gender; balloons round their bodies so you have no idea what shape they're in, not allowed to talk so timbre and pitch of voice can't distract. Neither would have the slightest idea whether the other is short, tall, fat, thin, black or white, man or woman, deaf or hearing; all they'd be allowed to do is write things down and mime. In that way, each one would have to relate to the other on the basis of *content*—not on external appearance.

SHEP: Write and mime—doesn't that give unfair advantage to good penmanship?

D'RALEIGH: We'll give them laptops, silly. The technology's just around the corner.

AUNTIE PRAM: So the ones who'll really make out are Marcel Marceau and Red Skelton—

D'RALEIGH: *(Impatiently)* Oh, we'll handicap them somehow. But see my dream? We'll do away with all artifices: cocktail chatter, sports opinions, senses of humor, ease in social situations, charm and fake charm—

JACQUES: What's left?

D'RALEIGH: Compassion, Jacqueoline! That's what should distinguish one person from another! Compassion and the most microscopic human behavioral differences—

VI: Sounds kind of wonderful! And incredibly dull...You think you can do that?

D'RALEIGH: I can with your help, Vi. Jacques, Pram, I need you now— need your prayers and good wishes and votes. We have an amazing chance here to do good.

VI: What can we do?

D'RALEIGH: Have your surgeries, return to your home chapters, convince the others who've flown here and been so ruthlessly rejected by Mister Diedricksen—

SHEP: Well, not ruthlessly, D'—

D'RALEIGH: —that equality of physical appearance is an idea whose time has come—than which, as we all know, there is nothing more powerful. And then...send me to Washington.

ROZ: As if we're not in enough trouble.

D'RALEIGH: I've got the issue; I've already raised half the money; I'm working on being a low-key charismatic personality with a regional flavor. All I need are a few surgical conversions—think about it, Vi—and a little television exposure.

SHEP: We can help you with that.

D'RALEIGH: Oh yes. Shep Bradley's decided to do an entire show with me as the only guest.

SHEP: Maybe two if it goes well.

D'RALEIGH: Whatever you say, Shep. My life is expectantly in your hands.

ROZ: You'd do that for her? Give her one full hour of network air time and just let me, who can really help people, crash and burn like Icarus?

SHEP: But she has a proven system! Yours was exploded in ten minutes. She's a very strong woman, Roz.

ROZ: Strong? You call paying a team of surgeons to make up for her lack of character strong?

SHEP: She changed her whole life!

ROZ: She didn't change it—they did! She isn't strong, Shep! She's as weak as my poor flock here....

D'RALEIGH: Oh ho, you think your own members are weak?

VI: What—us?

JACQUES: Weak?

ROZ: Of course they're weak. What do you think they are?

SHEP: I prefer to believe every human being has dignity; and they deserve respect for their dignity and their humanity.

ROZ: You don't believe that. Every human being doesn't have dignity; there're too many creeps running around. Nor is every woman who lives to be forty a "survivor."

SHEP: You're a survivor.

ROZ: Where do all these sentimental, self-glorifying melodramatics come from? Who dreams them up? Whole professions pop up overnight for the sole reason of making excuses for people's weaknesses!

SHEP: But have a heart, Roz—you were like them once.

ROZ: Oh, I was like them, all right—seventy pounds of bulging *pulkes*. But I never needed a group or an encounter session or anybody else's help. And I never needed gimmicks like D'Raleigh Pugnose here.

SHEP: Wait a minute— you mean you didn't go through the Fat Fighters program yourself?

ROZ: No.

VI: What?

JACQUES: You didn't?

SHEP: But how did you lose seventy pounds?

ROZ: By not eating. By figuring out what made me fat and not putting it in my mouth. By exercising like mad. Period.

D'RALEIGH: Why, the world will be delighted at your hypocrisy, Roz.

SHEP: No food governesses, no sexual relationships, no smashing jams and jellies jars?

ROZ: Nope.

SHEP: Maybe it was just easy for you.

ROZ: It wasn't easy—it was damn hard. I sweated like a pig—for months. But I did it, and on my own. I just didn't need coddling like everybody else.

SHEP: Will you go on the air and say that?

ROZ: Nope.

SHEP: Of course not—it would mean an end to fraudulently flim-flamming millions off those poor helpless stooges!

ROZ: I will not go on the air and say it because it won't help; people don't want to be told "You know how to get thin? Buy a NordicTrack and don't eat so much. You know how to stop smoking? Don't light any cigarettes." I tried that in the beginning—one hundred percent failure.

SHEP: But she decimated you, Roz! I'm sorry, but I have to find the truth, you know me...

ROZ: The truth. I love your sanctimony, Shep—it's so ennobling.

SHEP: Look, I've had about enough of you and your little narcissists—

ROZ: You're calling *us* narcissistic?

SHEP: Yeah, why not?

ROZ: A thousand guests every fiscal year compelled to go on national television and confess their most personal, private sins to millions of people they've never met, and you call losing weight narcissistic? Tell me, Sheppy, just how was she?

SHEP: What?

ROZ: How was she? Since you have no shame running off with her in public, why not just tell us all how exciting her factory-manufactured flesh is—how her tendrils heave and sigh, buds moisten and twitch, skin pulsates with epidermal thrombosis—

SHEP: We don't have to put up with this slumgirl talk. Let's go, D'Raleigh. We can scrape together another six hundred women, get this thing going *now*.

D'RALEIGH: Whatever you say, Shep. I am total putty.

ROZ: (*To* SHEP) You're a professional dazzler, aren't you: spend all your time and imagination polishing up your Lothario technique for the perfect one-night stand; and for one night you *are* brilliant. But you can't ever repeat yourself—you lose interest. No wonder you have to go from broad to broad. Your poor wife must be furious!

SHEP: That's it, don't forget to remind me I'm married.

ROZ: Somebody should.

SHEP: And my wife isn't furious. She doesn't get jealous.

ROZ: Who's talking about jealousy? She's furious because she's bored stiff! 'COME ON, HOW WAS SHE?

SHEP: She was great!

ROZ: Seemed pretty quick to me.

SHEP: (*Stung*) Boy, if you're ever looking for work, Roz, you can scratch P R.

D'RALEIGH: Vi? How you coming?

VI: I don't know, D'Raleigh....

D'RALEIGH: It'll change your life!

(SHEP *opens the door S L. We hear six hundred women shouting. He calls to them.*)

SHEP: Hey! Hey! This is Shep Bradley Diedricksen! Stop yelling for a minute!

OFFSTAGE MURMURS: (*V O*) Shep Bradley Diedricksen?

SHEP: It is!

(*Several sounds of women fainting*)

WOMAN #1: (*V O*) Hiya handsome!

WOMAN #2: (*V O*) It's really him—and his flesh!

SHEP: Please, ladies, I know we've kept you waiting, but it's because of the strike, and if you can just wait a few more minutes, I promise you you'll see one of the most exciting programs we've personally ever prepared. Just a couple of minutes more...okay? (*Silence*) Okay?

SIX HUNDRED WOMEN: *(V O. In unison)* Okay!

(SHEP closes the door, the noise subsides.)

SHEP: *(Indicating* AUNTIE PRAM*)* Oh, Jacques, would you do me a favor— help cart out the deadwood, would you? I've got to put my make-up on.

ROZ: Make-up? You're already wearing make-up.

SHEP: Are you crazy? Do you see blush? Do you?

VI: Wait, wait! Shep—I'll do it!

SHEP: Do what?

VI: I'll do the surgery, get the Ohio local of I F F behind D'Raleigh, renounce Obsessional Therapy.

D'RALEIGH: Hallelujah!

ROZ: Oh, Vi...

VI: I'm sorry, Roz, but if you were like me, you'd see I have no choice. Now can I do the show? The degradation and epiphany are built in: The pizza I just wolfed down.

SHEP: You figured it out, Vi! Yes, you can do my show. What made you change your mind?

VI: D'Raleigh's right—eating is sublime! Psychiatrists have the priorities all wrong—food isn't sexual. Sex is culinary!

AUNTIE PRAM: She's right for a change—the tart! For the first ten and the last twenty years of the average life there's no sex unless you're Nelson Rockefeller; but you've gotta eat!

VI: I loved my wastrel days! Six thousand dollars—I could get a bypass *and* look like someone else.

AUNTIE PRAM: Who would you choose—Judas Iscariot?

VI: Oh, that's so nasty, Auntie Pram! No, I've always wanted to look like Elizabeth Barrett. Before she married Robert Browning. Long-suffering, brilliant...

D'RALEIGH: Well, with my bill you can!

ROZ: Poor Vi.

(D'RALEIGH opens her arms, VI crosses to her.)

D'RALEIGH: You can too, Auntie Pram!

AUNTIE PRAM: Oh no—the Pram ain't goin' nowhere.

D'RALEIGH: But you can at least fantasize...

AUNTIE PRAM: Oh no, I'm a goner. Just have them put on my tombstone, "Author of the Declaration of Independence, Designer of Monticello, and Founder of the University of Virginia." Nothing more.

D'RALEIGH: Surely there are ways you've always wanted to change your life...

AUNTIE PRAM: What's the country where they respect old people?

JACQUES: China.

AUNTIE PRAM: That's it, China. I'd like to be a much older me and live in China. Could I use the six thousand for travel?

D'RALEIGH: Maybe...with an amendment...

AUNTIE PRAM: China...and expire.

(D'RALEIGH *and* VI *cross to* AUNTIE PRAM.)

ROZ: You don't need dreams like that—

D'RALEIGH: These aren't dreams, this is action. Jacques?

JACQUES: Can they juggle organs for six thousand dollars?

D'RALEIGH: Sure!

JACQUES: Well, I look okay, but I would like a new pancreas. Pancreas is the organ of aggressiveness.

D'RALEIGH: You've got it!

(*She opens her arms,* JACQUES *comes to her.* D'RALEIGH *now stands over* AUNTIE PRAM *with one arm around* VI, *the other around* JACQUES.)

ROZ: Don't you get soft on me, too, Jacques! Don't be afraid of a little discipline...

D'RALEIGH: This is discipline, Roz—the discipline of permissiveness!

SHEP: I'm swung. All right, what I'm going to do now is pure TV magic. And raw ratings power. I'm going to do an emergency interrupt of our Vietnam Vets who were children of so on and so forth and snap this country to! Wait till they see D'Raleigh's surgical converts. It'll make the Bobbit Trial look like *Cop Rock*. You know why? WE'RE GOING LIVE! (*He picks up the phone.*) Morosini? Prepare for an emergency interrupt. We're going live in five to seven minutes! We've set national and foreign policy before, phone the White House, tell 'em we've got their platform. And warn the affiliates we may go over. Oh, and get the six hundred banshee women back. They never left? They never do. This is even better, D'Raleigh. We'll do two shows on you—one with them testifying, one with you solo.

D'RALEIGH: You're the boss, Shep Diedricksen, lean and strong as a wedge.

ROZ: The White House? Isn't that a tad presumptuous?

SHEP: Haven't you been watching? We set national and foreign policy all the time. The Year of the Woman didn't just happen, you know. See how twelve years of hectoring the American people five hours a week finally paid off? Well, today we begin a new chapter. *(Gesturing to* AUNTIE PRAM*)* Anybody know C P R? Can we get the Nielsen Box back?

(No one knows C P R.)

SHEP: Better take her downstairs. She'll depress the viewers. More will switch away than her Nielsen box represents. *(Lifting her arm, then dropping it)* She hasn't got the strength to turn on a radio!

*(*SHEP *puts a tissue in his collar, faces upstage and applies make-up.* JACQUES *and* D'RALEIGH *carry* AUNTIE PRAM *right.* LILLIAN *crosses to* ROZ.*)*

LILLIAN: Oh, Roz, I'm so sorry.

ROZ: Is it really that attractive? All your problems solved by magic? They don't understand—everything they're unhappy about now will still be there when the surgery's over.

LILLIAN: We can rebuild I F F. With Izzy's help—

ROZ: I don't know—I feel so tired. The thought of rebuilding...

*(*JACQUES *and* D'RALEIGH *carry* AUNTIE PRAM *to the elevator door S R.)*

D'RALEIGH: Just get her to the elevator, we'll be fine.

JACQUES: Just prop her up and run, eh? They open the door downstairs, the old person falls out! I have a million funny elevator stories! I even got laid in an elevator once.

*(*D'RALEIGH *drops her half of* AUNTIE PRAM; SHEP *wheels around to face the action.)*

D'RALEIGH: What!

JACQUES: I got laid in an elevator. It was the most sexy. Power failure five years ago in Saint Paul, Minnesota.

D'RALEIGH: You!

SHEP: You!

JACQUES: Hoo, it was quite wild. Never seen her before or since; it was something, okay.

D'RALEIGH: *(Dramatically)* It was me.

JACQUES: Huh?

SHEP: Yeah!

D'RALEIGH: Don't you recognize me?

JACQUES: No.

D'RALEIGH: Of course not! It was dark and I was three hundred pounds! I was the one you pummeled with your bearded hairy love in the blackout! I've been searching for you for forty-nine months!

JACQUES: Yes? Well, but, oh no! How funny!

D'RALEIGH: That was the most intensely pleasurable sexual experience of my life!

SHEP: Hey, buddy, I got to talk to you.

JACQUES: Well, yes...you were the dynamite chick.

D'RALEIGH: God, if you thought so then, when I weighed three hundred pounds, what must you think now! *(A pause)* Right?

JACQUES: Well, to be the very honest person, I liked you better then.

D'RALEIGH: But I weighed three hundred pounds! Face like a scar!

JACQUES: I know, but....

SHEP: What is it, Jacques? You married?

JACQUES: No.

D'RALEIGH: Going with somebody?

JACQUES: Not really.

D'RALEIGH: You like women....

JACQUES: Oh yeah.

D'RALEIGH: Well then?

SHEP: Yes, what is it?

JACQUES: I...I—

ROZ: Jacques only likes fat women.

D'RALEIGH: What?

ROZ: Tell her, Jacques. Tell her why you joined I F F.

JACQUES: I only like a fat woman.

LILLIAN: I had a brother like that once. Watch out.

D'RALEIGH: But wait, wait a minute, there's something you don't understand, Jacques LaFace. Look at me—look at me! People foam at the mouth over me; the most popular host in the history of daytime television went off his rocker in ten minutes over me right in front of your eyes—didn't you see that?

SHEP: Well, not off his rocker—

D'RALEIGH: Oh, what do *you* know! Jacquie?

JACQUES: *(Quietly)* I am very touched by your love for me, Miss Bell-Blower, and I only wish I could reciprocate. But Roz is right—I am attracted to the fat woman.

D'RALEIGH: This isn't possible! No one likes fat women!

ROZ: Actually, the statistics are very high.

D'RALEIGH: You're lying Roz, lying through your totally defeated, craven teeth! No men like fat women!

VI: Oh no, Roz's right. I got my first husband because I was so huge. He loved me till my thighs got too fat to let him in.

LILLIAN: Izzy never loved me more thin than fat; Roz did, but Izzy didn't.

ROZ: Thousands of case histories.

SHEP: We've already done two shows on it.

D'RALEIGH: But this is insane!

JACQUES: Oh no, the hey—just because I wish to be thin myself doesn't mean I fail to admire the fat in another person.

ROZ:Put on a couple of hundred pounds, maybe he'll change his mind.

VI: Yeah, what about that?

D'RALEIGH: I can't.

ROZ: *(Not surprised)* Oh?

JACQUES: What do you mean?

D'RALEIGH: I can't put on weight. It's not possible.

ROZ: Richen up on butterfats. Eat some oil. Buy health food, that'll get you fat in a week!

D'RALEIGH: Don't torture me like this, Roz, you know I can't! Don't you see, Jacques? It's my surgery—it's irreversible! All I can do now is *lose* weight! I have to put away eighty-five hundred calories every day just to stay alive.

JACQUES: Yeah? Gee, that's tough, doll...

ROZ: Yeah, that's tough, doll.

D'RALEIGH: Shuttup, Roz! But surely we can work something out! Surely you have room in your aesthetic for other types of women.

JACQUES: Uh, not really.

D'RALEIGH: But true love allows for little physical deformities—it should enable you to see past the superficials and into the sensitive caring soul that truly is D'Raleigh Bell.

ROZ: Stick to your feelings, Jacques.

JACQUES: *(Thinking it over)* No. No. No.

D'RALEIGH: But this is so sick! No one loves fat women!

JACQUES: To be honest, it's why I joined this group—I thought I'd meet more.

D'RALEIGH: I'm going to be sick! You mean all along Mister Right was out there skulking around, and I coughed up two hundred and ninety-five large and went under the knife thirty-six times anyway? You—you...you would have grovelled after me like a cat after herring had I been my pudge-ugly old self, and now...nothing?

JACQUES: No, not nothing. But not much.

SHEP: I still want you, D'Raleigh.

D'RALEIGH: So what! This man gave me the one true religious experience of my life and you say *you* want me? Fooey! This is impossible! Insane! My holy stars! WHY DIDN'T I KNOW ABOUT THIS!!!

ROZ: With International Fat Fighters, you wanted to stay fat, you could have. My graduates can be anything they want. You can only be thin.

D'RALEIGH: Be charitable, Roz, for once in your life! People need help!

ROZ: Help, not magic.

D'RALEIGH: But none of this is their fault—or mine! Surely you can see that.

ROZ: Freud said nothing was anybody's fault—it was all our parents, the neighborhood, and the unconscious; to Marx everything was inevitable economic force. Bingo—individuals were off the hook forever. These people are weak. They need groups.

D'RALEIGH: No they don't—they need surgery! Like me!

ROZ: Sure that's not too hard on them, D'Raleigh? Sure you don't want them to wait a couple of years till a pill's invented? Then there'd be no sacrifice whatsoever. *(To herself)* People need groups just to get out of bed in the morning.

D'RALEIGH: My man, my man! I'm going to throw myself off various buildings, tear my hair out strand by strand till my head's a-blood, breathe CO_2 from a paper bag!

ROZ: Here's your future, folks! A cancerous, rotting soul trapped in a bombshell facade. A life of toilless ease, Jacques, no free choice in sight! Can you see that far ahead, Vi, six months after your scars have healed?

VI: No, no—it's almost tragic, isn't it?

ROZ: You're happy *now*, Vi. You've testified to that a hundred times— and for once you were telling the truth. Nobody wants to look like Elizabeth Barrett—particularly before she married Browning and could get up and walk around! Forget this bogus cure-all, get back over here! Jacques, she'll sculpt you like a harsh Pygmalion!

JACQUES: *(Crossing to* ROZ*)* Acccchhhh...

AUNTIE PRAM: *(Feebly)* If I could walk I'd come over, too, Roz. I'd never make it in China, who'm'I kidding?

D'RALEIGH: Jacquie, maybe with a little brain surgery you could like beautiful women—

JACQUES: What? But the oh no!

D'RALEIGH: Listen, Jacques, what if I wore pillows under my dress?

JACQUES: Eh?

(She demonstrates frantically.)

D'RALEIGH: Sure!

JACQUES: No, no. Besides, what about the jowls?

D'RALEIGH: *(Puffing her jowls)* I could puff them out like this—

ROZ: Watch her scrape and wheedle. That's what she's really like, not Scarlett O'Hara! Scrape and wheedle, D'Raleigh!

D'RALEIGH: Give me a break, Roz! Look, Jacques, see—pillows here, I could put chestnuts in here. Bits of rubber hanging from my arms like flab—

JACQUES: *(Impatient at last)* No, no, come on, lady, it's got to be real or no soap—

D'RALEIGH: I cannot believe this! Trapped! A poet's soul in the skin of a beauty! Beauty, beauty, beauty!

*(*D'RALEIGH *pummels the floor.* SHEP *crosses to* JACQUES.*)*

SHEP: *(To* JACQUES*)* Hey, I gotta talk to you.

VI: I'm kinda glad—she deserves it.

ROZ: Poor thing. Take it easy.

D'RALEIGH: Don't you poor thing take it easy me! You think because I have nothing to live for I won't live? Never. If I can't live for beefy love, I'll iive for well-roiled hate! Hatred of you, you leather-hearted, bitch goddess WASP! I'll make you eat dust, and in front of twenty million people!

SHEP: *(To* JACQUES*)* What exactly did you do to her in that elevator?

D'RALEIGH: You'll see, he and I together're going to roast you on a public spit, turning you ever so slowly over hotbed coals of ridicule, humiliating you with testimonies and case histories—

SHEP: *(To* JACQUES*)* Yeah, but what exactly did you *do*?

D'RALEIGH: *(Building to a shriek)* —revel in your sexual inadequacies, make your children hate you, the audience will stand up and cheer when you cry! You'll bleed from the ears! Come with me, Vi! Jacques, allons!

JACQUES: You are too scary.

D'RALEIGH: NO MAN CAN LOVE FAT WOMEN! EVERYTHING I'VE LIVED FOR, EVERYTHING I'VE EVER WORKED FOR, GONE IN TEN SECONDS OF WILD MISCALCULATION! I'M DOOMED, MY GOOSE IS COOKED, MY LIFE'S A FIASCO! WHERE'S THE ELECTRIC SOCKET!!

(She unscrews a powerful T V light, inserts her fingers, and fries in front of our eyes. When the lightning and smoke clear, all that remains is a puddle of goo. Everyone is stunned.)

ROZ: My God...

LILLIAN: *(Looking at the goo)* It's all...Teflon...

JACQUES: Holy—!

AUNTIE PRAM: Atta boy!

VI: Omigod! She's melted....

LILLIAN: And her blood. It's...green.

SHEP: *(Falling to his knees)* Oh my God, my God...D'Raleigh, dead! Such a lovely...in the flower of her...she could have been the second Mrs Diedricksen! This is terrible! I feel terrible!

ROZ: You'll get over it.

SHEP: But I lived for that woman! Or at least that kind of woman. How will I ever get over it?

ROZ: Why don't you do a nice television show, Shep? Broadcasting always makes you feel so much better. Girls are waiting, your henchpeople are all ready.   •

SHEP: Oh my God, you're right, Roz! You really do know me like a book! But what'll I do about guests? I was just figuring how great'd it'd be to have you and D'Raleigh on together—you know, a real adversary show, Norman Mailer and Gore Vidal, Ed Murrow— Joe McCarthy, Stanley Siegel—Marlo Thomas! We'd bring back the days of Joe Pyne! And now she's gone....

ROZ: Yeah.

SHEP: But we could still do it! Tell me somebody else who hates you.

ROZ: I don't think so, Shep.

(JACQUES sweeps D'RALEIGH's remains into a garbage bag.)

SHEP: Look, look, Roz, am I kidding, it should have been this all along! Me interviewing you! Simple one-on-one classic. Frost and Nixon, Cavett and

Olivier, Joe Franklin and Noam Chomsky! I'll ask you questions about your incredible success, your amazingly effective diet—forget about the food orgy! Your diet works best, the stats show that. You'll be the envy of every woman in America, totally self-made, working within the system but bending it to you. It'll be exciting, vibrant, thrilling! You're a monument to your sex, Roz, to my sex, to sex in general. And we'll pack the audience with all of them— Jacques, Vi, Lillian, the Pram. What do you say? We'll make television history!

ROZ: You've got a deal.

SHEP: Oh, Roz, I'll never forget you for this! You're a beautiful person. I've got to get to wardrobe—back in a flash, with the cash! *(He exits.)*

LILLIAN: You really going to do it?

ROZ: Not a chance.

JACQUES: How can I ever give you the thank-yous?

ROZ: That's all right, Jacques. Just stick to your guns.

VI: Gosh, that was exciting, wasn't it?

AUNTIE PRAM: You ought to be ashamed, Vi Wickers!

VI: Oh, I am ashamed, so ashamed! Whatever made me do it? Just because I wanted to go on television?

ROZ: What she was promising was pretty seductive.

VI: How can I ever repay you for her death?

ROZ: Go home with Auntie Pram. See to her from now on. Make sure she's not alone when she doesn't want to be. Make sure she's warm.

VI: But Auntie Pram hates me!

AUNTIE PRAM: Don't flatter yourself. To hate you, I'd have to be aware of your existence. I don't like you, but I don't hate you.

VI: What should I do?

AUNTIE PRAM: Make me aware of you. Then I'll decide whether I like you or hate you. Get your things. We'll trudge to a hotel in Passaic, make plans tomorrow how to get west.

VI: Okay.

ROZ: Come on girls, let me help you.

VI: I'll take her, Roz.

(VI helps AUNTIE PRAM.)

AUNTIE PRAM: *(To* VI*)* Why thank you, dear. You're really quite a scrumptious human being, little girl. Like my niece. Sort of like my daughter, too.

VI: Why, thank you, Auntie Pram.

ROZ: I'll phone you this time.

AUNTIE PRAM: Thank you, but if she works out it won't be necessary.

*(*PRAM *and* VI *exit,* JACQUES *picks up the garbage bag.)*

JACQUES: What should I do with this? Send her to DuPont?

LILLIAN: I'll give it to Izzy. He can always make something valuable out of carbon. Ready to go, Roz?

ROZ: Yeah. Break a leg, Sheppy. Only really. *(She calls offstage.)* Girls! In here! Showtime!

(They exit. Lights fade, come up on SHEP *as he runs into the studio. Cameras and monitors appear from the flies. A neon sign reads, AT LARGE IN DEPTH STARRING SHEP BRADLEY DIEDRICKSEN.* SHEP *is out of breath.)*

SHEP: Hey, where is she? Morosini, where's Roz?

MOROSINI: *(V O/O S)* Oh, she left.

(The six hundred banshee women stream in screaming and ooh-ing and aah-ing. SHEP *runs to stay out of their way.)*

SHEP: Left? But I don't have any guests! Roz, where are you! Listen—you don't have to talk about fat—talk about anything! I can make a show out of anything you want—just give me a couple of heartfelt confessions! Roz! You, you in the aviator glasses, what about you? Or you—surely at one time or another you must have stolen money, set fire to a neighbor's barn, been revenged on your parents, come on now! Think of the millions of viewers out there hanging on your every word—housewives, shut-ins, layabouts... and, hey, confessing in front of twenty million people makes you feel great—why do you think so many people kill to get on this show? Hey!

MOROSINI: *(V O)* All right, ladies and gentlemen, Shep...rolling!

(His theme music swells, stage lights dim except on SHEP*, where they intensify to a blinding whiteness.)*

SHEP: No, no, wait! I haven't got any guests! Any show!

MOROSINI: *(V O/O S, rolling over* SHEP*)* And now, direct from our studios in New York, live on tape, broadcast before a living audience partially augmented in post-production, it's the award-winning, totally unrehearsed-but-stories-edited-for-general-suitability Shep Bradley Diedricksen Show, AT LARGE IN DEPTH STARRING SHEP BRADLEY DIEDRICKSEN!!

(Enormous applause and whistles. The stage never looked darker than it does now around the edges of the spot on SHEP, who has never looked whiter. The applause stops, and the silence is deafening.)

SHEP: *(Scared stiff)* Well. Any questions? *(Silence)* I mean it ladies—women. Questions! *(After a pause)* Well, uh, today, we've decided to do without guests—as a sort of experiment...and instead we're going to do a show about...about.... *(He doesn't know what to say.)*

WOMAN #1: *(V O/O S)* About what, Shep?

WOMAN #2: *(V O/O S)* Yeah, what's the show about?

SHEP: Today the show is about...me! Yes...yes...me. Who is Shep Bradley Diedricksen? What does he want, what are his hobbies, his favorite color, why is he on this earth. Sound like a good idea? *(Silence)* Let's see...got it! Does Shep Bradley Diedricksen have a foreign policy? We fervently...he... *I* fervently believe we need to give aid and comfort to our former enemy and anyone else in pain globally, unless they're fascist dictators—except in Africa, where they are fascist dictators, but where we should help them anyway. We must learn to respect one another's humanity—not to mention dignity. In fact, I believe in our new president and his ethic of a New Altruism. That should be controversial enough for openers. Okay, who's got a question? *(Silence)* A comment? *(Silence)* Oh. Well, now uh, many of you may wonder, what is Shep Diedricksen's position viv-a-vis abortion and women's rights? Well, you all know we're in favor of abortion if that's what the woman wants. Actually, whatever she wants, I'm in favor of. Also as you know, I've long been on record against the White European Male, particularly the Dead White European Male, the one responsible for thousands of years of persecution—and our present oppression. I firmly believe that without the Dead White European Male, many more women movie stars would be making twenty mil per picture instead of twelve-five. *All* the major villains throughout history have been White European·Males: who invented nuclear waste? How about chlorofluorocarbons? And who thought up pornography? As we've shown many times on earlier broadcasts, not only was Jesus either black or Hispanic, Shakespeare was a member of the Cherokee Nation, Rembrandt was a Filipino, and the wheel was invented by a woman named Nancy. There, that should get things brewing. *(Silence)* How about a comment? Jesus, where's the right wing when you need them? *(Silence; he is increasingly nervous.)* Death penalty and sex changes. We believe—uh, he, *I* believe—there should be no death penalty for even the most heinous crimes and sex changes should be given to anyone who desires them *on demand*. In fact, prisons are an outmoded notion and all of them should be abolished. No more jail sentences. We'll handle crime through *counseling*. Caring, sharing, nurturing counseling, of course. Now come on, you can't get much more controversial than that, so let's hear some comments and questions! *(Silence)* Look, what is it with you—every day you ask so many questions I scream in my nightmares—today when I need you, you clam up! IS THE CALLER THERE? *(Silence. He is approaching hysteria.)* All right, you want to know what Shep B Diedricksen really believes? He longs for the return of the neutron bomb—it just destroys people, not buildings, and it's people who ought to be wiped out, not good archiecture! He's in favor of abortion whether the gal wants it or not—population's too high, and mandatory abortion for ten years would level that off. Besides, you gals always screw up your kids anyway, and the world'd be better off without most of them. He's really not in favor of equal rights for you—it's hard enough to get a job without giving special advantage to a bunch of middle-class girls who've already had plenty of special advantage and who're no good at getting things done anyway! All blacks should be detained in camps in time of peace; Mexicans should be shot at the border and Ricans never allowed on the plane—only the English should be allowed to immigrate; any and all creep sex deviates should be harassed and sterilized; all Muslims knived, Jews kicked out of show business so they'll stop destroying our kids' minds, and rock musicians should be taxed in the ninety-seven percent bracket—they'd still have six million a year each! John Adams was right—you have to have three acres of land to vote in an election, subways should cost more than taxis 'cause they get around town faster,.Microsoft should be Pope, and lookey here, I've got my ballot X'd for Pat Buchanan! There—you wanted Shep Diedricksen, that's vintage Shep Diedricksen! Now come on, give me a question! *(Silence)* Did I ever show you my picture of Felix the Cat? *(He opens his wallet.)* Forty years ago in a suburb outside Chicago, a five-year-old boy has a dream. Every night—

WOMAN #1: *(V O/O S)* We've heard it, Shep!

(He sits down in his chair, defeated, and mumbles.)

SHEP: I never thought when I had breakfast this morning I'd wind up like this.

WOMAN #2: *(V O/O S)* *(After a moment)* What?

SHEP: *(Only slightly louder)* I never thought when I had breakfast this morning I'd wind up like this.

WOMAN #3: *(V O/O S. After a pause)* What did you have for breakfast?

SHEP: *(Still dejected)* What? A cup of coffee and a donut.

WOMAN #4: *(V O/O S)* What kind of donut?

SHEP: A powdered sugar donut.

WOMAN #3: *(V O/O S)* Then what did you do, Shep?

SHEP: Then I put on my socks. One after the other.

(A few "Oooos" and "Aaaahs" from the audience. SHEP is amazed, looks out front.)

SHEP: Suddenly a million hands go up. Yes, the woman in fur.

WOMAN IN FUR: *(V O/O S)* What kind of socks?

SHEP: What kind of socks? Black, all cotton, mid-calf, nylon reinforced gold heel and toe, ribbing up the sides in a straight vertical pattern.

WOMAN #18: *(V O/O S)* Stop, my heart!

WOMAN BLEEDING FROM THE EYES: *(V O/O S)* How'd you do it?

SHEP: *(Warming to it)* First I pulled on the left sock, unrolling it as I went, then I slipped my left foot into a loafer and started the process again with my right. Woman euphoric in the hat!

WOMAN IN HAT: *(V O/O S)* Then what?

SHEP: *(Really rolling now)* Then I had a sip of the coffee and the last bite of the donut, bringing the deep-fried circle of dough to my lips and engulfing it with my mouth, chewing it to bits and washing it down with the last of the bracing brown beverage—bitter but buoyant. Sometimes I must admit, I slurp!

(Laughter)

SHEP: Woman bleeding from the eyes!

WOMAN BLEEDING FROM THE EYES: What about your shirt?

SHEP: Good question! I turned to the drawer: Which color would it be— and which collar? High tab, button down, straight tips or wing?

WOMAN #1: *(V O/O S)* Yes!

SHEP: I narrowed it down between a blue and a white with high collared tabs, held each in a palm, checking for fit, lint, dirt, spots—

WOMAN #57: *(V O/O S)* Yes, yes!

SHEP: *(Building)* Finally, mind racing ahead, I chose the white you see before you, thrust it on my talcummed body, one arm then the other, just like the socks, and— *(He walks to the edge of the stage, and addresses the audience—his arms stretched out—and bellows.)* Are you rolling Morosini!

MOROSINI: *(V O/O S)* Rolling, Shep!

SHEP: —then slid it on. Like silk it was, grazing the hairs on my chest, back, arms, neck, tickling the buttock and tingling my thighs with its drape.

WOMAN IN A MILLION: *(V O/O S)* Yes, yes!

SHEP: The buttoning took only moments, but what about the tie? And which suit? For a moment I forgot who gets the promo on the show. Then I remembered: Pohhh-lllll-ooo!

SEVERAL ORGASMIC WOMEN: *(V O/O S)* OH, GOD, YES!

SHEP: And wait'll you hear my toilette!

(SHEP *freezes, his light fades. After a moment,* ROZ *appears left, once again gnawing on a chicken wing, seventy again and dressed like the hag at the beginning of the play.*)

ROZ: Americans, they say, are always surprised by evil. Surprise at evil was the national response to Watergate, those quiz show scandals, the news that the Kennedy Brothers slept around, all our countless murders and assassination attempts, and of course nine-eleven. None of that ever surprises the Europeans much, of course—it's always seemed a sort of ingenuous, endearing, solely American trait. Naive and gullible, proof of our innocence, don'tcha know. Stupid, don'tcha know. Only our businessmen seem to understand how people really function.

I was surprised at the evil of D'Raleigh Bell, but I won't ever be again. We're seldom lucky enough to come face to face with everything we fear all at once—but if we do, once is enough. Groups now terrify me, whether at a stadium, in a voting block, or having upper east side cocktails. Any number more than one is unreliable, I see that now. Sociologists run everything, and all you can really hope to do is reinforce your cocoon and protect it with fire. Fire still seems to be the one thing that scares people.

Shep Bradley Diedricksen went on to become one of the greatest celebrities the country has ever known. He took over the game show and soap spots each day, knocked off all the other talk shows, then the Food Network and C N N, three hours of prime time at night on all the mighty networks and cable—blacking out all other programming—and never once had another guest. For two years he microscopically examined his life on the public airwaves, and Americans responded by the hundreds of millions, fantasizing that this attention might one day be lavished on each of them. The narcississm was unceasing; Shep really didn't need viewers to feel fulfilled, no true narcissist does. He just needed them to pay the bills.

And I? I left International Fat Fighters. I retain a stock position, but knew it would collapse without my relentless, admittedly anal, attention to detail. It languishes now, having been taken over by the Dutch and incorporating it with a tobacco company. Fat is nearly in style again, as I predicted, the justifiers smug that people really shouldn't have to suffer for health and beauty—they're really great just the way they are. Being in shape has become an embarrassing symbol of the upper-middle class, and more and more rhinoceroses are trying to at least *look* fat so they won't get carjacked.

In truth, I don't need I F F any longer. People need groups. Most individuals can't, by themselves, give up drinking, get a raise, or win a baseball game. That's why there's an Alcoholics Anonymous, a Teamsters Union, and the New York Yankees. I don't need them, but I'm unusual. I didn't need an International Fat Fighters—they do.

Shep Bradley and I became one and the same, though we never met again: We are both fulfilled without others—his vanity satisfied by his own internal, vigilant audience, my terror salved by the stones I continue to arrange around me in an ever-increasing cone.

May the spirit of D'Raleigh Bell never catch you unawares. That is my black lesson. And so, good night.

(Fade to black)

END OF PLAY

STONEWALL JACKSON'S HOUSE

for
William O Brasmer
Professor of Theater Arts, Denison University

and

Wynn Handman
Artistic Director, American Place Theater

Two Inspiring Water-Roilers

STONEWALL JACKSON'S HOUSE premiered at the American Place Theater (Wynn Handman, Artistic Director; Susannah Halston, Executive Director) on 17 February 1997. The cast and creative contributors were:

LaWANDA .... Lisa Louise Langford
JUNIOR .... R E Rodgers
MAG .... Katherine Leask
BARNEY .... Ron Faber
DEL .... Mimi Bensinger

Director .... Jamie Richards
Scenic design .... Henry S Dunn
Lighting design .... Chad McArver
Costume design .... Barbara A Bell
Sound design .... Kurt B Kellenberger
Casting .... Rebecca Taichman
Production stage manager .... Joe Witt
Production supervisor .... Jonathan Morrison

Note: During the run of the play, the role of LaWANDA was also played by Starla Benford.

CHARACTERS & SETTING

LAWANDA GAYLE. *Nineteen to twenty-three and daydreamy, costumed as a middle-class Confederate housewife, which is customary for a guide—except that* LAWANDA *is black and there were few middle-class blacks in the Confederacy.*

BARNEY GOSHEN. *Fifty-five to sixty-five, married to* DEL, *with a rich, seductive baritone voice and an extremely kind face and manner. Also wears classically tasteful clothing.*

DEL GOSHEN. *Fifty to sixty, a genteel WASP from Ohio with a soothing voice and calming demeanor. She wears classically tasteful clothing.*

JUNIOR NUCKOLLS. *Twenty-five to forty, married to* MAG, *also from the Deep South, and quick to lose his temper. In the north, he would be called a redneck. He might wear a straw cowboy hat, and sideburns.*

MAG NUCKOLLS. *Twenty-five to forty, opinionated, angry at the world, and from the Deep South. She carries two cameras, and her hair is highly teased.*

The same actors also play the following characters:

TRACY MUNSON. *Twenty-five, black, attractive, middle-class with trendy clothes. She is a grad student at N Y U, extremely articulate and passionate. She has no other life but her job.*

OZ O'CONNELL. *Sixty-five. Feisty, opinionated, wise, highly respected in his field, and devoted to his wife* GABRIELLA.

GABRIELLA KOHNER. *Sixty-four. A bravura, committed actress, with a surreal way of expressing herself. Easily indignant, she and her husband have been social activists since the forties.*

CLAIRE HENNOCK. *Twenty-five to thirty-five, British, and alternately cold and sensual. A keen sense of history, men, and the heart of an argument.*

JOE ROCK. *Thirty-four. An angry young man without much money.*

The action takes place in the house once lived in by Stonewall Jackson in Lexington, Virginia, and in the rehearsal room of a not-for-profit theater. The rooms of the house are decorated true to the period of 1863, the year Jackson died (or as described in the play). Each has a velvet rope across its doorway to protect it from misbehaving tourists.

The rooms may be revealed realistically (and expensively) on a revolving stage, or by one area behind a scrim that is changed in darkness, *or by any imaginative use of the stage.*

Gentlemen. We have a new foreman. Welcome to the foundry of lies.
—Lambert Leroux in *Pravda* by David Hare & Howard Brenton

ACT ONE

(At rise: LAWANDA *and the two couples stand in front of the Stonewall Jackson House kitchen, which is furnished with chopping tables, a stove, and other items mentioned in the dialogue.)*

LAWANDA: Good morning and welcome to the house of General Thomas Jonathan "Stonewall" Jackson. My name is LaWanda Gayle, and I'm your docent, or guide, through the Stonewall Jackson House. Now Stonewall Jackson owned only one house in his entire life, and this is it. Stonewall Jackson lived in this house two and a half years, from 1859 to 1861 when he went away to fight the Civil War. During the Civil War he only returned home twice, but this house stayed in his family many years after he was killed at the historic battle of Chancellorsville in 1863. Okay. Stonewall Jackson bought this house for his second wife, Mary Anna Morrison, in 1858, whom he loved very greatly. Stonewall Jackson had moved here to Lexington, Virginia, in 1851 to take up a teaching assignment at the Virginia Military Institute, or V M I, as it is more popularly known as. The first room we'd like to visit is the Stonewall Jackson kitchen. Now as we wander throughout the house, we would like to encourage you to take as many photographs as you want, but kindly don't touch anything and, please, no flash. Now here we have, first of all, some knives of the period and the kind of chopping table where Stonewall Jackson and Mary Anna might have done some chopping. Now Stonewall Jackson had chronic indigestion and probably an ulcer. And so he drank the natural spring water from Rockbridge Island Springs, Hot Springs, and Warm Springs, all in this part of Virginia, outta this demijohn. *(Aside)* Boy, I wish I could keep my mind on this. This is my eighth tour today, and I got a toothache split your head open Sunday. *(To others)* Now even though Mary Anna didn't like domestic chores, Stonewall Jackson *did* like domestic chores, and it's on the record that one day Stonewall Jackson canned ninety-nine heads of cabbage in one afternoon. It's hard but interesting to picture Stonewall Jackson, such a ferocious general in wartime, canning ninety-nine heads of cabbage, but he did.

(BARNEY *and* DEL *laugh pleasantly, surprised.)*

JUNIOR: I never heard that....

LAWANDA: *(Aside)* I can't believe how full of hate I am. *(To others)* Over here we have a one-hundred-percent authentic item owned by Stonewall Jackson and his wife Mary Anna, and it is called a rotor ruffler. And this is how the peoples of the time put ruffles or you might say pleats in their collars. The rods in here was taken out, put into the fire to get red hot, then the collars of the time was made damp, the red hot rods was inserted back into the ruffler, the collar was placed under the ruffler rotor, and the rotor of the ruffler would implant the ruffles.

BARNEY: Huh!

LAWANDA: It was considered very modern for the time, and they enjoyed it thoroughly.

DEL: Victorians were so clever, weren't they, Barn!

JUNIOR: This really belonged to them?

LAWANDA: Yes, sir.

(JUNIOR *and* MAG *take several photos quickly.*)

JUNIOR: How's it installed?

LAWANDA: With a screw. Two screws.

JUNIOR: Oh. Are they authentic?

LAWANDA: Well, they're authentic screws—

JUNIOR: No, no, I mean are they original with the house?

LAWANDA: No, they was put in last week.

JUNIOR: Oh. Modren.

MAG: Junior hates things that are modren.

LAWANDA: Oh. Now let's see, what else.... *(Aside)* I can't remember a thing, I'm so distract. That's why Calvin took off. And 'cause he say I'm so passive. Can't concentrate, can't make no decisions. Where am I? Oh, yeah, the pitcher! *(To others)* The pitcher on the shelf is the pitcher Stonewall Jackson drank lemonade and buttermilk from as a boy, so you can look at that. Now before we move on to the next room, does anyone got any questions?

JUNIOR: Did the stove belong to him?

LAWANDA: Okay. The wood-burning four-burner stove is from the period, and it is exactly the kind of stove it is believed Stonewall Jackson and Mary Anna had in his house.

JUNIOR: In other words—fake. Not like the bedroom, I hope!

MAG: That's what we really came to see—Stonewall Jackson's bedroom.

JUNIOR: That's really one-hundred-percent authentic, isn't it?

LAWANDA: Yes, sir, it is.

JUNIOR: But really the only thing that belonged to him in here is the rotor ruffler and the lemonade-buttermilk pitcher, izzat right?

LAWANDA: In this room that is correct, though there are several items in other rooms which belonged to them both. You mentioned the famous bedroom for one. Now there's a tour right behind me, so if you'd like to take some pictures, please go right ahead, and then we can move on to Stonewall Jackson's study.

JUNIOR: Oh, what the hell. Let's get some of this stuff, even if it isn't real.

(He and MAG *photograph wildly.)*

LAWANDA: *(Aside)* I never understand why peoples wants pictures of this place—we got professional ones outside in the gift shop. Do they show 'em off? Does their friends axe 'em, "Oh, please, can we see your pictures of the interior of the Stonewall Jackson House?" Does they stretch out in front of the fire and reminisce about all the good times they had in this house? *(To others)* 'Nuff light?

MAG: Oh, yes. We use A S A 400, kick it to a thousand.

(The Study reveals itself. En route:)

DEL: How did he get the name "Stonewall"?

LAWANDA: In 1861 at Manassas he was given orders to stop the enemy, and, even though the fire was heavy, his regiment stood so stock still, they was called a stone wall.

DEL: Oh, how interesting. Thank you.

BARNEY: He was killed by his own men, wasn't he?

LAWANDA: Yes, sir. He was returning to his troops from a meeting, and they shot him by mistake.

DEL: How awful for his family!

LAWANDA: Yes, ma'am. Stonewall and Mary Anna Jackson had only one child while he was alive, though he only saw her twice or so before he died.

DEL: Oh, how sad for them...

BARNEY: Was he pretty much thought to be a good general?

LAWANDA: Didn't lose a battle.

JUNIOR: Well, not quite—won ten, lost one. Kernstown, 1862, first battle of the Shenandoah Valley. But he whipped 'em everyplace else!

LAWANDA: *(Aside)* Uh-oh. Somebody here has read a book.

MAG: And though he was ferocious and bloodthirsty in war, he was the sweetest, most considerate husband—

JUNIOR: One of the great love stories of all time, isn't it, guide.

LAWANDA: Oh, yes, I'm surprised it hasn't been made into a H B O Special Projeck by now. *(Aside)* Both of them has read books. I hate that, when the tourist know more than the guide.

JUNIOR: I ain't sorry those H B Os ain't done a show about him. Hollywood always turns our heroes into buffoons. 'Cause, really, it's a pretty unanimous fact the Civil War would've been won by the South if he'd of stayed alive.

LAWANDA: *(Aside)* Just what I want to hear—that the Civil War would've been won by the South. What am I doin' here in this house? Put a handkerchief on my head and call me Aunt Jemima! The man owned slaves!

BARNEY: You mean if Stonewall Jackson had lived, we'd still have slavery?

JUNIOR: Ho, that'd be just the beginnin'!

MAG: I'll say!

BARNEY: Terrible thing, slavery. We're from Ohio, so we know.

DEL: Awful, awful.

LAWANDA: *(Aside)* Yeah, right. Ohio? Where is that 'zackly? *(Aside)* Okay. Now we are coming to the liberry. Okay. Now the one thing you got to remember is Stonewall Jackson and Mary Anna Jackson loved each other very much. This was one of the great love stories of all time.

JUNIOR: We just said that!

LAWANDA: *(Aside)* Nothing goes right for me. We had such a happy family till I was born. *(To others)* Now Stonewall Jackson prepared for his class at V M I every night. He often spent three to five hours a night working on his lectures right at this handsome secretary.

BARNEY: Goodness—three to five hours!

JUNIOR: He memorized them word for word. Taught physics and artillery tactics.

MAG: He memorized 'em by rote. If he ever forgot something in class, he'd have to start right all over at the beginning.

JUNIOR: Students didn't like him. He wasn't much of a teacher.

LAWANDA: *(Aside)* Damn, next they be telling me the color of his horse's eyeballs.

DEL: How tall was he?

LAWANDA: Stonewall Jackson was five feet, eleven inches tall.

MAG: Five-nine.

LaWanda: Oh. Uh, according to our manual—

Junior: Your manual? Ha, ha, your manual?

Mag: Your manual?

(Junior *and* Mag *break up.*)

Junior: Oh, no. Current scholarship contradicts that. In addition to Mary Anna's letters, Naomi Burtin's scholarly work, *Random Measurements of Confederate Generals*, she says he was five-nine, and if he was five-eleven, he would have had to stoop over to write on that there secketary. That proves it.

LaWanda: Not necessarily. That there secketary isn't authentic.

Junior: It isn't?

Mag: Oh, no, not another fake!

LaWanda: *(Aside)* That was dumb, LaWanda. You ain't supposed to volunteer that unless they *axe* you if it's authentic.

Barney: Slavery must have been really terrible. The crass inhumanity! Goes against my grain so...

LaWanda: *(Aside)* Oh, I don't know. Compared to taking a couple of rednecks through this house, it wasn't so bad. We was kept warm, they give us clothes, everybody sure 'nuff had a job...

Junior: It wasn't that bad. They was taken care of.

LaWanda: *(Aside)* Somehow, for me to say slavery wadn't so bad's one thing; when he does it, all *I* see is guys hanging from trees.

Junior: Look, little lady, LaWanda, I don't mean to be rude, but this is pretty damn frustrating. My name is Junior Nuckolls, and my wife Mag and me—

Mag: Each year Junior and me has a special projeck in American history—

LaWanda: Oh.

Mag: Last year we did "James A Garfield: Ambidexterous Classicist."

Barney: He was ambidexterous?

Mag: He could write Greek with one hand and Latin with the other— simultaneously! Sort of stood for his whole administration. Which by the way only lasted one year.

Barney: How interesting!

Junior: Year 'fore that, it was James K Polk. Nobody remembers it, but he was sorta responsible for America bein' so big.

Del: Polk?

MAG: "Our manifest destiny is to overspread and possess the whole of the continent which Providence has given us."

DEL: So that's when it started.

BARNEY: Polk...Polk. I sort of forget what he did.

JUNIOR: Poor Polk had two problems: first, he didn't have his own nickname. Had to settle for "Young Hickory" cause evvybody hoped he's gonna be like "Old Hickory," Andy Jackson, which never happened. Second, school kids always mix him up with Franklin Pierce. Damn, history can break your heart.

MAG: We spent the whole year reading up on Polk, then took the Greyhound to Pineville, South Carolina, where he was born. A log cabin, by the way, long before Abe Lincoln and his P R spinmeisters ever heard of one!

JUNIOR: '94, we was so short of cash had to stay home and do Oglethorpe of Georgia, which was pathetic. So this year we saved for our dream and it's him.

DEL: What a grand idea! How long have you been doing this?

JUNIOR: Oh, six, seven years.

MAG: It can be anyone, as long as it's American and as long as he ain't modren.

JUNIOR: Oh, no, no modren! None of that modren furniture, houses, none of that Nelson Rockefeller bidness—

LAWANDA: Are you teachers?

JUNIOR: Oh, no, I'm in the bait bidness.

BARNEY: The bait business? What's that?

JUNIOR: Bait. I sit by the water and sell bait—gubbets, mungos, special whippies, you know—

MAG: And I'm his wife.

JUNIOR: On the Alabama side of the Peasman River, between Focus and Grand Libbit, Alabama.

BARNEY: Oh.

JUNIOR: So we're expecting quite a bit. We've read everything about him.

BARNEY: Is there a great deal written about him?

MAG: Oh, hundreds of things! *I Rode With Stonewall, The Stonewall Brigade, Stonewall Jackson: This Big Hat.*

JUNIOR: *Stonewall Jackson: The Last Few Minutes of the First Few Days—*

MAG: I'd say the best text for the general reader is Mary Cotton Brigoon's *Tiny Metal Objects of the Civil War.*

JUNIOR: Then there is *Stonewall Jackson: What He Ate—*

MAG: *His Hair and Why—*

LAWANDA: Wow! *(Aside)* They's scary. We only get a twenty-five-page manual for this whole house; not like Colonial Williamsburg, where they get two hundred pages for each *room.* My tooth is killing me!

JUNIOR: Did you know he said, "You may be whatever you resolve to be"?

LAWANDA: Yes, sir, that's the first thing they teach us here.

JUNIOR: Well, at least they taught you something, guide!

LAWANDA: *(Aside)* This is what I left Richmond for? Hate that big city. Thought I'd like a small town where there's no competition—'steada all them politics 'bout how everybody hates us. But this ain't no better. And now I got some kind of skinhead *Jeopardy* champs on my tour.

BARNEY: Are you all right, LaWanda?

LAWANDA: *(Snapping out of it)* Oh, uh, yes, Mr—

BARNEY: Goshen. But please call me Barney. This is my first wife Del, and we're on our way to Monticello. I think you're doing a splendid job.

LAWANDA: Yeah?

BARNEY: We live in Granville, Ohio, a small university town filled with white, high-steepled churches, students in varsity sweaters and sorority pins, much quiet jogging on the footpaths....

DEL: It's a comfortable life; we're not ambitious, but we worked hard and made a lot of money anyway. Always wanted a son or a daughter.

BARNEY: A daughter, really. Sons, we feel, are mean.

DEL: We own a six-hundred-acre farm in Granville, tilled by sturdy toilers. Barney sells insurance on the phone.

BARNEY: And Del's one of the town librarians. Monday, Thursday, and Saturday, eleven to three. It not only stimulates her, it's good for the community.

DEL: Our feet are almost the same size.

BARNEY: Sweat gathers slowly but meaningfully for Del and me. Summers we go for vacations together. We always talk in low tones to each other. I smooth her hair.

DEL: I rub his hand.

BARNEY: In Granville, summer grass is green and spiky, snow clean and thick in winter; we treat the people who work for us very well.

DEL: They're entitled; they have our respect, our loyalty. Once they're there, they never leave us.

LAWANDA: Gee, that sounds nice. *(Aside)* Spiky grass and thick, clean snow, the honest work of a farm. I never knew a life like that. Never knew anyone who had a life like that. I never knew anyone who knew a *cousin* who'd had a life like that.

JUNIOR: You folks really got it cushy, don't you...

BARNEY: We've been very fortunate, as I'm sure you have been in the bait business.

MAG: *(Disgusted)* The bait bidness... Stinking hands—

JUNIOR: —two fires with no insurance—

MAG: —hot, long hours, Peasman's all toxic—

JUNIOR: —gummint's all over us dawn to dark. And for what?

MAG: Dollar bills! That's what we live for. Sweaty little dollar bills.

BARNEY: Come visit us up North. We'll make you feel right at home. Go for long walks, rake and burn leaves in the fall; most of my friends smoke a pipe.

LAWANDA: *(Aside)* That sounds so...seductive. So trouble-free...

JUNIOR: Who can afford to go to Ohio? Whole year's allowance out the window comin' to this clip joint.

MAG: I mean, six hundred miles plus gas and so far outta two rooms we got a thing that makes ruffles in collars, a buttermilk pitcher, and a housefula fakes, that right?

LAWANDA: Oh, uh, well, technically, yes'm, but—

JUNIOR: "Yes, but technically"? Don't you give her no "Yes, but technically"!

LAWANDA: Well now, sir, but wait till you see what's next. Here is the parlor, where Stonewall Jackson used to teach Sunday school class every week to the colored children. He was very devoted to the little children and was an elder in the Presbyterian Church. *(Aside)* What am I gonna do with these snarlin' hillbillies? Now I got a *headache* and a toothache. *(To others)* Okay. In this room, Stonewall Jackson and Mary Anna would spend their evenings after he finished preparing his lectures. He'd read to her every night, 'cause he knew the candlelight would hurt her eyes.

JUNIOR: These books his?

LAWANDA: All Stonewall Jackson's books is in the Museum of the Confederacy in Richmond.

JUNIOR: I can't stand it! I'm gonna go faint like a woman! Ain't nothing authentic in the whole place!

LAWANDA: No, you in for a happy surprise, Mister Nuckolls. Set your gaze on this horsehair sofa. It is one-hundred-percent authentic.

JUNIOR: It is?

MAG: Oh, thank God!

(They prepare to photograph it. LAWANDA *moves between them and the couch.)*

LAWANDA: However, I am sorry to report, Mister Nuckolls, that that sofa is the one object in the house you're not allowed to photograph.

JUNIOR: What! Why not!

MAG: What kind of a shyster hell-hole is this!

LAWANDA: The light waves absorbed by your camera's lens could do irreparable damage to the upholstery.

JUNIOR: What!

MAG: The light waves?

LAWANDA: *(Aside)* This is a lie. This is such a lie, and it feels so good. *(To others)* I'm sorry, sir, that is not my decision, it is the policy of the United States Government and the Commonwealth of Virginia, which owns and operates us.

JUNIOR: But I've photographed things much older'n this sofa! Much!

MAG: James K Polk's stuff was all older!

LAWANDA: It's not my fault, sir. But I will have to confiscate you and your wife's cameras if you don't quit takin' pictures.

JUNIOR: What?!

LAWANDA: *(Aside)* I'ze in heaven.

JUNIOR: You think this is some cheap disposable? You lay one hand on this camera, and I'll—

MAG: You know somethin', sister? I never heard of no policy about light waves hurtin' no furniture, and me and Junior've had just about enougha you and this devil-ugly house!

BARNEY: Now just a moment. Junior, Mag, these rules aren't LaWanda's fault. And I happen to think this house is beautiful.

JUNIOR: Well, you're wrong!

MAG: Beautiful? I've seen compost prettier'n this!

BARNEY: *(Soothingly)* Sometimes we have disputes on the farm in Ohio. I take the men out among the sheep. We talk things out in low, rumbling *timbres* that can't be overheard. There's something soothing about a flock of sheep—especially if they're not jumping.

DEL: They have a glass of spring water right at the spring—just as Stonewall may have done here.

BARNEY: We always come back revived and heartened.

LAWANDA: Sounds like paradise...

JUNIOR: Oh, no you don't. You're going to be looking for a new job by the time my dear Mag here gets my supper on the table! A new job without no kind of gummint quota crutch!

LAWANDA: *(Aside)* How am I supposed to deal with those two—I can't get no new job! Should I tell him he can photograph the sofa?

(The lights go out around LAWANDA. She is in a pin spot.)

LAWANDA: My whole life's been like this. Abandoned by my father and mother at three, raised by a blind sister with diabetes; an early smoker and crackhead; flunk out the tenth grade. They had to scrape me up off the sidewalk in Richmond one morning after I been beat up by some pissed-off tricks. I got every V D you can think of. Only reason I ain't in jail now is cause of a judge couldn't keep his eyes offa my butt. No direction, no purpose—didn't got no goal then, don't got one now. And now this: a toothache through my brain and a nasty bait salesman from Alabama just waiting for Lurleen Wallace to come back from the dead. Last night I got my sixteenth parking ticket, and in June some gangstas killed my dog. Oh, and I'm being audited by the U S Government! Me! Only twenty-three and I'm being audited! What's next? I couldn't get into no schools with two times affirmative action; no friends, no job, no future. Who's ever looked out for me but me?

(Lights fade on LAWANDA, come up on a beautiful dining room. It is 1861. BARNEY, dressed in the handsome gray and gold uniform of the Confederacy, sits at the table eating partridge with DEL, who is dressed in luxurious red velvet. Without missing a beat, LAWANDA serves them dinner.)

BARNEY: My dear, it looks as though Joe Johnston and Sam Hood's got 'em on the run! And Stonewall at Manassas! And Harper's Ferry—we captured twelve thousand Yankees! If we can just lick 'em at Fredericksburg, I think we may be able to preserve this emerald land free and independent forever.

DEL: That's wonderful news, Mister Goshen. A short war would benefit us all.

BARNEY: Yes, indeed. What else is for supper, LaWanda? That partridge was mighty tasty, wasn't it Mrs Goshen?

DEL: Mighty, Mister Goshen.

LAWANDA: We got the lubbol, halves of chicken with the dowdy, parboiled muffins, liver pudding, sausage and apple toddy with molasses....

BARNEY: Ahh, delicious. But then you and Calvin always feed us so well.

LAWANDA: Thank you, Marse Goshen.

DEL: How are the chirren? Claiborne? Little Ninna? How is Little Ninna?

LAWANDA: Claiborne's cole's all better, and Little Ninna, her infections healed straight up. What you did work puffick.

DEL: Bless your heart. What about yo' eight other chirren?

LAWANDA: They's fine, ma'am.

BARNEY: You look as though something's botherin' you, LaWanda.

LAWANDA: Oh, it's just a little toothache. It don't matter....

DEL: *(Getting up)* Let me have a look.

(She forces LAWANDA *over the table and examines her.)*

LAWANDA: Oh no, missis, it's not important, not during yo' supper—

DEL: This is more important than our old supper, good as it is. Now open up—I see it. This won't take a second.

LAWANDA: No, no, missis, I got to get the lollop fuh you—aaaahhhh!

*(*DEL *pulls her tooth dramatically.)*

DEL: There—got it. Here, bite down on this.

LAWANDA: Gee, that didn't hurt a bit! It feels better already. You surely does take care of us, Marse Goshen, Miz Goshen—clothes, shelter, taxes, nussin', da Bible—

BARNEY: Well, you're family, LaWanda. We love you. And y'all work so hard for us.

DEL: We're a team. Your life is our life.

LAWANDA: You even name our chirrun for us sometimes. I bet them Yankees don't look atter they own families good as you do atter mine.

BARNEY: I don't know about their own families, but they surely do 'spise us.

LAWANDA: Excuse me, suh, Marse Goshen, but if the Yankee hates us so much, how come he so hongry to hold onto us?

BARNEY: They made a fortune importing and selling slaves, but now that there's no profit in it, they get all righteous and demand that we—whom they took the profits *from*—gotta give 'em up. For free!

DEL: Envy and meddlin' started this war—not this sanctimonious emancipation flag they wrap themselves in.

BARNEY: Tell you what, let the Yankees reimburse us what we paid them, I'll be glad to free every one! 'Course you know you and Calvin and your ten children can be free anytime you want....

LAWANDA: No suh! You be good to us, take care of us...what would we do? Where'd we go?

BARNEY: Why up North, do whatever Nigras do up North. Be free!

LAWANDA: *(Frightened)* Don't you talk like that, Marse Goshen! No, sir! We don't want to be free! You too good to us. You ain't thinkin' about doin' that, is you?

DEL: No, LaWanda, we're not thinking about doing that, not if you don't want it.

BARNEY: You tell Calvin not to worry about a thing. We'll take care of all of you.

(Lights go down on the supping Goshens, pin spot up on LAWANDA.*)*

LAWANDA: *(Aside)* All cream and sugar on the outside, maybe. *Then* they beat you. Be a fool to live like that. I be just as passive as I is now. "Yassa, nossa," jump when they sneeze. I don't make no difference now, didn't make no difference then. Nobody need me now, nobody need me then. Or did they?

(Lights come up on BARNEY, *now in a torn and filthy Confederate uniform, and* DEL, *her burgundy velvet dress in tatters. It is 1865. They are exhausted from years of fighting.)*

BARNEY: They burned Miz Holcomb's to the ground!

DEL: If only they'd leave us the cotton—so we could get back on our feet, have a chance at least.

BARNEY: Never thought this war would go on for four years. Sherman wasn't as bad as this new man Potter. Sherman just took the horses.

DEL: Ever since Stonewall was cut down at Chancellorsville, we've been a ship of state without a rudder. He was so strong, gave us such hope. The whole Confederacy seemed cut down with him.

*(*LAWANDA *rushes in with a baby.)*

LAWANDA: Marse Goshen, Miz Goshen, they right at the gate! Hurry, massa, hurry—they kill you or take you prisoner! Into the cellar!

BARNEY: No, LaWanda, this is my home, my land—

LAWANDA: You ain't got no time to be prideful! I won't let them downstairs! Go, go!

(In the background flames glow. LAWANDA *gives* DEL *her baby.)*

LAWANDA: An' you, ma'am, take my baby Hippolyte. Maybe they won't bother you if you got a baby. Just don't let them see she's colored. Here!

DEL: Where's Calvin?

LAWANDA: I sent him downstairs with the babies and the silver. If they see him, they be enlistin' him in the Yankee army!

BARNEY: I'm not budging!

LAWANDA: Then you let LaWanda bandage your leg, Marse Goshen. Maybe the Yankees ain't so low, they let a wounded man alone. I use the sugarbeet for blood. *(She bandages* BARNEY's *leg.)* Now you limp, Marse Goshen, you limp fo' yo' life!

(There is much racket. The flames glow redder in the background. JUNIOR *enters, dressed as a mangy Union officer. He carries a half-eaten mutton chop in his hand; his mouth is smeared with mutton grease.)*

JUNIOR: Well, look what we have here! Caught you red-handed. *(Yelling offstage)* Shoot all the animals—I want all of 'em dead, just like the place across the river! *(To others)* All right, where's your silver? *(No answer)* Hey, you know who we are? We are Potter's Raid! Already burned your cotton—

DEL: Oh no!

JUNIOR: —already set fire to your stables and all the outbuildings, took your horses, butchered your animals—

LAWANDA: Oh no, sir, no, sir—

JUNIOR: And we're gonna burn this pretty building here to the ground—

DEL: No!

JUNIOR: —unless you tell us where your silver is!

DEL: But that's everything we've got! You've burned all the rest! We'll never get back on our feet....

JUNIOR: Why should you? You lost. They lost, didn't they, mammy?

LAWANDA: Yes suh.

JUNIOR: Well now, you're free and all, you comin' with us?

LAWANDA: No suh.

JUNIOR: Going up North with family and friends?

LAWANDA: No suh.

JUNIOR: Well, whatta ya gonna do?

LAWANDA: I stays here.

JUNIOR: Stays here? With them? But you've missed the point of the whole war! Don't you know? They treat you like trash! Beat you, abuse you, rape you!

LAWANDA: Only ones done that was the Yankees comin' through.

JUNIOR: What! Oh you're one of the bad darkies. I heard about Negroes like you—just bad through and through. Well, I don't care what you do— none of you will have a place to live when I'm through with you. Now where's the silver!

(No answer)

(JUNIOR smacks BARNEY in the leg with his sword. BARNEY shrieks and falls to the floor.)

BARNEY: Ohhhhh! My leg! *(JUNIOR whacks him once more. DEL faints; LAWANDA picks up the crying baby.)*

LAWANDA: Stop this, Mister Yankee man! Is all of 'em up there like you? Beat an ole man got nothin' left outta his life, make a woman faint with a babe in her arms, and she already two months carrying?!

JUNIOR: She's gonna have a baby? But she's fifty-five!

LAWANDA: Is you what all Yankees is like? Kill animals, burn crops, whup people who ain't had nothin' to eat in four days? Kill women and unborn chirrun? Is all Yankees without honor?

JUNIOR: Well, no, I didn't mean to—

LAWANDA: An' here we waited so long for you to come liberate us and treat us like humans, and this is what's meant by Yankee justice? Scold, scold on you, Massachusetts shame!

(He holds his head low.)

JUNIOR: I am a shame. And a disgrace! We'll let you be. *(Calling)* Men! Put out those fires! Leave that cotton alone! You really ain't had nothing to eat for four days?

(She nods. He hands her the greasy mutton chop.)

JUNIOR: Here. *(Calling)* Morosini! Carvalho! Put everything back! Tie up those drapes! I want this place like new when we leave! You know what I've always said: "Leave the interior space looking better than when you found it for the sake of the next fellow!"

(He exits. They wait until he's fully gone, then jump up and embrace each other.)

LAWANDA: He's gone!

DEL: Oh, LaWanda, LaWanda! You saved our lives, our home!

BARNEY: We owe you everything!

LaWANDA: Hush now, Marse Goshen! What you think family is for?
(They hug and laugh. Lights back up on the tour. JUNIOR *is changed back into his contemporary clothes;* BARNEY *and* DEL *change in front of the audience.)*

JUNIOR: Know what I think? I think this is just a greedy gummint trap for innocent out-of-state tourists!

LaWANDA: *(Aside)* My toothache's gone....

JUNIOR: I ain't lettin' you get away with this, guide!

LaWANDA: *(Aside)* I know what I have to do now.

MAG: And if you're an example of a guide, I'd ruther buy a book!

LaWANDA: *(Aside)* It's so clear, so shimmering. Why didn't I come to this before? I did make a difference! History will teach us everything.

JUNIOR: Come all the way up from 'Bama for this? Get by the frost, get by the drought, pay off the inspector, and for what, guide?

LaWANDA: *(Aside)* I want to sip cold water from a spring like Stonewall, pound the bread with purpose, roll around in the snow, dance naked on the spiky summer grass, sing till my bosom burst from joy....

JUNIOR: Are you listening to us? Are you?

LaWANDA: *(Aside)* Because underneath this confused and battered exterior beats the heart of a swooning romantic. So it's either kill myself or...or.... *(To others)* Mister Goshen, Mrs Goshen, do you have any openings on your farm?

BARNEY: *(Surprised)* What? Well, we do have openings from time to time....

LaWANDA: Could I fill one?

BARNEY: Fill one? As what exactly, LaWanda?

LaWANDA: I want to be your slave.

JUNIOR: Huh?

LaWANDA: I want to go with you and work your farm.

JUNIOR: Maybe you ain't so bad after all.

LaWANDA: I'm a good housekeeper, I can cook, serve you dinner, I can even work the fields—it's in m'blood!

DEL: Well, we could certainly quite possibly employ you, yes, but—

LaWANDA: No ma'am, thank you, but I'm not talking about employment, I'm talking about slavery—uncruel but abject. You can't beat me or be mean to me, but aside from that I want to be your property. My whole life is some kind of permanent bone cancer, and I got to get out of it else I'm gonna die—today. I'll work hard for you, ma'am, hard as you want. And in return you handle my money, decide what I want to do in life, do my concentrating fuh me, get me to a doctor when I needs it, figure out which sexuality I like, pick out my clothes and friends, and bury me when it's over. I don't ever want to figger out taxes or parking tickets, hafta choose a H M O, keep track of no frequent flyer miles, go to school, hunt down no jobs, or decide if Jesse Jackson's right or not. And mainly what I don't want most is to make any more decisions! You own me—the lock, the stock, and the barrel.

BARNEY: Is your life really that bad, LaWanda?

LAWANDA: Yup.

DEL: But all those things are part of the growing-up process. You'll get over it.

LAWANDA: Growing up is knowing what you want and going after it. I want to be your slave, and I'm going after slavery. I won't get over it.

JUNIOR: But what if they beat you, treat you bad, whup you like in the old days?

LAWANDA: I thought you said they never did that.

JUNIOR: They didn't! Well, not unless someone deserved it. What if you deserved it?

BARNEY: Mister Nuckolls, how dare you!

DEL: My God, you're a dark rascal!

JUNIOR: Yeah, yeah, but well...?

LAWANDA: They won't beat me or treat me bad. I can tell by their eyes.

BARNEY: (Red in the face) May my hands be cut off if ever I raise one finger 'gainst this girl!

DEL: (Angry, too) Is that clear, Mister Nuckolls?

JUNIOR: Yeah, yeah, I was just asking.

LAWANDA: Please, Mister Goshen!

JUNIOR: You really want to be a...a slave?

LAWANDA: Yes, sir!

JUNIOR: Well, come be our slave! Come dig up worms in the mud for us.

MAG: What a dream...our own property! Just like we was promised!

LAWANDA: Uh...no thank you, sir. Mister Goshen—?

BARNEY: Well, I don't know....

DEL: We'll have to talk it over, LaWanda.

(They confer upstage.)

JUNIOR: What do you mean, "No thank you, sir"? How come you'll slave it up for them but not for us?

MAG: We not good enough for you? Why, you uppity—

LAWANDA: Mister Goshen, please hurry!

JUNIOR: Maybe we just oughtta take you out back—

BARNEY: All right! We'll do it. We'll be responsible for your life.

LAWANDA: Oh, thank you, Mister Goshen!

JUNIOR: What? You actually gonna let her be your slave?

DEL: That's what she wants. And that's what we want.

BARNEY: Of course, we're not going to call you slave...

DEL: What if we called you an "associate"?

LAWANDA: Nope. Slave.

JUNIOR: Actually, we didn't call 'em slaves. We called 'em servants.

BARNEY: Well, what if we called you a servant?

LAWANDA: Well...all right!

(They cheer and embrace. JUNIOR and MAG are thoroughly disgusted.)

JUNIOR: I never seed such stuff.

MAG: Very trashy personnel.

BARNEY: When would you like to start?

LAWANDA: Right away. But first I want to show Mag and Junior here that this house ain't no rip-off. We have yet to see Stonewall Jackson's famous bedroom. In that room, everything's authentic.

MAG: Oh my God, I almost forgot!

JUNIOR: Hurry up, guide, hurry up.

LAWANDA: The bed is an authentic canopied four poster, with Victorian ropes instead of springs, all the spreads and pillows, the dresser, his shaving bowl, commode, razor, and strop are authentic, the entire room a hymn to Victoriana!

JUNIOR: This is more than I ever thought! Dreamed!

MAG: I can't wait—my knees is trembling!

LAWANDA: Voilà!

(The Stonewall Jackson bedroom reveals itself. There is not a Victorian piece in it. It's all modern. In the center is the modernist bed Nelson Rockefeller donated to the United States when he was Vice-President. JUNIOR *and* MAG *are stunned.)*

JUNIOR: That ain't his bed!

MAG: That ain't his room!

JUNIOR: That didn't belong to Stonewall Jackson!

MAG: Never!

JUNIOR: Didn't belong to Stonewall Jackson, Andy Jackson, or Reggie Jackson!

MAG: That's Nelson and Happy Rockefeller's bed!

JUNIOR: What! Lied to again! Where's my ax?

MAG: We been clowned out again! This is all Bauhaus!

JUNIOR: Gropius chairs, Breuer tables, Corbusier chaise!

LAWANDA: How did this happen?

BARNEY: You mean it doesn't usually look like this?

LAWANDA: No sir! Usually Stonewall Jackson's bedroom!

JUNIOR: *(Falling to his knees and crying)* Why does this always happen to us? So much torture, so much despair!

MAG: *(Crying too)* We plan, we work, we scrimp and save, everything goes wrong!

LAWANDA: *(Kindly)* Is it just bad luck, maybe?

JUNIOR: Sometimes luck, sometimes we just ruin it ourselves.

MAG: Peoples always against us—gummints send lawyers, our friends don't like us—

JUNIOR: We walk down a street, people get mad just lookin' at us!

MAG: We can't get anything to work!

JUNIOR: Couldn't even have chirrun! I'm sterile, she's barren.

MAG: Ain't easy bein' white trash.

JUNIOR: If I didn't have her, I'd be dead by now.

MAG: If I didn't have him, *I'd* be dead by now.

JUNIOR: This century's too hard, God! First kudzu, now this furniture—!

BARNEY: Come live with us.

JUNIOR: What?

BARNEY: We'll take care of you.

DEL: We'll lift care from your shoulders like a cloak.

BARNEY: You'll feel as if you're floating....

JUNIOR: You mean...like her?

DEL: Yes.

MAG: Be slaves?

BARNEY: You'll have to work—but we'll take care of everything else. Come and enjoy the rolling hills.

DEL: Summers in Granville are humid, but our spring water salves and cools.

JUNIOR: You mean...slave it up with her?

DEL: Well, you *will* have to work that out. But it shouldn't be so hard. Your needs are the same.

JUNIOR: I haven't seen a lamb since 1982!

BARNEY: We'll wait outside.

(BARNEY, DEL, *and* LAWANDA *exit.*)

JUNIOR: God, sounds like heaven, don't it?

MAG: Like heaven...celestial cherubim and everythin'...

JUNIOR: What do you say, sugarbus?

MAG: Whatever you say, Junior. I'd like to....

JUNIOR: So would I.

(*They kiss.*)

MAG: I love you, Junior.

JUNIOR: And I love you, sugarbus.

JUNIOR & MAG: We're coming, Stonewall!

(*They exit, music swells as in the ending of a play, lights dim...*)

(*...and pop back up on a Rehearsal Room in midtown Manhattan.* OZ, TRACY, GABY, *and* CLAIRE *are in shock over the play they've just seen.*)

OZ: Lights!

TRACY: Jesus!

GABY: God!

OZ: Now, now—

TRACY: (*Angrily*) Who funded this?

GABY: It is infuriating!

TRACY: What a waste of a workshop!

GABY: It's absurd, just absurd—

CLAIRE: But not Absurdist—

GABY: Why on earth did you approve this, Tracy? Why is it even under consideration?

TRACY: Oz never let me read it.

OZ: Now, that's not exactly true—

GABY: This is the play you've been talking about for three weeks? Why on earth did you want to direct *this?*

CLAIRE: *(Looking at a script) Stonewall Jackson's House* by Joe Rock.

GABY: Just how many grants do you want us to lose?

OZ: Now, Gaby—

GABY: It's a goddam sitcom!

OZ: It is not a sitcom—

TRACY: It sure as hell is not a sitcom!

OZ: I think the guy's a good writer, and we're here to help writers.

GABY: My God, this is supposed to be the theater, man!

OZ: Come on, give it a chance, will you? I think what we have here is a very imaginative play, gutsy, very theatrical, with a great deal to say—

TRACY: I'm so mad I can't sit down!

GABY: Really, Oz, let's just move on to the next one.

TRACY: Ho no. I want the son-of-a-bitch who wrote this downstage center—preferably at the end of a rope!

OZ: That's not how we do things, you know that, Gaby. *(Shouting into audience)* Joe!

GABY: In the theater you need to be moved, shaken, enriched and ennobled—

JOE: *(O S) (Surly)* Yes!

GABY: —have the eyes forced open with tent pegs if necessary!

OZ: *(To* JOE*)* Would you come in, please?

JOE: *(O S)* No!

OZ: *(To* JOE*)* But it's your play!

JOE: *(O S)* Nope!

GABY: I don't blame him. You always go off on tangents like this, Oz. Two or three hits, then you get *avant-garde*.

OZ: Well, I'm not backing down on this one, Gabriella.

GABY: That's what you said about all those Irish plays. Remember when you wanted to do an entire season of Irish plays?

OZ: Well, the one we did do won an Obie.

GABY: *One* Obie.

OZ: *(To* JOE*)* Now, Joe, we want you to have your say. Constructive criticism is the foundation of the Kaplan Macklow Theater. Don't you want your play in the Festival?

JOE: *(O S)* But they hate it!

OZ: No, they don't! Now, Joe, we're not here to rewrite your play. Such may be the ways of fascist government, but that's not our way at the Macklow. We respect each playwright for the singular voice with which she or he has been gifted. Kap Macklow was a very great critic, which is why we named the theater after him, and if he were alive today, he would applaud your play, because it epitomizes what we call our Vision 2000 Program—

GABY: 2010.

OZ: We agreed on Vision 2000.

GABY: But what happens in 2001? We'll be behind the curve again!

OZ: But Vision 2010 sounds so clumsy. Look, could we leave this for the board meeting, dear? *(Back to* JOE*)* You see, in order to bring the Macklow into the Twenty-first Century, we are committed to making over seventy-five percent of our productions nontraditional. People of color, women, the sexually precarious—

TRACY: Plays of controversy—

OZ: We certainly don't shy from controversy—

JOE: *(O S)* I know all this shit!

CLAIRE: Seventy-five percent?

OZ: Long been a dream of Gaby's and mine, Claire.

TRACY: A two-million-dollar grant kicks in if we do.

CLAIRE: Ahhh.

JOE: I'm not coming up there!

OZ: Well, we'll begin without you, then.

(Seating GABY*)*

Oz: You had some problems with *Stonewall Jackson's House*, didn't you, Gabriella?

GABY: Some problems? That's like saying I had "some problems" with my chemo. It's an appalling, distasteful little comic book, littered with characters who are just pure—very pure—one-and-a-half dimensional. And so mean-spirited. You have a highly developed spleen, young man.

Oz: Sometimes people *are* mean-spirited.

GABY: Well, they shouldn't be. Strindberg would be produced every day if he weren't so mean-spirited. You don't really want to put this on in the Festival, Oz—

Oz: Well, I think we should at least discuss it, Gaby. Just because there's nothing for you to play in it—

GABY: There's nothing for anybody to play in it! The characters are all one-and-a-half-dimensional cartoons! I could play any or all of them if I wanted to, but I wouldn't go near them with...with a barge pole! *(To* JOE*)* What you should do, young man, is go check out *Nothing Is Anybody's Fault* or *The Crucible.* Those are plays!

Oz: But the playwright has to have his own process. You do the same thing to me at home all the time! We've only got two hours, and we have four more one-acts to see.

GABY: All right, if you want to wear your Mister Trains-Run-On-Time chapeau, why did you want to direct it?

Oz: Well...it's bold, original, and, most important, speaks to our time. Here you've got a complex setup with a young girl who—

GABY: Bitch! Slut!

Oz: What?

GABY: I can't stand it, *Ms* magazine has been published for thirty years, and you're still calling them "girls"! Why don't you just call them bitches and sluts?

Oz: Are you questioning my politics after all these years? Yes, all right, the play's about this young *woman,* who's obviously unhappy, who's being taken advantage of—

TRACY: Goddammit, can't any of you see it? THIS PLAY IS RACIST!!

(There is a moment of silence. Everyone is uncomfortable.)

Oz: Yes, well, we discussed that.

GABY: *(Just occurred to her)* That's right—racist, too!

TRACY: A black woman who chooses to go into slavery? What do you think we were watching up there?

Oz: Now, wait a second, Tracy, you can't just jump to conclusions like that—

TRACY: Are you black?

Oz: That's not the point—

TRACY: Are you black?

Oz: Tracy—

TRACY: You're not black, you never will be, and you have no conception of what it means to *be* black.

Oz: Of course I can't ever know *exactly* what it means to be black, but that doesn't mean I can't tell whether a play's racist or not.

GABY: I am a Jew.

(This stops everything.)

Oz: We know that, dear. Why is that important now?

GABY: Because when a play's anti-Semitic I know it right through to my bones—much more than anyone would who's not a Jew. And I'm offended by this play.

Oz: Jesus, Gabriella. The one thing the play's not is anti-Semitic—

GABY: It would be if it were about a Jew.

Oz: But it's not about a Jew! It's about a young black girl—

GABY: Bitch! Slut!

Oz: —a young black *woman*, who's miserable, and everybody's picking on her, she's led a miserable life—

GABY: No African-American woman in today's South is going to dress up like a mammy to work in the house of a Confederate general, would she, Tracy!

TRACY: Well—

GABY: I mean, if the play's entire premise is unbelievable, how can the dramatic events which unfold thereafter be remotely plausible?

Oz: *(After a pause)* Well, aside from the racism, how'd you like it?

TRACY: There *is* nothing aside from the racism!

Oz: Now, Tracy, don't be dogmatic. Surely if you were in front of your undergrads you'd explore your distaste in greater depth.

TRACY: *(Suppressing her anger)* All right. A, you don't like any of the characters. B, in terms of literary value, the, uh, the desperate attempts at stylization are derivative; they numb. False, neo-Stoppardian wordplay (in itself and by definition sub-Nabokovian) bewilders, leaving the spectator anxious for the genuine article. The author confuses, with an arbitrarily

Pinter-black segue here, a Beckett-bleak silence there. Provocative? I'll say.
Stimulating? Harumph. But the middle of the play becomes overtly
Ortonian, one is tempted to say even Fo-like. Where is the Mametian, the
Shepardite, even the Fugarditic? And the supposedly satiric scholastical
parodies—I E, the riff on Stonewalliana—while aspiring to a Shavian
astringency, fail to reach either the Wassersteinian, the Kushnerite, or
even an acute Guareness. And, in an effort to limn contemporary *angst* by
employing a quasi-Sartrerian, hopelessly post-Brechtical style, the fledgling
scribe reveals merely an unpleasant, Connecticut-inspired looking down his
nose at the characters which can only be described as a Cheeverian *snarl*
coupled with a Judeo-Protestant patriarchal *smile* in what I like to call a
postmodern, semideconstructionist, pseudopainterly
Sondheimeronianesque *snile*. How's that?

GABY: Who are all these people?

TRACY: And God knows the ending is unearned.

GABY: This has touched a nerve in Tracy few of us will ever fully appreciate.
Let's go straight to the surgery: it's not a play! It isn't theater! It wasn't
moving, there was no ennoblement, no enrichment, not a shred of dignity!

OZ: Oh, there was plenty of dignity. More important, it makes a profound
statement for our time—

TRACY: Which is what?

OZ: Well, in my view, the play is about the need for a welfare state.

GABY: A welfare state? Ha ha! A welfare state?

OZ: Yes—some people need to be taken care of. That's what the play's
saying.

TRACY: No, it isn't!

GABY: There's no one to sympathize with, young man, who are we
supposed to root for?

OZ: This isn't the movies, Gaby. You don't have to "root for" somebody.

GABY: It doesn't make any difference if it's the movies or the living,
breathing theater—you've got to root for somebody.

JOE: *(O S)* Who do you "root for" in *Oedipus at Colonus*?

GABY: What?

OZ: And I happen to think LaWanda is very sympathetic. I feel sorry for
her, I want her to change her life.

GABY: You feel sorry for her, Oz, or contempt? Isn't she really just a cliché—
though, admittedly, she's the first African-American crackhead I've ever
seen on a stage with Attention Deficit Disorder. This is just fodder for the

cannons of the fascist Right. No one like her exists, and it's racist and irresponsible of this author to put her on a stage!

(JOE *storms onstage from the house, crosses to each of them threateningly*)

JOE: Who are you people? What are you doing to me? I give you my passion, my brain, my guts, everything I have, forge it white hot on the anvil of my art, and you crucify me, crucify me!

CLAIRE: This must be the writer.

GABY: (*To* CLAIRE) I like them better when they're self-deprecating, don't you?

JOE: What gives you the right to trash my life to bits with your big black boots?

OZ: Now Joe, settle down. We were talking about your play—

JOE: Oh, yes, my play, my beautiful, poetic, racist play! The characters are unrealistic, situations unbelievable, and nobody black'd ever take a job like that, am I right so far? Well, do you want to know *how* I came to write this racist play? I was *in* Stonewall Jackson's house in Lexington, Virginia, where the tour guide *was* black and twenty-three, dressed *exactly* like I wrote, with a pitiful memorized spiel which I went back a second and a third time with a tape recorder to make sure I got right, who *hated* what she was doing, who kept losing her train of thought, who was bullied by a couple of sinister hicks from Georgia who knew a lot more about Stonewall Jackson than she did, and all I could see on her face was misery and despair and the desire to dig a hole, crawl into it, and die!

GABY: You mean everything in this play actually happened?

JOE: No, no, of course not!

GABY: Because just because something really happens doesn't make it art.

JOE: I know that! You can't knife me from both sides! She and lots of others like her do exist, and I know that doesn't make it art, *I* make it art!

CLAIRE: Or not.

JOE: (*This stops him.*) What's your name again?

CLAIRE: Claire.

JOE: Okay, Claire, how can it be racist—both LaWanda *and* the rednecks, as you call them, go into slavery.

GABY: So?

JOE: So, the rednecks are white! How can it be racist if both races do the same thing? And for the same reason?

TRACY: Which is what?

·JOE: They both hate their lives and want to be taken care of! It has nothing to do with race! It's just what Oz said—some people need to be taken care of.

CLAIRE: Oh, a closet liberal.

OZ: Yes, you see, the couple from Ohio represents the state, and everybody else're the people who need help.

JOE: Yes! He can see it, why can't the rest of you?

TRACY: That's ridiculous!

CLAIRE: She does go into slavery, Oz...

JOE: But not nineteenth-century slavery! LaWanda says, "You can't beat me, you can't treat me bad, can't be like the old days"—

TRACY: But that's not the point of the play! That's not what this is about!

GABY: Answer me this: What if the wonderful couple from Ohio loses their money or starts to hate each other or one of them gets Alzheimer's— everything changes, and now they don't love her so much. What if she gets married, and they split her up from her husband just the way they did two hundred years ago? What if they whip her for reading a map or lynch her for seeing her friends?

JOE: I didn't write *Mandingo*. These aren't those kind of characters! If they did that to her, I'd make her leave!

GABY: Tell him some of their indignities, Tracy.

TRACY: Well, punishment was very creative—nostrils slit, unuseful bones broken, teeth pulled out, toes cut off—anything painful that wouldn't keep them from working. And of course you know it was against the law for a slave to learn to read or to look a white person in the eye? We had to look down all the time or we were considered a threat.

GABY: Three-fifths of a person, Mister So-Called Rock! Her people were tortured for hundreds of years—you have no idea what they went through!

JOE: Everybody knows what they went through, come on! How could we miss it? We've all been bashed over the head since birth by fifty thousand books, movies, and miniseries telling us how wretched slavery was 'til everybody's practically in favor of it!

GABY: In favor of it? You are one young, repellent man.

JOE: But that's the point of this play—LaWanda's so miserable in her present life she fantasizes back to the worst period of her racial history and decides it was better than what she's got right now. The point is LaWanda's inability to cope with life—regardless of race.

TRACY: Regardless of race? Then why didn't you make it about a white girl?

GABY: Excellent point, Tracy!

JOE: What bud are you folks smoking? Where's the conflict in a white girl deciding to become a slave? There's no drama, no risk—

GABY: No, but see, see, I like this idea, you could turn this into a sort of exquisite political statement—we need to take care of others. But you've got it all wrong. Get rid of the rednecks, make what is her name, LaWanda? Make it Wanda or Wendy and make her white. A white woman learns about slavery firsthand—now *that's* a play—and a part! How slaves live, eat, sleep, suffer, suffer, how their masters beat them, and so forth. They have to bring in the corn.... Now there's a role. Could be very moving.

TRACY: Not exactly what I meant—

GABY: It would make a great play!

JOE: It would not—no bitches or sluts would come see it! And it's not the play I want to write.

GABY: How about this—keep her black but have her played by a white woman.

OZ: Gaby, in blackface?

GABY: No, no, she stays white, but you *tell* the audience she's black. Like *The Elephant Man*, played by a handsome young boy, you know, "Sometimes I think my head's so big because it's so full of dreams."

OZ: Gaby!

GABY: Actors should not be limited by race, gender, age, imagination, nationality, or any of the body prisons! African-Americans should be able to play Anglos, and Caucasian-Americans should be allowed to play *them!* And why shouldn't Latinos and Latinas and Chicanos and Chicanas be completely acceptable as Iraquis or Poles or Pacific-Rim-Islander-Americans; men should happily play women, women men, oldsters youngsters young as pups, and so on without limit! A great actor is a great actor, period.

TRACY: Yes, yes, of course we agree, but what about the one-sidedness of the play?

JOE: Whadda ya mean "one-sidedness"?

TRACY: Your darky volunteers to be a slave, which to you means an idyllic life talking to sheep and running her hands through spring water—

GABY: Now there I agree with Tracy one-hundred-fifty-one and one-half percent—there's no balance. You've got to show the negative side of something like this, too.

JOE: This is a play, not a newscast! A work of art is supposed to be biased! A play's gotta be passionate, and you can't have balanced passion. I mean, should Picasso have made a *pro*-Franco painting to balance *Guernica*? You think the audience has to be shown the positive aspects of witch-hunting to properly balance your beloved *Crucible*?

GABY: I don't like the way you said, "beloved."

TRACY: But you glorify slavery! The Civil War wasn't some kind of spa experience, and there weren't any Walt Disney plantations like yours, everybody one big happy family!

JOE: But that was her *fantasy* about the Civil War! Besides, there were plantations like that—

TRACY: Next you're going to tell us that some slaves needed their masters just as much as the masters needed them!

JOE: Some did!

TRACY: You're saying some slaves actually enjoyed being slaves?

JOE: Some *were* happy! I did research!

TRACY: What's your source material—*Gone With the Wind*? Or Vachel Lindsay! And where did you get that line, "At least we all had jobs"?

JOE: Louis Farrakhan! Direct quote!

GABY: I knew this play was anti-Semitic! You are a highly twisted boy, young man—a sort of cross between Uriah Heep and Jean-Claude van Damme.

OZ: Joe is very eager to get his play on.

JOE: Eager? I'm desperate, man! This is my *life* you're talking about, and you're treating it like a pair of socks! You've all lost the wonder that, hey, first, hey, somebody *made* those socks, and they're amazing! They're a great color, they don't shrink in the wash, and not one of you could ever have made any pair of socks, not one!

GABY: Socks? What is he talking about?

CLAIRE: Murky, highfalutin' similes.

TRACY: The play, Joe—

JOE: Oh, forget my play! I'll just go back to my garret and rip my heart out, ventricle by ventricle.

CLAIRE: Ah, Christ on the cross, just where artists feel most comfortable.

GABY: Where do you live?

JOE: Hand-to-mouth, eating scraps, sleeping with worms—

TRACY: Come on, come on—

JOE: In a ten-by-fifteen loft in Hoboken. Yes, I do carpentry, yes, I watch television news twelve hours a day. And you know what else I do that's really degrading besides writing? I mop out at the morgue when I'm not baring my soul for you brownshirts to stomp on.

TRACY: Oh, please...

JOE: That's it, send me away, send the poet back to his cadavers! I knew I should have been a pianist!

CLAIRE: Orchestras have artistic boards, too.

JOE: Then I should have been a painter! No one collaborates with a painter, no one tells them what to do.

GABY: I hate painters. They never *listen.*

JOE: What I have to remember is it's me who matters, not you! I'm the artist! I don't need you!

TRACY: Oh stop it—there are thousands of you out there, and how many of us? Twenty?

CLAIRE: Quite invigorating dealing with creative people, isn't it—as long as you've got the control.

TRACY: Invigorating?

CLAIRE: Yes. You can spot it a mile away—whether they're any good or not depends on whether they're sufficiently selfish to shut others out so they can work—and obnoxious enough to shove their work in everyone's face despite its constant rejection.

JOE: Do you really think we're that bad?

CLAIRE: Not at all. Artists stand for something—unpretentious selfishness. Conservatism so intense it would bring Disraeli to his knees. Always puzzles me they aren't all right-wing fascists, since that's how they deal with their work. And they do have an admirable potential for violence.

GABY: Violence is admirable?

CLAIRE: It's passion gone crazy and proof of life. I adore that about them. It's what I adore about America.

JOE: Are you one of those gorgeous Brits who'd rather lance the boil than soak it? Cut through the clutter and chaos with brutal insight and wit?

CLAIRE: Yes.

JOE: I knew it! Hey, would you like to go to a club later? Dance? Or the fights? I can get passes.

CLAIRE: No.

TRACY: Oh, stop it—nobody's interested in your white male testosterone—

(JOE *advances on* TRACY *threateningly.*)

JOE: And just what do you do?

OZ: Tracy's the dramaturg here.

JOE: The dramaturg? So you choose what plays get done?

OZ: Not yet. Tracy filters them; Gabriella and I decide what gets done.

JOE: Just what the arts in America need—a bureaucrat to filter the thickmeat just in case our creations might accidentally have an impact on somebody's life! Tell me, what's the difference between you guys, the government, and a bunch of television execs?

TRACY: I also student teach at N Y U, and I'm going for my master's in the history of theater.

JOE: Oh, couldn't get into the *film* school, huh, Trace?

OZ: Now just one minute, boy! You can say whatever you want on our stage, but you cannot disparage Tracy's devotion to this theater! She spends thirty-six hours every single day down here! She has no other life besides this theater, if I'm not being presumptuous, Tracy.

TRACY: You're not being presumptuous, Oz.

OZ: When I had my bypass last year, she ran this entire operation single-handedly, mounted the entire one-act play festival herself! She is a loyal friend, practically our daughter, and a dazzling administrator. Which is why Gaby and I intend to make her the new artistic director next year.

CLAIRE: You're both retiring?

OZ: Just have to send out the press release.

CLAIRE: And the plan is, Tracy will take over your role?

OZ: The youngest African-American woman to run a major not-for-profit theater in the land.

CLAIRE: I had no idea your profile with the artistic community was so high, Tracy. Congratulations.

OZ: Absolutely. What do you mean?

CLAIRE: Well, our important theaters are all run by artists—actors, writers, directors—gives them more credibility with·the artistic community.

OZ: (*Defensively*) Well, Tracy's written plays. Nothing produced, but she's well aware of the artistic process.

CLAIRE: Never been produced? Well, I'm sure they'll make allowances in this case. She has shown no lack of finesse with Joe Rock here.

JOE: Who are you? So beautiful... Wouldn't it be great if you were a lesbian. Who'd let guys watch. I'd give half my ribs to make clutching, passionate, skin-damp, vicious love to a lesbian.

CLAIRE: You'd be burned to a crisp. *(Meaning* OZ *and* GABY*)* I'm a friend of theirs. I run the Hazlitt Theater in London.

JOE: The Hazlitt? Another theater named after a critic? Oh, I see, you think they're all going to give you good reviews because you name a theater after them? Why don't you just call this place "The New York Times Theater"— then you'd always have the critic in the palm of your hand no matter who it was. *(To* CLAIRE*) Are* you a lesbian?

TRACY: Focus on the play, Joe—

CLAIRE: Why do men find lesbians at play so sexually exciting? Women don't find gay men sexually exciting. I'm unavailable to you, if that's what you're asking. Do all playwrights in your country write plays just to get laid, Oz?

OZ: Don't be naïve, Claire. Aeschylus wrote plays just to get laid.

CLAIRE: Might be quite fun to run a theater in America. Rather intense, but certainly keep one alert.

OZ: Really? You'd consider running a theater here?

CLAIRE: Well, it is still Mecca, isn't it.

GABY: You should hear Claire's plan for the Hazlitt. Tell Tracy, Claire.

CLAIRE: Not so much a plan as a dream, really. Long been a fantasy of mine to have a place in the country where all the artists could live—writers, actors, directors, designers—where honest work could be done without the competition and stress of London.

GABY: Doesn't that sound exciting, Tracy? Maybe you could do it— the Berkshires and Bedford are underpriced—

TRACY: Sounds a little impractical to me...and just how high is your profile with the artistic community?

OZ: Oh, Claire's won two *Evening Standard* awards for her directing.

CLAIRE: I try to keep the odd hand in.

OZ: Well, what's your take on this *Stonewall Jackson*?

CLAIRE: Well, as a foreigner, I may be totally off base here, but I think if you put this on you'd be lynched. Though that, of course, is not reason not to do it.

GABY: Really...

CLAIRE: There is a small matter of moral dishonesty, of course. But the chief problem I see—through years of running my own theater—is one of public relations.

TRACY: What moral dishonesty?

CLAIRE: Well, the whole crime of your peculiar institution—whether slaves were treated badly or not—was that they had no choice in the matter. And the girl in your little play does have a choice.

OZ: That is so perceptive!

GABY: What public relations problem?

CLAIRE: Well...here you have a white male playwright...writing about— and demeaning—a black female...

OZ: Oh, my God, oh, my God, of course...oh, my God...!

GABY: We'd be excruciated! Ostracized!

OZ: Oh, my God, my God, let me clutch my head. They'd hang us out to dry....

TRACY: But you knew all along he was a white boy!

OZ: Al Sharpton and the boys'd be down here with fifteen cameras in five minutes!

JOE: You mean if it were written by a Guatemalan señorita you'd put it on?

GABY: We've never had a Guatemalan playwright. Probably make the short list. That, you see, would give it resonance. A racist play written by a minority.

JOE: Well, get out the burnt cork, folks, I'ze a white boy!

OZ: That's right, this is out of the question. We gotta get moving, Tracy, only thirty minutes left—

TRACY: Joe—

JOE: That's it? You're throwing me out because I'm not Guatemalan? Well what do I care—my life is over, my career is dead! Where can I get a six-pack? I'm going to get beer. So much beer, I'll float back to Hoboken! Did you know this week it cures cancer? And you petty dictators—I'm sorry people don't exist as you hope they do, I'm sorry everyone isn't admirable and sympathetic, but as long as you demand sentimental and platitudinous mendacity, all the arts in this country will always be a hypocritical foundry of lies! May all you playground bullies be burned to death on the pyre of your own piety, aflame in the bowels of your own spirit-crushing megalomania! *(He starts to exit, stops.)* Unless, of course, you wanted me to make some changes.

TRACY: *(Astonished)* Changes?

JOE: *(Hustling)* I mean, suppose, instead of having such a demeaning job as tour guide, LaWanda was—hold on—a lawyer.

TRACY: What?

GABY: Go on...

JOE: She hasn't won a case in twelve years, because the criminal justice system is rigged against her. So the Goshens are her new clients—

TRACY: *(Seething)* What are you talking about?

JOE: Just hear me out on this, Tracy. The Goshens are her new clients and decide to retain her as head of their legal staff. Change him from a folksy insurance salesman to head of a racist corporation. Like Texaco!

GABY: Right on!

TRACY: Stop it, Joe—

JOE: I extend the play into two acts, and the second act takes place in the Goshen's corporate headquarters, Oklahoma City or wherever Texaco is, and a contrite Barney apologizes to his wife for the years of oppression and gives her the keys to the business.

TRACY: STOP! STOP! KEEP YOUR MOUTH SHUT, STOP TALKING RIGHT NOW!

JOE: But...

TRACY: NO ONE'S MAKING ANY CHANGES IN THIS PLAY WHATSOEVER! NOT A WORD, NOT A COMMA, NOT AN INTERABANG! Except the author.

OZ: Except the author? Who do you think we're talking to?

JOE: Don't do this to me, Tracy.

TRACY: Ladies and gentlemen, I hadn't planned it this way, but now is as good a time as ever. Joe Rock did not write *Stonewall Jackson's House*.

OZ: What?

GABY: What are you talking about?

CLAIRE: Really...?

OZ: He didn't write this play?

TRACY: No.

(This sinks in for a moment.)

GABY: Well, who did?

(A beat, then...)

TRACY: I did.

(Blackout)

END OF ACT ONE

ACT TWO

Scene One

(Setting: The Rehearsal Room)

(At rise: TRACY, GABY, OZ, CLAIRE, *and* JOE *are frozen in the same positions as they were at the end of* ACT ONE.*)*

GABY: Tracy!

CLAIRE: You wrote this?

OZ: Wait a minute, wait a minute—you wrote this play...he didn't?

TRACY: Joe Rock doesn't even like this play—

GABY: What?

JOE: I hate this play! Everything I've ever stood for, my middle-class upbringing, my tortured adolescence, every political stance I've ever taken, I have always embraced people of color. I'd be a member of the A C L U if I could afford the dues! Please don't judge me, everybody!

CLAIRE: I've never heard of such a thing...

OZ: You're a...a front for Tracy?

GABY: I haven't heard the word "front" since the blacklist...

CLAIRE: How Byzantine! But who are you then?

JOE: Just an actor. You have seen me before, Gaby. With a beard. I auditioned for *Breakfast Resonance*. Didn't get it, of course, but we met, and—

GABY: I knew I knew that voice! You're...you're—

JOE: Neal Rellini. Maybe you saw my Edgar in the Park, the coked-out punk in *Douglas Fir* at Playwrights Horizons, I've got that Coffee Tree commercial running—

OZ: I feel completely tricked—made a fool of!

JOE: It wasn't my idea. Tracy promised me I could play Junior if you did it, be on the regular audition list next year—

GABY: Tracy, how could you?

CLAIRE: You actually...rehearsed all that?

JOE: Yeah, by attacking her own play she thought Oz would defend it and become more convinced to put it on. I've got to know—does everybody hate me?

TRACY: Only those who know you.

JOE: She said, "Attack anyone you want, I'll protect you." I didn't want to, Gaby, not you and Oz in particular. I have so much respect for everything you've—

TRACY: Oh shut up, you pussy.

GABY: This is the most shocking literary hoax since Clifford Irving tried to smoke one by us with Howard Hughes!

JOE: She told me what to say when you called me a racist and how she went down to Virginia and saw this girl—this woman—and she told me to get mad when you brought up nontraditional casting. But there I drew the line!

GABY: And you told him the Louis Farrakhan thing?

TRACY: Yes.

CLAIRE: Well, I have to say, on the basis of his performance this afternoon, I'd hire him for anything he wants to play. Brilliant.

JOE: Yeah?

CLAIRE: Don't get any ideas. I only hire actors, I never date them.

JOE: How come?

CLAIRE: They steal the light.

OZ: Well, yeah—you were damn good.

JOE: Oh, thanks, Oz. I mean, it wasn't like all scripted you know—most of it was my own improv.

GABY: Very believable.

CLAIRE: And about me?

JOE: That wasn't acting. That was inspiration. My muse really kicked in there.

TRACY: Oh, anybody can act with a hard-on. Once this boathead started believing he actually wrote it, I realized we were tiptoeing into Lithium County. He couldn't keep his face out of the British vixen's lap, and he kept getting the point of the play wrong!

JOE: I did?

TRACY: Yes! It's not about wanting a welfare state—I told you that. This play is about us being indentured *now*. *To* a welfare state.

OZ: I just...don't believe it.

TRACY: Don't you see? We're just as indentured now as we were then—and it's precisely because of Claire's smug but unperceptive observation that it's so reprehensible: We do have a choice now, and what we've chosen is to be unbeaten, voluntary slaves.

CLAIRE: Smug *but* unperceptive? I should have thought it would be smug *and* unperceptive.

TRACY: You'll never get this place.

CLAIRE: And you'll never get to heaven.

JOE: That's why I kept gagging—I had to keep saying these vicious lies about African-Americans wanting to go into bondage! I just couldn't say it again with any integrity.

TRACY: No disrespect, Gaby, but over the last thirty years we've had more time, energy, good will, and money dumped on us than all the assets of the Fortune 500! And what did we get out of it? *New owners!* Instead of belonging to plantation fat cats, now we're the property of the United States Government and the Civil Rights Industry, Inc. You said you wanted controversy in the theater, Oz. Well, lookee here.

OZ: *(Flustered)* Well, yes, but by controversy I meant something like...like that picture of Jesus Christ in the glass of urine—

TRACY: Oh, Oz, the piss-Christ was out-of-date protest ten years before it happened. Who'd that offend—two nonagenarian Southern Senators and the Pope? Criticizing the Catholic Church stopped being dangerous in 1951. *This* is dangerous.

CLAIRE: Something I don't quite get. Why did you need him? Why didn't you just write the play and submit it under your own name instead of going through this elaborate charade?

TRACY: Every play I've written here gets a "Very exciting, dear, some of it is really quite innovative" brush-off. And then you tell me, "Please, please find us a playwright of color or we'll lose that damn grant". Hey, *I'm* a playwright of color! I had to show them how alive the play is without their knowing I'd written it.

GABY: Tracy, you didn't need to do this. We would have told you what we thought!

OZ: We're known for our candor!

TRACY: All right, tell me now.

GABY: *(Thrown)* Well...well...it's, uh, extremely interesting—

OZ: *(Helping her out)* —Rather bold, very exciting—

GABY: —Parts are very innovative...really makes you think....

TRACY: Exactly.

JOE: She wanted me to come back in later all drunk and criticize the next play you're reading. I drew the line!

GABY: *The Sweetness of Sammy Sadd*? I thought you liked that one—

TRACY: "You wounded me, Pop" "Wounded you, wounded you, son? Oh son, whadda ya, whadda ya—" "Oh, Pop, whaddo I, whaddo I?" Not a complete sentence in the entire play.

GABY: It is the poetry of the inarticulate.

TRACY: A father comes to grips with his gay son one neverdawning night over a bottle of Scotch.

GABY: We feel it has a shot at the Pulitzer.

TRACY: I'm sure it does.

JOE: She said you'd decide it was terrible compared to hers!

GABY: Tracy, that is despicable! Trashing another writer's work for personal gain!

TRACY: Yeah, like I'm the first one ever to do that....

OZ: I...I...just don't believe it....

TRACY: *(Furious)* I want the job! Now do you believe it?

(A moment while this sinks in. GABY sees TRACY clearly for the first time.)

TRACY: I got so sick of reading all those self-pitying *mea culpas* we get over the transom about how we been wronged. I mean, we *have* been wronged, but it's over, folks. Or worse, all those fake "I am a proud dyke of color and some kind of indomitable." Isn't there anything else to say about us? Are we forever to be defined by slavery and Jim Crow? That just makes us look wretched, like a permanent class of psychiatric patients. "Hey, we went through slavery, we went through Jim Crow, we gotta be dysfunctional." I want to change that, give us a new identity! I want to change this theater, change the culture, change the world! Shake things up—just like you, Oz. I know you'd be more confident in my being artistic director if one of my plays had been produced—well, produce this one. This is what I want the Macklow to be in the next century—a place that makes people think!

JOE: Oh, God, I am so loathsome, so swinish, a complete and total fishspine! How could I sell out the very things I've believed so passionately my whole life? I've gone against everything I've ever believed in. Won't somebody please hold me?

TRACY: Jesus, my casting sucks. Send out for Mickey Rourke, and I get back Richard Simmons.

JOE: Gaby, Oz, I was actually getting sick—I just couldn't say one more word about people of color begging to be slaves! No one would ever beg to be a slave!

TRACY: *(Turning on* JOE*)* You know what slaves found? The one percent who fought back got beat least!

JOE: Yeah, so?

TRACY: So that leaves the ninety-nine percent who didn't fight back. They had to get along somehow. You think there's no complicity in subjugation? Try this!

*(*TRACY *whips off her belt, loops it around* JOE's *neck like a dog's leash, and shoves him onto the floor. The others are stunned.)*

OZ: What are you doing?

GABY: Tracy—!

TRACY: Taking responsibility for your life—just like Barney Goshen. *(To* JOE*)* How do you feel?

JOE: Scared shitless.

*(*TRACY *kneels and affectionately musses* JOE's *hair.)*

TRACY: *(Seducing him)* Of course you do, what am I thinking? Just let me calm down for a second. Oh, Joe—Neal—what would you like to be called?

JOE: Well, I'm actually sort of beginning to like Joe Rock.

TRACY: Killer name—very strong. Very you. I'm not going to hurt you, Joe. I want to comfort you. You did such a wonderful job, see how you impressed all these important people? Do you think you could help me out just one more time?

JOE: You're not mad?

TRACY: I got a little upset when you started making changes in my play, but I understand how hard it was for you. I'm really incredibly grateful for your performance. You were so good we could have gone on for hours!

JOE: Oh, thank you, Tracy, thank you! And I can still audition next year?

TRACY: I gave you my word.

JOE: What would you like me to do?

TRACY: Just an acting exercise. Put this back on.

*(*JOE *closes his eyes, and* TRACY *leads him around by her belt gently.)*

TRACY: Close your eyes. Follow me around. Now heel...sit..lay down... play dead...how do you feel?

(She plays dog tricks with him—roll over; beg; play dead. She tosses him an invisible treat. It's quiet and playful.)

JOE: A little nervous.

TRACY: *(Kneeling and caressing him)* Of course. But it's sort of fun when the threat's gone, isn't it?

JOE: Well...yeah...

TRACY: Kind of liberating?

JOE: Yeah...a kind of very nice sort of surrender.

TRACY: You're a very trusting person, Joe. I love that about actors. Not so bad having your life defined by someone else, is it?

JOE: *(Luxuriating)* I have friends who'd never want to take this off!

TRACY: *(Softly)* That is so sweet! Oh, I'm going to take such care of you next year, Joe. Six productions...won't it be nice to have your rent secure? No more morgue...move into Manhattan? All tension vanished...uncertainty gone.

JOE: Ohhh...ohhh...

TRACY: You'll be appreciated at last, just as your friends've told you you should be....

JOE: Mmmmmmmmmmmmmmmmmm...

GABY: Claire, you're breathing through your mouth.

(An excited CLAIRE blows down her blouse. TRACY rubs JOE's thigh.)

TRACY: Just give yourself up to a greater power, Joe. No decisions— like a Charismatic or a Shiite. Always know where you stand, what your place in the world is. Isn't it safe?

JOE: Mmmmmmmmmmmm...

GABY: This is obscene. Pornographic!

TRACY: *(Holding out her belt)* Anybody else want to try this? Oz?

OZ: No, no, I'm a director. I do that master-slave thing all the time.

TRACY: Fergie?

(CLAIRE shakes her head, "No".)

GABY: *(To JOE)* Get up! Have you no self-respect whatsoever?

TRACY: Yeah, but see how seductive subjugation can be? In my play, LaWanda makes it clear hers is voluntary. She is seduced just the way we've been seduced!

JOE: You mean this was all just to prove some racist point in your play?

TRACY: Victimization is always at least somewhat voluntary. Isn't that worth putting on a stage?

JOE: *(Exploding)* You just humiliated me again!

TRACY: Well, yes.

JOE: You can't equate one minute of sexual titillation with two to three hundred years of enforced bondage! I don't want to be anyone's slave, and I don't want to be anyone's owner, and maybe you're some kind of professional victim, but, hey, baby, I'm not. In real life slavery isn't voluntary!

GABY: Of course you have grievances, Tracy dear, many, many grievances, but you're not really a slave—

TRACY: Look, it's easy to call Hitler and Mao and Pol Pot butchers, but they must have offered something in return or they wouldn't have been in power so long—safety, national pride, a better future. One man can't do it alone. "S and M" is never referred to as just "S." You have to believe either there's something inherently subservient in some human beings or that these systems actually offer payoffs pretty beguiling to both sides.

GABY: You have no idea what you're talking about with Hitler! He had guns, the police, the government on his side!

TRACY: I'm not saying I want it that way, I'm saying it *is* that way. Why are you all too frightened to at least ask why enormous numbers of people like being told what to do?

JOE: Boy, they'd love you over at *The American Spectator.*

OZ: I don't think I like this play.

TRACY: Oz, how can you say that? You were so eager to direct it! I saw you skipping in the hall on your way to rehearsal! You told me you were going to surprise and thrill us—

OZ: I think you misunderstood what I meant by "controversial"—

TRACY: Don't you remember all those things you told me over drinks at Sabu's night after night? "If Marx were alive today in America, he'd say it's not religion that's the opiate of the people, it's the arts!" Don't you remember saying that? "The chief responsibility of the artist has become to not hurt anyone's feelings." And you weren't drunk. Our audience needs to be stirred up—that's what you said!

GABY: What you don't seem to understand, Tracy, is that audiences don't really like controversy. Unless they agree with it, of course.

OZ: Well, I meant something else—

CLAIRE: Tracy, surely you've been here long enough to distinguish between after-hours rhetoric and public policy.

TRACY: *(Exploding)* That's not what you said, Oz! You said you wanted to blow the roof off the theater—off all culture in the country! I said, "But what about Gaby, she doesn't want to blow the roof off the theater, she wants to do *The Sweetness of Sammy Sadd,* how will you get it by her?" And you said, "Tracy, if only somebody would give me the ammo, I'd not only stand up to Gaby, I'd make that bully fall to her knees!" You said!

GABY: What?

OZ: Never did!

TRACY: Yes, you did!

OZ: Did not! After what she and I have gone through all these years, you think I'd say something like that about my own wife? *(To GABY)* I never said that, dear. You're not a bully!

GABY: Of course you didn't. Or if you did you didn't mean it. We all have to vent from time to time.

OZ: Tracy, I just got this whole thing wrong.

TRACY: No, you didn't, you got it right, or nearly right, you were so brave about it! But you're caving now because you're afraid—

OZ: I am not "caving"! It really, really went right by me—

GABY: It's all right, dear. You're on the right side now.

OZ: Thank you, dear.

TRACY: *(Exploding)* Oh, you've never been on the right side of anything, either of you, just the comfortable one!

OZ: What?

GABY: Excuse me?

TRACY: Sentimental, self-centered Old Lefties whose well-meaning, stubborn politics have wrecked this century—trying to stuff real, complicated anguish into simplistic theories!

GABY: What real, complicated anguish?

TRACY: All of it! Racism! Welfare! Nam! Stalin!

GABY: Stalin?

TRACY: Yes, even him! You were told and told what he was doing and refused and refused to let the sunlight in even when it pierced your bulletproof sunglasses! While he murdered and tortured more of his own citizens than Hitler and Pol Pot and Idi Amin combined, you protected yourself with lies so you wouldn't have to admit you were wrong—and instead focused on a bunch of mediocre movie writers martyred by a blacklist!

GABY: They were not mediocre writers!

TRACY: Well, mediocre martyrs then. I mean, what was your response to finding out about the gulags? To turn Solzhenitsyn into a crackpot for exposing them and ruining your lives!

GABY: He is a crackpot!

TRACY: Of course he is—he broke your heart! Well, it's about to be broken again.

GABY: Oh really? By who?

TRACY: By me! You and your Upper West Side reformers were told and told just passing laws wouldn't eradicate racism, but you wouldn't listen and when racism didn't go away, you buried your head in the sand and said, "I dont get it. Why aren't they happy?" Your noble theories don't have anything to do with real life. They are just as distant and idiotic as nontraditional casting! I mean, face it—nobody believes men playing women except in Vegas, and women playing men is just silly.

GABY: Not silly and completely believable!

TRACY: It's saying everybody's not only equal, they're the same! Theory!

GABY: What's wrong with theory? Really, dear, didn't you take *any* Black Studies in college?

TRACY: I wasted two entire semesters sleeping through that baloney—never heard so much made-up history in my life. That's all they teach in there— fictions about our past supposed to make us feel better and self-esteem exercises straight out of Big Sur. Spend hours lecturing about the greed of your slave traders—and none at all about the greed of our homey chieftains so eager to sell us. And in the end if you have the nerve to praise Booker T Washington instead of W E B DuBois, they give you an F.

GABY: I had no idea you felt this way about things, Tracy.

TRACY: I'm afraid there are lots of things you have no idea how I feel about, Gaby. You look at me and all you choose to see is a child of racism. What if I'm more than that? What if I'm less? What if maybe I ain't black after all, ever think of that?

JOE: What the hell does that mean?

TRACY: Perhaps I don't fit the code. You can't be black, if you date somebody white; can't be black if you don't blame all your problems on racism; can't be if you think some of our brothers in jail actually belong there; and you can't *no way* be black if you don't see that Clarence Thomas has two heads.

GABY: (*Coldly*) Tracy, dear, you are about *this* far from crossing a very precarious line.

JOE: I've never heard such blatant racism in my life!

TRACY: Your idea of a racist is anyone who won't spend twenty-four hours a day fighting for our God-given right to get free handouts from the government—

JOE: Racist!

TRACY: Why is everyone who doesn't want to give us things a bigot?

JOE: Racist!

CLAIRE: Your constant use of the word "racist" is really quite a brilliant rhetorical device—anything troublesome can be dismissed by calling it racist; the other person stands paralyzed with fear, defeated, his career and argument in tatters. Quite like being one of your Salem witches, or a Lutheran in 1520, isn't it? You've successfully trivialized the word into meaninglessness.

OZ: Racist this, racist that. I don't even know what the hell it is anymore. Nobody does.

GABY: I'll explain it to you after six.

OZ: Used to be so clear-cut: slavery, lynching, people as property. That's racism! Can't vote, segregated schools, stupid rules about drinking fountains—*that* was racism. But now...what is it exactly? A taxi won't pick you up? You get a bad table at a restaurant? Somebody calls you the "N" word? Is this what all the fuss is about? Hell, they call me a Mick, I start laughing.

GABY: How long have you been camouflaging your feelings, Tracy?

TRACY: Since I've known you. I'm such a different person from who you think I am. You don't have a clue what's on my mind, and you never will, 'cause most every time I see you, I lie. Most black people do. We say what we think you expect; and every time one of us tries to break through and act like an individual, clang, you close the jail bars on us.

JOE: All they've tried to do with their whole lives is make up for everything done to you for the last three or four centuries.

TRACY: Well, please get them to *stop*. White people believe two things about race: one, that all people are created equal, and two, that blacks are inferior to whites. And now our massa-pleasing demagogues and your dilettante press have sprung to your aid, focusing on stupid distractions like reparations and was Beethoven black, theories about melanin dumb as phlogiston. I don't want reparations for some injustice done three hundred years ago! What if everybody demanded that? How far back should the blame go? Christians and lions? Ostrogoths and Vandals in 330 B C? "I'm an Ostrogoth, and I demand reparations for—"

JOE: Quit trivializing your own struggle!

TRACY: I'm not! You are! Quit giving us stuff!

CLAIRE: "Massa-pleasing demagogues"—interesting turn of phrase.
Just who might they be?

TRACY: Why, the chief public relations arm for white racism—our very own
leaders.

JOE: That's the thanks they get for trying to solve your problems?

TRACY: How can they solve our problems—they *are* our problems! Don't
you get it? Listen. Everybody—regardless of race—is unhappy most of the
time, for all sorts of reasons, most of them having nothing to do with race.
But our loudmouth leaders want to simplify the human experience by
saying it's all because of racism.

JOE: Wait a minute—you're saying racism doesn't exist?

TRACY: Of course, it exists. It's just that, in this country anyway, it doesn't
matter much anymore except to our rabble rousers who'd be out of a job
without it. If our victimization-hustlers didn't play the race card, they might
actually have to be elected on merit.

JOE: So your leaders "fool" you into believing racism matters? Horseshit!

TRACY: You saw the L A riots, didn't you? The night less than a hundred
homeys gleefully set fire to several buildings, killing a few Koreans in the
process? The next morning a few thousand nonhomeys strolled through a
rather cheerful and clearly multiracial shopping spree. The event resembled
little more than an extremely expensive college prank—we all saw with our
own eyes the fun everyone was having.

JOE: That wasn't a shopping spree! Those people were furious!

TRACY: Oh, please—you saw their faces! That wasn't anger, it wasn't
revenge, it was exhilaration. Riots are exciting—at least to the rioters.
Imagine the adrenalin pumped at the Boston Tea Party. And the moment all
the multiculturals finished picking up their new appliances, you didn't see
white folks or Mexicans or Pacific-Rim-Islanders grabbing the mike. But *our*
glorious politicians practically tripped over each other in their eagerness to
tell the television cameras that it was *our* riot. And thank God for the riots,
so our Maxines and Cecils and Godfather Jesse flying around in some white
man's plane could remind everybody, "HEY! DONT FORGET US! WE GOT
POLIO! WE NEED MONEY! WE NEED PITY!" And Washington, duped
again, clambered in like Pavlov's dog with its usual condescending bags of
moolah, once again allowing our spokeshumans to explain criminality away
with excuses of "black rage," when everybody could plainly see from the
never-ending T V coverage that, A: most of the rioters weren't black and, B:
nobody seemed particularly angry.

JOE: That's your take on the rebellion?

TRACY: Rebellion? Rouge it up anyway you want, it was a riot.

JOE: The white European male has had his thumb in your eye since 1607!

GABY: Now, that's true! No one has been tyrannized like women and African-Americans!

TRACY: Women? Women?! Who'm I supposed to feel sorry for first? All these complaints about a glass ceiling—anybody here have any experience looking at a *cement* ceiling? Yeah, yeah, women have gripes, too, but compared to what we went through it's Gripes LITE. Your suffering is to ours as decaf is to regular. "We could have painted the Mona Lisa if only they'd let us."

GABY: You have just crossed the precarious line, Tracy.

OZ: Is this some kind of Pirandello thing where it turns out this guy really *did* write this play and rehearsed you?

JOE & TRACY: No!

OZ: But, why are you so pissed off at your white sisters—you should be working together.

TRACY: 'Cause you need a bunch of guilty white men to make any progress, and there aren't too many of them left. "My white sisters" are splitting up the resources. Let 'em come up with their own agonies for a change instead of always stealing ours. "Well, actually, with a little imaginative use of metaphor, we've been slaves, too." Well, kiss my black ass, they weren't beaten, not like us, and they have never since the beginning of time for thirty seconds been a minority.

GABY: You're not only burning your ideological bridges, you are digging your grave.

JOE: Maybe affirmative action for some people is a bad idea.

TRACY: What's affirmative action ever done for us? One tenth of The Talented Tenth move into the middle class, and a couple of guys get to go to Yale. Yeah bo! All we ever got from affirmative action was bad publicity. White girls got all the jobs.

OZ: Look, godammit, everybody's had a thumb in their eye at some point! What about us? Do you know what the Irish endured during the years of slavery? We did all the back-breaking, life-threatening work that was too dangerous for Africans to do, because Africans were property, and Massa didn't want to risk damage to his property. But potato-eating Micks were completely expendable. For a penny an hour we did all the high-risk work sixteen hours a day until we were either buried or sent to the hospital or allowed to go home to four-foot-high, tin-roofed huts, eight to a room, with

inside, open sewers and cholera seeping through the floorboards.
The eighteenth and nineteenth centuries were barbaric to everybody—
but we didn't have enough angry historians, so nobody remembers what
happened to us.

GABY: I don't want to get into competitive misfortunes, but you weren't
actually slaves, dear.

OZ: Look, I know African-Americans had it rough, okay, but they weren't
the only ones who did, and it burns my ass to hear all this sanctimony as
though they were the only people on earth who did! Burns my ass when I
see how far the Irish have come since then, and the Jews, and the Japanese,
and the Chinese for Christ's sake, and the Scandinavians in the midwest,
and the French, the Germans, the Italians, Rellini—your people! Even the
goddam Spanish! And then how far you've come! Your progress is
appreciable only in the intensity and volume of your complaint. I'm sick
of it! Everybody else has made America work for them but you, Tracy.
Everybody! Why?

GABY: Oz!

OZ: Oh, God, I am so sorry, Tracy, I—

TRACY: No, no, it's refreshing to hear you say something you actually
believe, Oz, though if I know Gaby, you won't for long. We can't make
America work because we've been told since birth we couldn't hack it—
first by your people, now by our people. How could we possibly function
like normal human beings? We went through slavery! How much longer
are you going to allow us to feed off our historic victimization?

OZ: You think all your political leaders do that?

TRACY: Not Dr King. He was the only one with vision. He saw the long-term
goal was harmony, not just getting a lot of laws passed. He saw that *how* the
laws were passed was just as important as the laws themselves. But, no,
our hot-hormone boys opted for their Raps and Stokelys and the most
adolescent of Mister X's many personalities and went around getting
everybody mad so they'd feel good for about five minutes but lousy for
the next two hundred years.

OZ: But what about all your mayors, governors, the Black Caucus, look
what they did in Haiti. Articulate, powerful leaders—

TRACY: That's the trouble with you farty Old Lefties, Oz—you condescend
to us by pretending rhymed couplets and rap slogans are powerful and
articulate. Our leadership has no credibility, because they're too busy
defending our criminals. They spend all their time making excuses for Colin
Ferguson instead of bragging on Colin Powell. You ever hear white boys
coming up with excuses for Gary Gilmore and Jeffrey Dahmer? Can you

name a black astronaut? Most people can't name a black entrepreneur besides Famous Amos. Can you?

OZ: Well...uhh—

TRACY: Did you even know there were any?

JOE: Of course there are!

CLAIRE: Goodness, you people are self-important.

TRACY: *(Viciously)* What does that mean?

CLAIRE: You really haven't a clue, have you, that the rest of the world watches your age-old little dance with such amusement. You just go round and round, don't you, the Great White Father and his misbehaving adolescent. If you could get your head out of your own collective rectum, you might notice that there's much greater prejudice in almost every country in the world—and considerably less justice. The crimes that Arabs do to Jews, Jews to Arabs, Tutsis to Hutus, Brahmins to Untouchables— all are much worse than what goes on here. But you people are so self-involved, so self-important, your ingrown toenail becomes more critical than the rest of the world's terminal cancer. And since you own most of the satellites, we all have to hear about it!

JOE: At least we're working on it—

CLAIRE: But you're not working on solving it, you're working on keeping it going. Don't you see how you feed off each other? You *want* the dance to continue. Without it, Tracy's right—your public figures would have no employment—not to mention income. Without the dance, you'd be like Europe now that the Soviet Union's collapsed. There's nobody to be against. That was part of Hitler's genius—and why Tracy's politicians keep racism alive.

TRACY: Maybe we should pay reparations to the U S for getting us out of West Africa in the first place.

GABY: How dare you say that! You think your great-great-grandmother was lucky to come here?

TRACY: She wasn't. But I am. I've been to Africa. Hated it.

JOE: Oh, I get it—you wish you were white!

TRACY: You're not just a knee-jerk, you're a full-body-jerk. No, I am not a self-loathing nigger, and no, I don't wish I was white. I wish I was more important than I am—and I wish you'd do my damn play.

JOE: You wish you were a dead white European male.

TRACY: No, I wish *you* were a dead white European male. And seventy-five percent of my wish has already come true, so watch your step.

JOE: No, no, you hate yourself so much, you despise everything about your own heritage!

TRACY: I do not! I just don't want to live in it!

CLAIRE: You seem to forget, Joe—or Neal—that loathing one's own heritage was precisely what was unique about the founding of your country. And what's ironic is how much of your republic is now banding together in separate, self-interested little groups which romanticize the very customs and cultures they risked their lives to flee. But don't you see, in two decades or so the debate may not even involve Tracy's people: it'll be over which four southwestern states to give to the Hispanics, or whether the whole month of Ramadan should be a federal holiday or just the feast at the end. Your citizenry seem intent on returning the United States of America back into the Squabbling Villages of Europe. Your goals, once the envy of the world, have deteriorated from daring and radical visions of unifying the planet into narcissistic little...dustballs.

GABY: *(Indignant)* Oh, really? And what are our goals now?

CLAIRE: Why, clearly, to be the best-entertained nation in the history of the world.

JOE: That is so kicking! Could we at least have dinner?

CLAIRE: Yes...but not together. The real villain of your Twentieth Century isn't Hitler or Stalin or Jesse Jackson or Gloria Steinem, it's Joseph Campbell.

JOE: Joseph Campbell—the myth guy? Why him?

CLAIRE: Because Joseph Campbell, in rebellion against his own Catholic upbringing, taught that each one of you is God—not an outside force—and he believed it right up until he died, when he chickened out and asked for last rites. Joseph Campbell and Luke Skywalker and Presidential adviser Anthony Robbins made it comfortable for you Americans to believe that the force was within each of you—and, therefore, that each one of you was the center of the universe. For all your religiosity, that's what you really believe, and that will be your ruin. No other country is so obsessed with obliterating spirituality and the presence of death with the trivialities of sport and show business.

JOE: That is so profound! What should we do now?

CLAIRE: Let your women run things for a while. Your men are all fagged out and deserve a rest. Thank them for twenty-five thousand years of faithful service, give them all cigars and melatonin and magazines and point them toward the pool. If that fails, reestablish the monarchy, that'd give you something to unite against. Perhaps have someone invade you—that always pulls people back together. And, Tracy, you can produce a prowar play about it when you take over the Macklow next year.

GABY: Assuming we step down.

TRACY: Assuming you step down? Gaby, for a full year you've been saying you were retiring at the end of this season! Just ten minutes ago—

GABY: What Oz said, and here I wholeheartedly support him, is that *when* he and I decide to step down, *that* will be the time to search for a new artistic director.

TRACY: But you said you were grooming me to be the youngest African-American woman to run a not-for-profit theater in the country!

GABY: But, Tracy dear, then you wrote this play...

TRACY: You mean...you might turn me down...because of this play?

GABY: Well, you meant what you wrote in it, didn't you?

TRACY: Well, yes, yes, but...

GABY: Well, you obviously have a strong creative drive, and what we really need is an outstanding administrator. Perhaps you should pursue your writing career.

OZ: Gaby—

TRACY: But Oz said I was a dazzling administrator!

GABY: Sometimes Oz gets a bit overzealous.

TRACY: Wait a minute, wait a minute, am I hearing this right? You're not only not going to do my play, you're going to can me?

GABY: No need to be melodramatic. Nobody's going to "can" you. I'm sure whoever takes over for us—Claire, for instance—would be happy to keep you on as dramaturg. Well, perhaps I shouldn't speak for her—

TRACY: Claire? But she's British!

GABY: That's racist, Tracy.

TRACY: But you said if this play wasn't written by a white boy, you'd do it, and it isn't, and it fits exactly into our mission statement of Vision 2000—

GABY: 2010.

TRACY: 2010.

GABY: I said if it were written by a Guatemalan, it would probably make the short list. Well, you're not Guatemalan, and the short list is full.

TRACY: Gaby, no—!

GABY: No, I'm afraid you can't unring this bell.

OZ: Can't unstir this porridge.

TRACY: *(Desperately)* Well, well, then I'll change it!

GABY: Really, how?

TRACY: *(Increasingly desperate)* Well, what if I, uh, made LaWanda more admirable, more sympathetic, just as you said, Gaby. She aspires to great things, but the world won't let her breathe, her folks beat her, she's a victim of society!

OZ: Now that's an interesting tack...

TRACY: I could get rid of those scenes where she's treated so well during the Civil War—no, better still, keep the scenes, but what if the Confederate family tortures her?

JOE: More believable than what you've got now, but—

TRACY: I could cut the cast in half, maybe get rid of the rednecks altogether—

GABY: No, I'm beginning to like the rednecks—

TRACY: —or, or keep them, beef up their parts! Give them all dignity, make it a little less sitcommy and and—

GABY: Get rid of that lovey-dovey stuff between Stonewall and his wife.

TRACY: But they were devoted to each other!

GABY: Doesn't really work for me, though—

TRACY: Well sure, yes, yes, of course, that wouldn't be much of a change, do all that, and make it a little more like, a little more like—

OZ: Yes?

TRACY: —*The Crucible.*

GABY: Bravo!

TRACY: Cut out all the mean-spiritedness and the academic jokes, get rid of the anti-Semitism—

GABY: Thank God.

TRACY: Insist on nontraditional casting!

OZ: Well, we could give it another look... .

TRACY: Think of the resonance the play will have, the actors' arcs!

GABY: I don't think so...

TRACY: BUT I'LL CHANGE EVERYTHING YOU WANT!! Why not?

GABY: *(Thinking it out)* A little too insincere. Too opportunistic, wouldn't you say, dear?

OZ: *(Uncertain)* Well...

TRACY: Please...please, Gaby...

GABY: (Suddenly ferocious) You liar! You coward! Take everything we hold dear and shit on it! You little thief in the night! Truth-mugger! Betrayer of my trust! Dissembler! Fake! Ingrate! Slippery, ill-bred, self-satisfied, condescending cunt! You have the hubris to believe you can break my heart? You resentful...whimpering...elitist! You think after this I'd let you *tear tickets* at a theater I had anything to do with?

OZ: Darling—

GABY: After all we've given you! Took you on vacations, showed you off to friends, confided in you...and you trick my husband into turning against me in a bar! A bar!

TRACY: I didn't, I didn't, no, Gaby—

GABY: Yes, yes, you didn't, you didn't. Solzhenitsyn *is* a crackpot! (Calming) Maybe it is better if we let you go now.

TRACY: No!

GABY: For the sake of the theater. Of all the arts. (She dismisses her, turns away.)

TRACY: I'll never lead the life I dreamed of. I'm shaking...my eyes are floating...I'm suicidal....

CLAIRE: Yes, you're quite like the guide in your play, aren't you.

TRACY: But...but...I worked so hard...I've been such a good girl...I thought I had crystallized our entire racial predicament in twenty-nine pages. I thought this was a *Waiting for Lefty* for the new century...I thought you'd be thrilled....

GABY: I am thrilled. Thrilled to see the self-loathing fascist you really are squirm before us. I won't pretend to know where we went wrong.

OZ: Let's get going! (Yelling offstage) Places for *Sammy Sadd!* We'll never finish by six.

JOE: (To CLAIRE) Look, just in case you take over, can I still audition for all the plays?

CLAIRE: Well, you *were* brilliant—

TRACY: But my heart is sinking, my head's all puffy, Gaby, you're spinning—

(Everyone ignores TRACY, hurrying for the next play. Even JOE helps move chairs.)

GABY: I'm leaving it to you, Oz—cut the next discussions short, or we won't even finish by seven.

TRACY: Little snowflakes in front of my eyes, Christmas songs, it was simple then. Momma, there's no floor under me, what should I do? I'll have no place to go, no reason to get up in the morning...what if all my friends liked me just because of my job?

JOE: *(To* GABY*)* I think that play about the gay guy and his father sounds fascinating!

TRACY: I don't have any friends outside of this theater! I can't just go to school, I can't stare at my walls. I'll wind up like Joe, spinning in a studio, sweeping up after cadavers. My folks'll say, "I told you so, serve you right."

*(*JOE *makes* CLAIRE *dance with him.)*

JOE: See?

CLAIRE: I do admire your persistence.

JOE: You can't be that busy later...

TRACY: Everybody always says, "Tell the truth," and when you do, they insist you compromise. But I did both!

CLAIRE: *(To* JOE*)* Well, maybe.

TRACY: I can't stand it, I'll lose everything—dreams, work, friends, the paltry salary I make here, everything! Am I really just wrong about the works? *(Suddenly shrieking)* Yahhhh!

CLAIRE: What is it?

TRACY: I'm so scared!

JOE: What of?

TRACY: We're going to die if you keep us trapped like this!

OZ: What do you mean?

TRACY: Where do we fit into all this? Are we just going to be a permanent beggar class living off your largesse? Fifteen I Q points—what if that's true? What if Claire's right—in twenty years we're no longer the most important minority? I mean, when all races are all over, cheek by jowl, and we're just a sidecar on your motorcycle—what'll happen to us? The Hispanics everywhere, Indians from India, the Chinese don't give a shit about us, and we know how the Japanese feel about a diversified culture! What'll happen when the Jews turn on us, and the grandchildren of the Baghdad Scud survivors become citizens, and the murderous Koreans—well known for being the most violent people on earth—what if they get to be...more? The *Times*es of New York and L A, what if they turn on us, the networks, Larry King, all those women—

GABY: Not quite so arrogant now, are we?

OZ: She's trembling, Gaby—

TRACY: They'll all be so furious! And you won't let us out of the cage!

OZ: What are you talking about?

TRACY: Us! Me! The black American!

OZ: What about you?

TRACY: WHAT'LL HAPPEN TO OUR LEG UP?

GABY: (Sudden revelation—sincerely) Why, you poor thing! That's all we've been talking about all along.

JOE: Jesus, you poor kid, you're terrified.

(TRACY is on her knees and shaking. GABY crosses to her, puts her arms around her to comfort her.)

GABY: There's not going to be any revenge. We'll take care of you, Tracy. We always have.

OZ: (Crossing to TRACY) Is that what you're worried about? What kind of people do you think we are?

(CLAIRE smooths TRACY's hair. OZ follows quickly.)

CLAIRE: Come on Trace, pull yourself together. We're here for you.

JOE: She's freezing! Let me rub your hands, Tracy.

GABY: The human heart is most fulfilled when it forgives. (They surround her, touching and holding her.)

CLAIRE: You know, Tracy, I think your play is on a very grand theme. Brilliant, really. It just needs some rethinking, a little shaping. Perhaps we can help.

OZ: It's such a timeless subject...

GABY: Perhaps I overreacted. I do respect your passion, dear, misguided though it may be. But we've handled that before.

TRACY: We're only twelve percent....

GABY: That's why you need us to take care of you.

OZ: Open your eyes. We'll lift care from your shoulders like a cloak...

OZ, GABY, JOE, & CLAIRE: Mmmmmmmm...

TRACY: Who's we?

GABY: We. Us.

(GABY puts her arm around CLAIRE, beckons to TRACY. JOE and OZ are left out and worried.)

GABY: Oh, come on, Oz, Joe, you can be honorary women...

(JOE and OZ cross to GABY joyfully, as if at the end of a very sentimental play. Arm in arm, they coax TRACY to join them. They hold this very pleasant tableau for a moment as....)

(End of Scene One)

Scene Two

(Fanfare!)

(A large mock Playbill flies in with the title and graphics for the play The House of Mary Anna Morrison-Jackson, Survivor. *Across one corner a yellow banner reads "PULITZER PRIZE WINNER!")*

(We hear the voices of the actors. The men play women and the women play men. GABY is LEWALDO GAYLE, a twenty-two year-old African-American male tour guide; JOE is MAG NUCKOLLS; OZ is DEL GOSHEN.)

GABY: *(As LEWALDO, O S)* And here we have the rotor ruffler of Ms Mary Anna Morrison-Jackson, Survivor, an item she loathed but which she was forced to use as a subservient female by her husband and tormentor, General Stonewall Jackson, domestic batterer and abuser.

OZ: *(As DEL, O S)* Young man, is it true Stonewall Jackson was killed by his own men?

GABY: *(As LEWALDO, O S)* Absolutely not. He was killed by his wife in self-defense. A close reading of history by the scholars here at Ms Mary Anna Morrison-Jackson, Survivor's house prove that Mary Anna dressed up like one of his soldiers and set him on fire while he slept, but that male historians thought this made him a sissy and so invented the fiction that he was killed by men.

JOE: *(As MAG, O S)* Excuse me for interrupting your powerful and convincing thesis, but I'd like to know if that rotor ruffler is real.

GABY: *(As LEWALDO, O S)* No, but it is the exact *kind* of rotor ruffler that Jackson so savagely demanded.

(As soon as the actors have changed costumes, The Playbill flies out, revealing GABY dressed as a man in nineteenth-century overalls, JOE and OZ in MAG's and DEL's costumes from ACT ONE.)

CLAIRE: *(As JUNIOR)* Oh, no, another fake! Listen here, sonny. My name is Junior Nuckolls, Junior, and my wife and me have come all the way from racist Southern Georgia and even more racist Alabama, and there isn't anything in this house that's authentic!

GABY: *(As LEWALDO) (Flustered)* Well, well, uh, we've tried to make it look nice even if inauthentic, but— *(Aside)* —oh, I am so distraught and alone!

OZ: *(As* DEL*)* *(Arm around* GABY'*s shoulder)* Are you all right, lad?

JOE: *(As* MAG*)* Yes, I, too, wonder why you are so melancholic, LeWaldo.

GABY: *(As* LEWALDO*)* It's genetic. As you know, it is common knowledge that the chief cause of the Civil War was the lack of self-esteem among the white male population of the time.

OZ: *(As* DEL*)* But how does this affect a virile African-American male youth like yourself, LeWaldo?

GABY: *(As* LEWALDO*)* Our scholars here at The Ibsen-like Doll's House of Mary Anna Morrison-Jackson, Survivor, have discovered that virtually every single American born before 1720 south of the Mason-Dixon line was a victim of child abuse.   ·

JOE: *(As* MAG*)* Mercy!

GABY: *(As* LEWALDO*)* The Eighteenth-Century Epidemic of Child Abuse caused the Nineteenth-Century Outbreak of Poor Self-Esteem. This in turn caused a genetic orientation to warfare among men, and a genetic orientation to be date-raped among women.

OZ: *(As* DEL*)* Really...

GABY: *(As* LEWALDO*)* But here's the important asterisk: while the litigious gene was passed on to the men, it was NOT PASSED ON TO THE WOMEN.

CLAIRE: *(As* JUNIOR*)* So basically, LeWaldo, you're saying that the abuse of women and men in the eighteenth century caused a lack of self-esteem and a plethora of date rape in the nineteenth century, which caused the Civil War...because the women were not yet litigious?

GABY: *(As* LEWALDO*)* That's right. And had it not been for the perseverance of Mary Todd Lincoln and Julia Dent Grant, who planned the winning strategy of the last eighteen months—these United States of America would still be the Squabbling Villages of Europe.

OZ: *(As* DEL*)* Ah.

GABY: *(As* LEWALDO*)* And, because litigiousness is not genetic in women it explains why women have had to play catch-up in that area over the last hundred thirty years, and why they deserve larger settlements.

JOE: *(As* MAG*)* And that's why so many of us are looking forward to the Johann Sebastian Bach Retroactive Rape Trial.

OZ: *(As* DEL*)* What's the Johann Sebastian Bach Retroactive Rape Trial?

CLAIRE: *(As* JUNIOR*)* The Attorney General's final argument this morning left no reasonable doubt that the two Mrs. Bachs would never have had twenty children voluntarily.

JOE: *(As* MAG*)* But, the Attorney General didn't say it was because of Bach's cross-dressing—I mean that's genetic and hardly his fault.

CLAIRE: *(As* JUNIOR*)* In fact, it was used in his defense, and his estate may receive reparations.

JOE: *(As* MAG*)* But the rape evidence is clear and verified by Beethoven's European-Caucasian mistress in a letter written as she ghost-wrote his Seventh Symphony while Ludwig was away celebrating Kwanzaa.

GABY: *(As* LEWALDO*)* But even Bach's justified conviction will not transport my misery! *(She breaks down and cries.)*

OZ: *(As* DEL*)* Now, now, LeWaldo. We all feel your pain. My partner Barney and I have a beautiful resort in the free-thinking state of Ohio. Sometimes we take walks among the calming sheep and run our hands through the clear brooks burbling everywhere. How would you like to come back and live with us, and we'll take care of you?

GABY: *(As* LEWALDO*)* Oh, how my head swims in anticipation of your wooded offer! How trouble-free and race-neutral it sounds!

OZ: *(As* DEL*)* Barney and I will help you make up your mind about everything. You'll never want for food or money, clothing or friends or T V. You can stay as long as you want, go when you like...what do you say?

(A pin spot finds LEWALDO's *face. The rest of the stage is black.)*

GABY: *(As* LEWALDO*)* But, no, you want me to be your slave, Del Goshen, I can tell! Yes, I want to be protected from the cruelties of the world, yes, I want to be taken care of as in some welfare state—and Lord knows I deserve it after the millennia of racist, sexist, looksist, classist, homophobic, unfair shampoo and dry-cleaning oppression we males of all races have enforced—but what about my dignity? For I am a survivor just like Ms Mary Anna Morrison-Jackson, Survivor, and I need not your patriarchal suffocation, nor the attendant heartbruise and arrowsling! If it's the hatin', cussin' world versus your fascistic prison, I'll not the latter, I'll not the latter, I'll not the latter! Give me my earth and my freedom!

(GABY's monologue concludes, and the pin spot fades. The unseen audience applauds and bravos wildly, then fades as country sounds come up.)

(End of Scene Two)

Scene Three

(Lights come up on TRACY *and* CLAIRE, *facing D S in a line of rocking chairs. Next to them in the sunlight are three empty rockers.)*

CLAIRE: Sold out again, Tracy! What a glorious feeling. Isn't Bedford exquisite? Beyond my wildest dreams for the Hazlitt. So much excitement around your play, Tracy, *The House of Mary Anna Morrison-Jackson, Survivor,* all the awards, every major film studio bidding for it as a possible miniseries, two operas, *Time* Magazine's Person of the Year. You are the New Voice of the American Theater. Of all the arts, really.

*(*JOE *enters, kisses* CLAIRE *passionately, puts his hand inside her shirt, feels her up. She moans and kisses back. He takes the chair next to her and rocks.)*

JOE: Hello, darling. Seven standing ovations last night, Tracy. Congratulations.

*(*OZ *enters, crosses to a chair, rocks.)*

OZ: Seven standing ovations, Tracy. Unusual for a Tuesday. Joe, you were superb and Gabriella transcendent—her greatest role. So much dignity in it.

(They rock in their chairs silently for a moment. GABY *enters looking like Rebecca of Sunnybrook Farm.)*

GABY: Hello, everyone. Tracy. What a beautiful sunset.

OZ: Tracy agrees your performance was transcendent last night, Gaby.

GABY: Oh my God, coming from the playwright, the creator! Your play is so fulfilling—my crowning achievement, capping a lifetime in the theater. Oh. I'm so at peace here. The splendid isolation, the ice-sharp perceptions of art....

OZ: Yes, and I feel so safe. Safe as...you Brits have an expression for it, "safe as..."?

CLAIRE: Safe as houses.

OZ: Right. That's how I feel. Safe as houses.

JOE: So peaceful. Secure.

OZ: Sort of like a gentle rain on a farm somewhere in Ohio. Hey, look at that rainbow!

GABY: Know what I'd like to do after all this success? Just sit here and rock. Reminisce—but not about the past. We can reminisce about the future. I'm so optimistic! From here, it looks lovely. Clean and hopeful and bright.

(They stare at the sunset, rocking peacefully.)

(Slow fade to black—)

END OF PLAY

AUTHOR'S NOTE

Discussing theatrical style is as frustrating as discussing acting, because so much of both are ethereal—but realization of a play's style on a stage is crucial and, in my opinion, the director's chief task. Some plays fit comfortably into traditional styles with which we're generally familiar— the sitcom, the kitchen-sink drama, the cinematic narrative, the theatrical musical. STONEWALL JACKSON'S HOUSE doesn't.

I am a verbal writer, and while I relish the visual and theatrical aspects of a production, still, first and last, the merit of my work excites or bores on the basis of what the characters say. As in all my plays, the characters of S J H are very real and should be played as such—but what they say is frequently not "realistic". Rather, it is the verbalization of their innermost, usually unspoken, thoughts and feelings. It is often spoken subtext. The characters believe passionately in everything they're saying—but are often unaware of its effect on others.

On the one hand, the play is silly; on the other, it couldn't be more serious. How does a director stage and how do actors play this seeming contradiction? On the one hand, if the actors distance themselves from the characters and smirk at them—or if the director allows them to be too broad—the whole things becomes a cartoon (and, not incidentally, won't be funny); on the other, if they play it "realistically," without comic sense, the production becomes deadly. The thin line that separates these two approaches constitutes the style of this play.

As for the longer speeches (particularly in Act Two), filling every moment becomes the actor's task. "But s/he wouldn't say that!" is an unhelpful exercise here. S/he *does* say it. The actors have no time off in this play. Almost all are onstage all the time—and all have plenty to say. In the New York production, they were generally wrung out after each performance— exhilarated when it went well, grumpy when it didn't.

I strongly suggest the director discuss the politics of the play with the actors *before* casting them. Although I welcome disagreement and outrage (it's why I wrote it!), this reaction needs to come from the audience—not from the cast. Obviously, this is not to say the actors should agree with everything the play says, but unless there is some uniform appreciation of its points of view—or at least the points of view being aired—the rehearsal process is liable to devolve into political harangue—"I buy this idea, but I don't buy

that one"—and the performances, which need to be so committed to the
characters, may be undermined.

www.ingramcontent.com/pod-product-compliance
Lightning Source LLC
Chambersburg PA
CBHW061303110426
42742CB00012BA/2039